The Rest of Wisdom
Eden's Ancient Path Unveiled

AMY MARIE LANGE

The Rest of Wisdom
Eden's Ancient Path Unveiled

ISBN (paperback): 979-8-218-89345-3
ISBN (ebook): 979-8-218-90820-1

This publication is designed to provide accurate and authoritative information regarding the subject matter covered. While the author and publisher have made every effort to ensure accuracy, no representations or warranties are made regarding the completeness or applicability of the content. The reflections and meditative practices presented are not intended to replace professional guidance. Readers are encouraged to seek appropriate counsel where needed.

Cover and interior design by The Overflow Studio
Cover art images used under license from Dreamstime.com

Published by Cloudrider Press
Kansas City, Missouri

First edition: February 2026
Printed in the United States of America

אֲנִי לְדוֹדִי וְדוֹדִי לִי
Ani L'dodi V'dodi Li

I Am My Beloved's, and My Beloved is Mine

"What delight comes to the one who follows God's ways!
He won't walk in step with the wicked, nor share the sinner's way,
nor be found sitting in the scorner's seat.

His passion is to remain true to the Word of "I AM,"
meditating day and night on the true revelation of light.

He will be standing firm like a flourishing tree
planted by God's design, deeply rooted by the brooks of bliss,
bearing fruit in every season of life.

He is never dry, never fainting, ever blessed, ever prosperous.

But how different are the wicked.
They are like chaff blown away by the wind.
The wicked will not endure the day of judgment,
for God will not defend them.

Nothing they do will succeed or endure for long,
for they have no part with those who walk in truth.

But how different it is for the righteous!
The Lord embraces their paths as they move forward
while the way of the wicked leads only to doom."

−Psalms 1−

TABLE OF CONTENTS

FOREWORD

There are books that inform. There are books that inspire. And then, every so often, there comes a book that awakens. Amy Lange has written that kind of book.

The Rest of Wisdom: Eden's Ancient Paths Unveiled is more than a study; it's a sacred journey back to the beginning in order to understand who we are becoming. From the whispering leaves of Eden's trees to the rainbow that arched over Ararat, from Lady Wisdom's house to the shimmering courts of Solomon's temple, Amy guides us along the ancient pathways where God first revealed His heart, His intention, and His eternal purpose.

With stunning clarity and poetic insight, she shows how every path leads to one Person, Christ, the fulfillment of every shadow, every promise, every longing. And more than that, she reveals how this Christ is not merely the destination but the very companion of the journey, the Living Ark who carries us, the Tree of Life who nourishes us, the Sabbath-rest who lives within us.

Amy writes with the rare combination of biblical depth and prophetic wonder. She does not simply explain the narrative of Scripture, she opens it like a doorway and invites us to step through. She reminds us that wisdom is not a concept but a Person, and that true wisdom is found when our lives intertwine with His. In her hands, ancient stories shine with fresh fire, revealing how Eden's design unfolds in the New Covenant reality of Christ dwelling inside His people.

This book will cause you to breathe differently. It will slow your pace. It will anchor your heart. It will call you back to the restful wisdom of walking with God in the cool of the day: no shame, no striving, no separation.

If you are hungry for union with Christ…

If you long to rediscover the simplicity of the Tree of Life…

If you desire to live from the inside out, from the indwelling glory of Jesus…

Then you are holding a treasure.

Prepare to be captivated. Prepare to be changed. Prepare to walk the ancient paths with new eyes and a renewed heart.

Amy Lange has given us a gift, a map, a melody, and a gentle invitation to return to the Rest of Wisdom Himself. Enjoy the journey. It's more than information; it's transformation.

Brian Simmons, *Passion and Fire Ministries*

ENDORSEMENTS

"This book is written in layers, each chapter building and revealing the intentionality of God and the building blocks of His creation. It draws us into understanding and truth, weaving the unfolding revelation as an invitation for others to step into, making this already accessible place easy to find!

You can hear the echoes of God's heart through Amy's skill as a writer; her heart entwined with wisdom as she reveals the relationship we were always intended to live from."

-Jane Gibbs, *Author*

"This book is a definite must read if you are looking for greater understanding into the Word of God. This book is born from a deep relationship of intimacy with the Father and it feeds the human soul and spirit at its deepest level. Amy's incredible insight into the meaning of the aspects of redemption is invaluable. She clearly draws the line between the fall of man and the redemption Yehovah God has worked into His eternal plan from the beginning. Redemption began immediately: the revelation of our Father's heart and the return to Eden's rest, if we have the eyes to see and the ears to hear."

-Cindy Rose Torio, *Missionary to the Philippines*

"In *The Rest of Wisdom*, Amy pulls the golden thread of Rest's mystery through the tapestry of Scripture. The unfolding of Rest's nature and function provides foundational truths that Kingdom establishers must shift into as the primary energy of Kingdom creation with God.

This was for us a book that did not just carry a priceless message; it drew us into encountering the message for transformation. God is establishing a New Kingdom which requires a different approach to building.

The Rest of Wisdom demonstrates how to move in surrendered engagement with God. It becomes clear that Rest is our inheritance, our identity, our joy and our oneness in moving forward. *The Rest of Wisdom* is a hidden treasure revealed."

-Ben & Lindsey Hankins, *Integrative Energy Therapist,*
www.youfullyyou.com

"Just a little while ago Bob Jones released a prophetic word he called *The Hundred-Year Prophecy*. In this word, Bob described the divine theme of each decade. The theme of God for the 2020's is THE REST OF GOD. At the time of this writing, we have just crossed over into 2026 and the message of rest has never been louder and more required. I know not everyone will enter this thing.

Rest is a choice (among many other things). Should you dear reader make the choice…this book will position you within the process and journey of Rest.

After reading this book I told Amy, '*You're really delightfully articulating from the Heart of God the reality He is calling us into!*' This is one of those precious works you will not be able to only read once. Emphatically and unilaterally do I LOUDLY ENDORSE THIS BOOK!!!!!!!."

-Joshua Stokes, *a son of God*

"This is one of the most beautiful works of heaven-sent manna I have ever read. Amy Lange writes exquisitely with unveiling light, with the quill of heaven, and with ink of rhema luminescence and revelation radiance. These words travel the contours of the heart and soul.

As you partner with the wisdom held within these pages, you inhale a deep rest drawn from the wells of divine revelation, a refreshing that is heaven-sent. What unfolds here is a gentle washing by the whisper of truth, poured out like a fragrant offering for all who will humble themselves and allow Jesus, who knocks at the door of holy communion to come in and sup with them."

-Wayne Biehn

PROLOGUE

There was a Garden where time did not lean forward.

Colors pulsed with life. Creatures drank deeply from the stillness that surrounded them. Plants blossomed without effort, giving and receiving beauty through the slow exchange of light and soil. Love moved through creation the way breath moves through a body, unnoticed only because it was everywhere.

Man and woman, hand in hand, moved in wonder, their laughter and breath filling the space between them. Delight was not something they pursued, but something they shared, unguarded and whole. As God walked among them, creation did not merely observe; it responded, answering His nearness with life, sound, and joy.

This was Eden.

Eden was not sustained by effort. Nothing strained to become, nothing reached beyond its place. Life unfolded because it was held. Wisdom did not need instruction; it entered with breath, received before it was ever named. Rest did not require permission. It was the ground itself. Creation did not strive to hear God because it lived within the sound of His presence.

And yet, somewhere along the way, a fracture entered the story. A different tree was chosen, and with it came a forgetting. Not of Eden's existence, but of how to remain within it. The ground grew louder. Time broke into measurements. Stillness became something to pursue rather than stand upon. Wisdom narrowed into information. Rest became a reward something earned instead of inhabited.

But Eden was never erased.

It did not vanish into history or dissolve into myth.

It withdrew, quietly waiting.

Waiting in covenants written into skin and stone. Waiting in breath and soil. Waiting in names and numbers, in trees and altars, in arks and temples. Waiting through generations until it could be revealed not as a place to return to, but as a life to be restored.

That revelation came in Yeshua.

Not as a system returned, but as a Person walking again among His beloved.

The Living Ark. The Tree of Life. The Rest of God made present.
The Gardener has not stopped walking.
The ground has not stopped listening.
And the way back has never been complicated.
The gate stands open.
The Gardener waits.
And the cool of the day has returned.

INTRODUCTION

Follow the Golden Thread

Imagine, for a moment, that you are standing in the first garden. Before words formed doctrine, before stories became chapters, before time learned to measure itself, there was only breath, light moving through leaves, and the quiet steps of God walking close enough to be heard.

The soil is warm beneath your feet. The trees carry a sweetness in the air. And there is an unmistakable nearness, the presence of the One who shaped everything you see.

This is where Scripture begins. And in a very real way, this is where this book begins as well.

Because the story of God can be traced like a single golden thread, running from the garden of beginnings to the garden of resurrection, and now into the inner garden He is restoring within you.

This book is an invitation to walk that thread.

Not as a scholar. Not as a spectator. But as someone who steps through the pages the way Adam once stepped into morning light, with a heart awake, with the Spirit near, with creation whispering all around.

The chapters ahead are not arranged as arguments or lessons. They unfold like landscapes.

Some will feel like wandering beneath trees where revelation waits quietly among the branches. Others will feel like kneeling beside ancient stone altars where the fire of covenant still glows. And some will feel like entering the hush of a holy room, where Yeshua lifts bread with hands that remember the dust.

Threaded through these moments are glimpses beneath the surface, where language, numbers, geography, and symbol reveal the structure of God's wisdom. Not to overwhelm, but to deepen what you already know.

At the end of each chapter, you will find a meditation. Each one is meant to be a clearing in the forest, a place to breathe, a space where the Spirit can settle truth into your heart the way morning dew settles on the earth.

Wisdom is not absorbed the way information is. It settles slowly, received rather than seized.

And rest is not achieved through effort. It is something we return to, the way the body returns to breath.

As you follow the thread, patterns begin to emerge. Eden echoes through every covenant. Mountains begin to speak. The earth responds to God's footsteps. Trees bend toward a shared memory. And the Messiah appears as the One who carries the whole tapestry within Himself.

Nothing here asks you to hurry. Everything invites you to become still and listen, as though you were standing in that first garden again.

So step in.

Let the story rise around you. Let the Holy Spirit guide your eyes to the golden thread woven through creation. Let the Gardener take your hand and walk with you, chapter by chapter, from dust to breath, from fracture to belonging, from exile to homecoming.

Follow the thread.

It knows the way back to Eden.

1

THE BEGINNING
The Breath of Wisdom

**"Then the LORD God formed man from the dust
of the ground and breathed into his nostrils the breath
of life; and man became a living soul."
Genesis 2:7**

The Garden of Fellowship

A moment in time when everything seemed to stand still.

A gentle hum shimmered through the air as God's breath exhaled, resting in the knowing that all was *good*.

The ground responded, opening beneath Him as He moved through it.

Grass rose to meet each step, holding and wrapping love around His presence. Color pulsed with life, glistening in quiet praise, radiant with hope yet unnamed. Everything leaned toward His nearness.

Eden was not merely a location. Its very name means delight. Not amusement. Not excess. But the deep pleasure of life aligned with God. Eden was the atmosphere of divine enjoyment. Creation flourished because it was held.

It was the first picture of harmony between Creator and creation.

1

Nothing in Eden was striving to become; everything already was. Every color, sound, and living thing existed within divine rhythm. This is what the rest of wisdom looks like: structure without tension, beauty without effort, purpose without pressure.

The soil of Eden had never felt sweat. The ground gave without resistance because it was responding to the same voice that formed it. Adam did not labor to earn life; he tended what already lived. His work was not toil; it was participation.

To name, to watch, to keep; these were acts of worship, not survival. He ruled by listening, not by forcing. That is dominion inside rest. God's breath was still moving through creation. The Holy Spirit, *Ruach*, that had hovered over the waters now moved through the trees.

When Scripture says God walked in the garden in the cool of the day, it means His presence was felt in every breeze. Adam and Eve did not wait for visitation; they lived in habitation. Rest was not a sabbath they observed but an environment they breathed.

Wisdom was visible in the order of everything around them. Rivers flowed within their boundaries. Seasons moved without chaos. Light and darkness knew their place. The same intelligence that built the cosmos was now the cadence of the garden. Every living thing responded to that wisdom instinctively. Harmony was the natural state of existence.

This is the pattern of God's world; the way life unfolds when *chokmah* (wisdom) builds and *nuach* (rest) fills. The Garden of Fellowship was the blueprint: God present, creation aligned, humanity at peace.

Made In His Image: The Fellowship Pattern

When God said, *"Let Us make man in Our image,"* He was revealing the reason creation existed at all. Everything He had formed, the light, the land, the rhythm of seasons, was waiting for a being who could live inside that rhythm. Humanity was created to mirror the fellowship already alive within God Himself: Father, Word, and Spirit moving in perfect harmony.

Wisdom At Work

Scripture later says, *"By wisdom the LORD founded the earth." (Proverbs 3:19)* That same *chokmah*, divine skill and understanding, was still shaping when God formed the man from dust. Every detail of the human body carried design: eyes to behold beauty, hands to cultivate, lungs to receive breath.

Wisdom built the framework, rest would fill it.

When God breathed into Adam's nostrils, the breath of life (*neshamah*) filled what wisdom had built. That breath was more than oxygen. It was presence.

In that instant, *nuach* (rest) entered creation's rhythm through humanity. Adam opened his eyes inside perfect alignment: the world around him ordered by wisdom, his own heart settled by rest.

The Fellowship of Two

But the image of God was not yet complete. When God said, *"It is not good that man should be alone,"* He was not pointing out loneliness but incompleteness. A single being could reflect the order of wisdom, but not the communion of love.

So, from Adam's side, while he rested, God built another. Scripture says, *"He built the woman." (Genesis 2:22)* That Hebrew verb built, *vayiven*, comes from the same root as *binah*, meaning understanding. Eve was constructed with the same intentionality as the world itself. She embodied relational wisdom; the insight that holds things together, that discerns, that nurtures what has been ordered.

Together, Adam and Eve became the full image of God: two lives moving as one breath. He carried the strength of rest; she carried the discernment of wisdom. Neither dominated the other; they completed the pattern.

In them, creation saw what divine fellowship looked like in human form.

Rest in Motion

Their relationship was the living demonstration of Eden's rest. They worked, but there was no striving. They governed, but without control. Every decision flowed from shared trust; the same trust that pulsed between the Father, the Word, and the Spirit. Where wisdom led, rest followed; where rest settled, wisdom built again.

That is why creation responded to them. The animals listened, the ground yielded, the air remained clear. Nothing resisted because nothing was dissonant. Humanity's harmony was the world's peace.

The Naming of Life

The Garden's order was not sustained by effort or rules, but by fellowship. As long as Adam and Eve remained aligned with each other and with God, moving within the rhythm of His wisdom and rest, Eden held its harmony. Creation mirrored that peace because relationship was intact. The moment communion fractured, the world itself would feel the tremor.

But when the serpent spoke, it did not tempt them with rebellion outright, it tempted them with independence. *"Has God indeed said...?"* *(Genesis 3:1)* The lie was not simply that the fruit would make them wise; it was that wisdom could exist apart from fellowship.

When Eve looked at the fruit, Scripture says she saw that it was good for food, pleasant to the eyes, and desirable to make one wise. She was reaching for something that already belonged to her. She was already created in the image of Wisdom Himself. But deception always disguises striving as enlightenment.

The moment they ate, sight fractured. They still saw, but no longer through God's perspective. The *ayin*, the Hebrew for word for "eye of perception," turned inward. Shame entered, and rest left. The ground had not changed, but the lens had.

Now, what had once been gifted felt like labor; what had once been peace now required effort to maintain. Yet even here, mercy was already moving. God did not curse Adam and Eve; He cursed the serpent and the ground. Creation absorbed the consequence so that humanity could still carry hope.

Then something remarkable happens.

After hearing of death, *"to dust you shall return,"* Adam turns to the woman beside him and names her Eve (חַוָּה, *Chavah*), which means life, to give life, to revive. (Genesis 3:20) It is the first time she receives a name of her own, and it comes not in innocence but in redemption. He could have called her "sorrow" or "loss." Instead, he calls her Life.

In doing so, Adam mirrors the heart of the God who had just shown mercy. As God redirected the curse away from Adam, Adam now speaks blessing over Eve. He becomes, again, the image-bearer, reflecting the nature of his Creator.

Eve's name becomes prophecy. Even as the world bends under the weight of broken wisdom, a new promise takes root through her. She will carry the seed that will one day crush deception and reopen the way to rest. Her identity becomes the bridge between fall and redemption, the lost rest of Eden, and the restored rest that will come through Christ.

In that moment, the pattern is visible again:

- Wisdom speaks truth into disorder.
- Rest begins to return where fear had entered.

Through a single act of naming, life begins to rise from dust.

The Ground and the Mercy

Before the fall, Adam's hands never broke soil. He lived from trees. Every need came from branches that reached upward, freely offered. Fruit appeared in its season; shade covered him in heat. This was rest in its truest form; provision without striving, wisdom providing before there was need. To eat from trees was to live inside divine rhythm: receiving what God had already caused to flourish.

When sight turned inward and wisdom was grasped instead of received, the rhythm shifted. The voice of God came again, not in rage but in order, setting boundaries that would hold creation until redemption. And in that voice, mercy was hidden inside judgment.

"Because you have done this,"

He said to the serpent, "you are cursed... on your belly you shall go,

and dust you shall eat all the days of your life."

"Cursed is the ground for your sake," He said to Adam.

Genesis 3:14-15

Two sentences, one thread. The dust.

The serpent would crawl through it and taste it every day, a continual reminder of the life he had tried to corrupt. Every movement across the ground would confront him with the substance of God's creation, Adam, formed from dust. The deceiver was condemned to consume the evidence of his own defeat.

For Adam, the same dust became both teacher and mercy. The ground would resist him, yet it would also sustain him. He would feel the ache of toil, but in every handful of soil he would remember his origin. He would remember the breath that turned dust into being. The struggle itself would remind him: You are not the curse; you are the creation I loved enough to spare.

God never said, *"Cursed are you."*

He said, *"Cursed is the ground for your sake."*

He diverted the weight from the man to the earth. Love carried consequence so that image could remain. Provision changed shape. Where Adam once reached up for fruit, he would now reach down for bread. What had been effortless became process; what had been given became grown. But even in sweat, grace was still present.

Every seed buried was a whisper of resurrection; life rising from the ground that bore the curse. The soil became the first altar: it carried the mark of substitution. The serpent was condemned to it; the man was sustained by it; God Himself would one day use it to heal what was broken. From that moment, the ground held the story of both judgment and hope.

When Adam turned to the woman and named her Eve, meaning "Life," he was acknowledging what had been revealed to him. God had not cursed humanity; He had covered it.

The ground would carry the weight of the fracture. The woman would bear the promise. Between them lay the pattern of redemption: dust, seed, and resurrection.

The Waiting Pattern

The story of the garden did not end in ruin; it settled into waiting. The ground carried mercy, and the pattern of rest waited to rise again. And standing amid that waiting were the trees; silent witnesses of both wisdom and rest, still rooted in the same soil that now carried the curse.

They reached upward as if remembering the rhythm of Eden. Through them, the next revelation begins.

Selah Meditation: Return to Your Garden

Close your eyes. Let your breath soften. Let the noise loosen its grip around you. For a moment, just pause and reflect. Imagine the stillness of the first morning in Eden. Before the ache. Before the striving. Before the world learned to hurry. Feel the coolness of the dawn brushing your skin. Hear the gentle rustle of leaves, alive with light. Sense the warmth of soil beneath your feet, steady and ancient, holding nothing but peace.

Somewhere in the distance, God's presence moves. Not rushed. Not hidden. Not demanding. Just walking. Footsteps that carry rest. Footsteps that know your name before you speak it. Footsteps that have waited for this moment with you.

Let Him draw near; not toward the version of you that strives, but toward the part of you that remembers. The inner garden. The quiet center. The place untouched by fear, untouched by shame, untouched by the long nights of wandering.

Breathe in and imagine His breath filling those inner places; the chambers of your heart where desire becomes prayer and prayer becomes communion.

Hear Him speak. He does not thunder but has the same gentle cadence that first moved through Eden's trees: *"I Am here."* This is the atmosphere He designed for you; not toil, but tenderness. Not distance, but nearness. Not survival but belonging.

Stay here a moment longer. Feel the garden opening within you; petal by petal, breath by breath, as Wisdom begins to build and Rest begins to reign. The Gardener has not changed. He is still walking. He is still calling. He is still planting.

And the place He most desires to walk is not far away, it is within you.

Return to your garden. It has been waiting for you.

Notes:

_____

_____

_____

_____

_____

_____

_____

_____

_____

_____

_____

_____

_____

_____

_____

_____

_____

_____

_____

_____

_____

_____

_____

_____

2
THE TREES
Living Conduits of Wisdom and Rest

**"And out of the ground the LORD God made to spring up
every tree that is pleasant to the sight and good for food.
The tree of life was in the midst of the garden,
and the tree of the knowledge of good and evil."
Genesis 2:9**

The Living Architecture of Creation

The garden did not lie flat.

Something quiet, patient, and alive arose from the soil. Trunks pressed upward through dark earth, branches stretching into light as though responding to an ancient call older than sound. Leaves whispered secrets to the wind. Shade gathered beneath their arms. The air itself seemed to breathe differently among them.

These were not decorations. They were witnesses.

Every step through the garden passed beneath their presence. Every breath was filtered through their stillness. Life did not rush here. It ascended, rooted and sure, drawing nourishment from depths unseen and lifting it toward the heavens.

Only then does Scripture name what grew there. It could have said "plants" or "vegetation," but the Spirit chose the Hebrew word עֵץ (ʿēts), tree.

In Hebrew thought, the tree is the living architecture of creation, the vertical structure that joins what is above to what is below. Every tree in Eden was more than bark and leaf; it was a living parable of divine order.

Roots buried deep in the ground, branches lifted high toward the heavens, sap flowing between worlds; each tree mirrored the design of the cosmos and of man himself: connection, circulation, balance.

It was wisdom (*chokmah*) embodied and rest (*nuach*) made visible. Each one silently declared the rhythm of the Creator: life flowing from rest.

"Pleasant to the sight, and good for food."

Two movements: seeing and receiving. Beauty and sustenance. Vision and nourishment. Both existed in perfect balance in every tree. That is what rest looks like in motion; a world that does not strain for its goodness but reveals it by simply being what it was created to be.

The Language of the Tree: Seeing and Reaching

The Hebrew word עֵץ (ʿēts) is formed by two Hebrew letters: ע (*ayin*) and צ (*tsade*).

Ayin, the eye, perception, revelation, the ability to see rightly.

Tsade, righteousness and the reaching upward, the connection between heaven and earth.

Together, they tell the story of the tree: to see rightly (*ayin*) and to reach rightly (*tsade*). The tree is both insight and alignment. It perceives the light, and it stretches toward it. It roots itself deep in the place of mercy, and it extends toward glory. This is why humanity was planted among the trees.

Adam and Eve were meant to be *ʿētsim* among *ʿētsim*, trees among trees.

They were living extensions of the same divine pattern: rooted in wisdom, reaching in righteousness, bearing fruit that nourishes others. They, too, were living conduits of wisdom and rest.

The Two Trees: The Choice Between Wisdom and Control

Two trees stood apart in Eden's center: the Tree of Life (עֵץ הַחַיִּים, ʿēts ha-ḥayyim) and the Tree of the Knowledge of Good and Evil (עֵץ הַדַּעַת טוֹב וָרָע, ʿēts ha-daʿat tov va-ra).

Both offered knowledge, but from opposite sources. One gave life through union, the other promised wisdom through independence. The first invited trust; the second offered control. The Tree of Life was divine *chokmah* (wisdom) made tangible. God's wisdom turned edible. To eat from it was to internalize His rest.

The Tree of Knowledge represented the Hebrew word *da'at*: information without intimacy, definition without dependence. It was the counterfeit of *chokmah*; wisdom seized rather than received.

The Hebrew verb for eat, אָכַל (*'akal*), means to internalize, to make part of oneself. When God said, *"You may freely eat,"* He was not giving dietary freedom; He was giving spiritual invitation. He was saying, *"Take My life into yourself. Let My wisdom become your inner substance."* The prohibition against the other tree was not about hunger, but about trust.

Would humanity live by revelation or by self-definition?

The Economy of Rest

Before the fall, Eden operated by what could be called the "Economy of Rest." There was no scarcity, no striving, no sweat. Work existed, but it was not toil. Work was participation in ongoing creation. Adam's labor was worship; his tending was delight. Provision came not from effort but from alignment.

To stretch out the hand toward fruit was to receive what wisdom had already prepared. Every harvest was a reminder that God's voice still sustained the world.

Eden's economy was a system of trust:

- Word produced fruit.
- Fruit sustained life.
- Life returned praise.
- Praise drew presence.

This rhythm was unbroken fellowship, the continual exchange between giving and receiving. That is why Deuteronomy 8:3 later echoes Eden's design:

"Man shall not live by bread alone, but by every word that proceeds from the mouth of God."

Adam and Eve lived by Word-made-fruit: wisdom turned to sweetness. They did not pray for daily bread; they walked among trees that produced it continually. Their rest was not inactivity but unbroken dependence. Eden's prosperity flowed not from effort but from communion. It was a world sustained by His Presence, not performance.

The Choice and the Shift

When the serpent entered, it did not begin by attacking appetite; it attacked perception. *"Has God indeed said…?"* The whisper targeted the *ayin*: the eye, the very letter that began *'ēts*. The temptation was not hunger; it was distortion. Genesis 3:6 says, *"When the woman saw that the tree was good for food…"*

In that moment, the eye turned inward. She saw the same tree differently. The fruit had not changed, but her sight had. She reached for wisdom outside of rest. They ate and their eyes opened, but they saw less. They perceived division where there had been union, shame where there had been reflection.

The *'ēts* that once connected Heaven and earth now marked their separation.

The conduit became a chasm.

Trees as Living Theology in Hebrew Thought

Even after Eden's fracture, the trees never stopped speaking. Throughout Scripture, they keep teaching. The ancient Hebrew sages understood them as living models of divine order rooted in soil.

Every righteous life, every act of covenant faithfulness, could be described as a tree.

"He shall be like a tree planted by streams of water…" Psalms 1:3

The man who delights in God becomes an *'ēts* of stability and fruitfulness, drawing life from a hidden flow.

"She [Wisdom] is a Tree of Life to those who lay hold of her." Proverbs 3:18

In Hebrew imagination, *chokmah* and the Tree of Life are interchangeable, both produce rest through order and abundance through alignment.

"They will be called oaks of righteousness, the planting of the LORD." Isaiah 61:3

The restored people become the new forest of Eden, living reminders that rest and fruitfulness return wherever righteousness takes root.

Even the Hebrew word for righteousness, צֶדֶק (*tsedeq*), shares its root with צ (*tsade*) which is the second Hebrew letter in *'ēts* (trees). To be righteous is to be tree-like: upright, rooted, fruitful, drawing unseen life from a hidden source.

So, when Scripture calls the righteous a "tree," it is not poetic imagery but truth in living form. To live in righteousness is to return to the design of Eden: wisdom rooted below, rest reaching above.

The trees remembered what humanity forgot. They became the quiet witnesses of God's covenants: the wood of vessels, the shade of altars, the branches that stretched across generations. Wherever God renewed His promise, a tree stood nearby.

The Forest of Promise

Even when the garden fell silent and the gate was sealed by flame, God's intent did not wither. What He planted in Eden was eternal; life cannot be unmade, only hidden. Though the first tree stood guarded, its pattern kept echoing through the earth like a memory that refused to die. Every seed, every root, every shadowed grove carried a whisper of the first breath: rest is not lost but waiting.

The world changed, but the rhythm of *chokmah* and *nuach*, wisdom and rest, still pulsed beneath the surface. It moved through seasons, through soil, through silent growth unseen. Wherever the wind of the Spirit moved, trees rose symbols of life holding on, witnesses of a covenant not yet broken.

They reached up from wastelands and deserts, standing as vertical prayers between heaven and earth. Even in chaos, the earth remembered how to grow toward rest. Creation does not forget its original song; it hums it quietly while the world learns to listen again. Somewhere, roots were deepening. Somewhere, sap was moving beneath bark. Somewhere, wisdom was preparing to rise once more; this time through covenant, through mercy, through a vessel built of wood.

The forest waited. Heaven waited. And when the appointed moment came, God spoke again to one man and gave him blueprints made of mercy:

> *"Make for yourself an ark of gopher wood…*
> *and I will establish My covenant with you."*
> *Genesis 6:14*

In that command, the first tree found its echo; wood once rooted in soil would now carry life through judgment. The *'ets* would float above chaos, bearing the seed of a new creation. And when the waters ceased, that vessel of rest would find its mountain, and the pattern would begin again.

Selah Meditation: Listening for the Roots

Close your eyes and step into the quiet between chapters, the silence between Eden's garden and the rising of the waters. This is not an empty space. It is the pause between heartbeat and breath, the thin place where

God rebuilds what has been broken. Let the world around you grow hushed. Let the noise fall away like leaves drifting to the forest floor. Feel the ground beneath you. Though it looks still, everything underneath is moving, roots threading through dark soil, sap rising in hidden veins, life gathering its strength in secret places.

This is how rest begins. Not in the visible, not in the sudden, but in the quiet below, where wisdom works patiently and unseen. Sit inside that stillness. Listen for the subtle shifts: the settling of earth, the faint hum of creation holding its breath.

When you cannot yet see fruit, remember this: forests are not born from branches, but from what happens underground. Let your spirit sink into the deep soil of God's rest, where nothing is rushed or wasted, and everything is becoming.

Remain here for a moment, in the holy calm beneath the surface, where God is already shaping what will one day rise.

Notes:

3
THE ARK
Rest on the Waters

"But I will establish My covenant with you;
and you shall go into the ark…"
Genesis 6:18

The Covenant Before the Rain

The day looked ordinary.

Fields were still worked. Tools still struck soil. Voices still filled the air. From a distance, nothing appeared broken. Life moved forward as it always had. But beneath the surface, something had shifted.

Strength was no longer used to protect but to take. Boundaries were crossed without shame. The vulnerable learned to stay quiet. The earth itself felt heavier, as if it were holding too much blood and too many stories it was never meant to keep.

This was not chaos born overnight. It was order slowly twisted.

Scripture calls it the Hebrew word *ḥamas* (חָמָס). A word that was not just violence but unjust gain. *Hamas* was power bent inward and life extracted rather than given. A corruption of the way things were meant to work. What had once flowed outward in generosity now collapsed inward in grasping.

And Noah lived inside it. He felt the weight of it in the ground beneath his feet, in the silences between neighbors, in the way the air itself seemed to press closer each year. Yet Noah did not join the acceleration. He did not harden. He did not retreat into noise. He walked with God. Quietly. Faithfully. Without spectacle.

His name, *Noach* (rest), stood like a living protest against a world that no longer knew how to slow. While everything around him strained and seized, Noah carried a different rhythm. His life became a pocket of stillness inside a swelling storm.

And it was into a day like this, before clouds gathered, before rain was imaginable, before judgment had a sound, that God gently whispered to Noah.

"I will establish My covenant with you."

The words did not arrive to Noah as threat, but as shelter. Not as response to repentance, but as mercy offered ahead of collapse. The Hebrew verb is *heqim* (הָקִים) means to raise upright, to cause to stand.

While the world bent under *hamas*, God caused rest to stand.

Covenant, *berith*, was not a contract negotiated after failure. It was an enclosure formed beforehand. A space where life could be held while judgment passed over the earth. Before the storm ever touched the horizon, God made room for rest to survive.

Noah did not yet know rain.

But he knew the voice that promised rest would outlast it. That knowing did not stay abstract. It became listening. And listening became form.

Blueprints of Mercy

"Make for yourself an ark of gopher wood; make rooms in the ark and cover it inside and out with pitch." Genesis 6:14

The instruction did not arrive as panic. It came as measured, calm, and deliberate precision. The word for ark, תֵּבָה (*tevah*), in Hebrew means container, chest, vessel for life. It is the same word later used for the basket that carried infant Moses across another flood. Every *tevah* in Scripture is a womb of deliverance; a small, sealed world where life is held while chaos passes over.

God gave Noah exact dimensions: three decks, one window, one door. Not because God measures by inches, but because rest begins with order. Wisdom (*chokmah*) sketches the framework so *nuach* (rest) can dwell inside it. The ark's blueprints echo Genesis 1 itself: boundaries, divisions, and structure were the architecture through which Eden first took form.

The Ribs of Mercy

The ark was made of trees; the same *ʿētsim* (trees) that once stood in Eden's light. Now they lay flat, humbled, their strength offered for another purpose. They became ribs, curving around life, holding breath in a world that could no longer breathe.

From Adam's side, God drew a bride. From the ark's side, He would draw a new creation. Both were shaped by His hands while the world slept; both were built as resting places for life.

Its pitch-covered planks glistened like skin anointed with oil, a body set apart for covenant. The word cover, כָּפַר (*kaphar*), later becomes atonement. Even the tar between the boards reflected grace: Covered within, covered without was mercy sealing every seam.

The ark's wooden ribs curved like a human chest, enclosing the breath of creation: the body of Adam reborn.

Waters Before Creation

When the fountains of the deep broke open and the heavens poured forth, the world returned to *tohu vabohu* (formless and void). Yet the Spirit hovered again, not to destroy but to re-create. The ark drifted between worlds, suspended between heaven's grief and earth's hope. Inside its ribs, creation slept in covenant; outside, creation groaned for rebirth.

This is what divine rest feels like in the dark: no steering, no striving, only surrender to the wind of God.

The Sabbath of Waiting

Forty days, then months more, Noah could not see what God was doing beneath the waters. He could only trust that wisdom was carving mountains in secret. Every creak of timber, every hush between waves became a liturgy of stillness and a worship service of waiting. The ark rocked like a heartbeat.

Noah rested because there was nowhere else to stand. This was Sabbath not as a day but as a dimension; the stillness that exists when nothing can be controlled. Inside, the family tended to life; outside, life was being remade. The covenant was a seed asleep in wood and water.

The Hidden Work of Wisdom

Time passed, measured only by waves. Under the flood, wisdom sculpted the new earth. Currents shifted; boundaries formed. The same Spirit who once hovered over the face of the waters still breathed beneath the surface. What was chaos began to take shape again.

Noah could not see it. He only felt the quiet weight of waiting; the hush between promise and fulfillment, the unseen labor of *chokmah* beneath the surface of *nuach*. It was the silence before the world exhaled.

The Ark and the First Adam

The ark was more than a vessel; it was a mirror of Adam: a body formed to cradle breath. Both came from the dust and the trees of the earth; both were sealed by the Spirit's breath; both carried every kind of living thing within. When Adam fell, the ground bore his weight and creation shared his ache.

Through Noah, God reshaped that same pattern: a body of earth and wood, closed by divine hands, carrying the promise that life would not end in dust. When the ark came to rest on Ararat, it was as if the body of Adam finally found its altar. The world that had fallen in a garden now turned on a mountain.

The breath that once brought death through disobedience now brought life through surrender.

Where the first Adam's rest was broken, God allowed the second Adam's image, Noah, the man of rest to lie still until mercy touched ground again.

Ararat became a threshold: the place where the memory of Eden met the mercy of renewal. The ark, like Adam, opened its side so that a new creation could walk into light.

Ararat: The Mountain of Reversal and Covenant

"Then the ark rested … upon the mountains of Ararat." Genesis 8:4

The Hebrew name *Ararat* means high place but carries in its root the sense of reversal (*arar*, to reverse a curse). This mountain was more than geography; it was theology in stone. Here, every element of judgment began to turn backward; the curse reversed, the flood undone, the world rising again from water as it had once risen from dust.

Death below, life above. Silence below, song above. Chaos underneath, wisdom resting over it.

This is the heartbeat of divine rest: it inverts what the world calls final.

The Mathematics of Mercy

*"And in the seventh month, on the seventeenth day of the month,
the ark rested upon the mountains of Ararat." Genesis 8:4*

*"And the waters decreased continually until the tenth month...
In the tenth month, on the first day of the month,
the tops of the mountains were seen." Genesis 8:5*

Between those two verses lies a span of seventy-three days: the hidden distance between resting and revealing. For seventy-three days the ark remained sealed while the waters obeyed wisdom's unseen command. Beneath the surface, creation was being remade in silence.

Even the numbers speak the same language of reversal in Hebrew:

- Seven (שֶׁבַע/*sheva*), completion, covenant, the rhythm of creation fulfilled.
- Seventeen (שבע עשר/*sheva-asar*), victory and restoration after loss.
- Seventy-three (ע"ג/*shiv'im v'shalosh*), the very same numeric value as חָכְמָה (*chokmah*/wisdom). Wisdom is the architect beneath rest.

The seventy-three days between Genesis 8:4 and 8:5 are not random, but the mirror of Genesis 1, the mathematics of mercy.

In creation, God formed order out of chaos; on *Ararat*, He reversed the chaos back into order. The pattern unfolds like a reflection:

- In Genesis, land rose from water.
- In the flood, water covered land.
- On *Ararat*, land rose again, this time under covenant.

Everything is restored, but inside-out, like the turning of a great mirror. Wisdom working backward through judgment, unwinding the curse until it ends in rest. So, the numbers speak the same truth as the mountain and the man:

Rest (*Noach*) lifted; Wisdom (*Chokmah*) revealed; Covenant (*Berith*) renewed.

This is creation replayed in reverse, the melody of Eden sung backward until it becomes whole again.

The Covenant of Stillness

When the ark touched ground, Noah did not rush out. He waited for the voice of the Lord; the same Spirit who had hovered over the waters now hovered over his obedience. That waiting was the covenant's test: *Can you rest even when the ground is beneath you?*

Then came the sending, first a raven, then a dove. The raven never returned; the dove did, carrying an olive leaf. That small leaf was the signature of peace, a covenant written in green.

The Hebrew word for dove, יוֹנָה (*yonah*), sounds like *nuach* which is Hebrew for rest. It was rest returning home, carrying the first leaf from the new Eden.

God looked upon that trust and sealed His promise with a bow of light. Never again would the waters cover the earth. Never again would rest need a vessel of wood to survive.

The First Altar: The Fragrance of Rest

When Noah stepped onto the new earth, his first act was not to build a house but an altar. No command had been given but his worship was instinct. The first man of rest answered covenant with thanksgiving.

And Scripture says, *"Then Noah built an altar to the LORD … and the LORD smelled a pleasing aroma." Genesis 8:20–21*

The Hebrew phrase "pleasing aroma" is רֵיחַ נִיחוֹחַ (*reiyaḥ niḥoaḥ*) and means the fragrance of rest. The same Hebrew root as *nuach*. The altar breathed, and God breathed in. It was the first time since Eden that heaven and earth shared the same air again.

Here, the curse began to reverse not by labor or sweat but by fragrance and surrender. The altar became the garden reborn, a place where life rose to meet the breath of God.

This was the first Sabbath offering: no law, no priesthood, no sacrifice demanded, only gratitude given. Rest, not fear, burned on that altar.

The Bow of Covenant: Warfare Turned to Wonder

Then the sky answered. *"I set My bow in the clouds, and it shall be a sign of the covenant between Me and the earth." Genesis 9:13*

The Hebrew word for bow is קֶשֶׁת (*qeshet*), the same word used for a warrior's weapon. When God placed His *qeshet* in the clouds, He was hanging up His bow or laying down His weapon. Judgment was over; mercy was enthroned.

The arc of color bent across the heavens like a bridge between worlds, a weapon turned to witness, warfare transformed into wonder.

Light itself became the language of rest: a spectrum of peace refracted through passing storm. The rainbow was not decoration; it was declaration. Every hue shimmered with covenant: Never again. The Creator who once divided light from darkness now fused them into color, turning wrath into radiance.

Noah's Offering: The First Sabbath

That altar smoke was the first true Sabbath act since creation. Sabbath is not idleness, but alignment that flows from rest, because the work is finished.

When Noah worshiped, he joined God's own rhythm again. The flood had erased the marks of toil; the ground beneath him was clean. The curse on the soil, *"Cursed is the ground for your sake,"* was now carried through water and washed in covenant.

From that day forward, humanity would till soil that had been baptized. Noah's altar was Eden renewed, not by fruit but by fire. The same ground that once resisted now released fragrance. Creation exhaled and God called it good again.

Generations of Rest

God blessed Noah and his sons and said,
"Be fruitful and multiply, and fill the earth." Genesis 9:1

The same words once spoken to Adam were spoken again. The covenant was generational; rest was meant to multiply. Every covenant that would follow with Abraham, with Israel, with David, and finally in Messiah would carry this same pattern: rest first, then fruitfulness.

From this mountain, all others would echo. Each altar, each temple, each cross would repeat the same rhythm: chaos stilled, covenant spoken, creation renewed. The bow, the altar, the fragrance, the blessing; each a note in the same song: wisdom rebuilding through rest.

Reflection: Wisdom in Rest

The ark teaches us that surrender is not the end of creation; it is where new creation begins.

Every time God begins again, He does so from a resting place: a womb, a promise, a covenant enclosed in mercy.

Rest is never passive in Scripture. It is purposeful containment. It is wisdom at work beneath the surface, shaping what will rise when the waters recede.

"And in the seventh month, on the seventeenth day of the month,

the ark rested upon the mountains of Ararat." Genesis 8:4

Before the world reemerged, rest came first.

Selah Meditation: Held Within Rest

Pause here. Know that you are held. Outside, things may still be moving. Inside, nothing needs to. There is space to breathe. There is room to rest your weight. Life is steady here.

You do not have to see where you are going. You do not have to make sense of the noise. You are already carried by Him. Let your shoulders soften. Let your breath find its own rhythm. Stay here for a moment longer than feels efficient. This is not escape. This is shelter.

Life is calm here. And you are not alone.

Notes:

_____

_____

_____

_____

_____

_____

_____

_____

_____

_____

_____

_____

_____

_____

_____

_____

_____

_____

4

ABRAHAM

The Covenant of Promise and Rest

**"Now the LORD had said to Abram:
'Get out of your country, from your family
and from your father's house,
to a land that I will show you.'"
Genesis 12:1**

The Night of Calling

It was quiet in Ur that night, but not silent.

Somewhere above the hum of idols and the firelight of human worship, another flame flickered: a whisper older than creation itself.

It spoke a name.

Not loudly, not with thunder, but with certainty that cut through the noise: *"Abram."*

He had known the stories of the garden, of the flood, of a God who walked with men and then hid Himself among stars. But that night, the distance between heaven and earth thinned. A voice moved through the stillness and said, *"Go. Leave what you have known. Walk toward what I will show you."*

No map. No guarantee. Only rest disguised as risk.

The stars shimmered like unspoken promises, a silent blueprint of something vast. And in the stillness of his tent, Abram felt the same pulse that moved over the waters in the beginning. It was not command that called him out, but covenant in seed form. A whisper that said, *"Rest does not end at stillness, it moves by trust."*

The Call to Leave: Rest in Motion

When God said, *"Go,"* it was not an eviction; it was an invitation. The Hebrew phrase *lekh lekha* (לֶךְ־לְךָ) means *"go to yourself,"* or *"go into your becoming."* This was not simply a geographical journey but a spiritual return.

Abraham was being called back into the pattern of *chokmah* and *nuach*, wisdom and rest, this time expressed as faith. To leave one's country, kindred, and father's house was to lay down every structure of human security. God was restoring Eden's rhythm in motion: walk with Me in trust.

In the garden, Adam lost rest by reaching for control. In the wilderness, Abraham found rest by releasing control. Rest was not a destination; it was obedience without striving. Faith was how wisdom now moved.

Lekh Lekha: The Journey into Becoming

When God spoke *lekh lekha*, the sound itself carried a mystery. In Hebrew, the words mean *"Go to yourself,"* or more literally, *"Go for your own essence."*

God was not sending Abram away; He was summoning him inward, into the part of him that had been waiting since Eden to walk again with the Creator in the garden. Rest always begins with return. Not to a place, but to the original design.

Abram's obedience was not merely a relocation; it was a restoration. The same breath that formed Adam in the garden now stirred Abram's soul in the wilderness. Every step was a heartbeat of wisdom drawing him closer to who he already was but had not yet become.

This is the paradox of divine rest: *You move not to strive, but to remember.* You go forward to come home. And as Abram walked, heaven began to whisper his future into his name. *Abram* (אַבְרָם) means *"exalted father."* It was a title of potential, a promise in waiting.

In *lekh lekha*, the journey inward becomes the birthplace of multiplication. Rest expands through revelation: the more you walk in trust, the more your true name is unveiled.

The Tent and the Altar: Rest Between Stones and Stars

Everywhere Abraham went, he pitched a tent and built an altar. A temporary dwelling and a permanent testimony. The tent said, I am passing through. The altar said, God is here. He carried no throne, no walls, no monument: only rest wrapped in obedience.

The Hebrew word for tent, אֹהֶל (*ohel*), comes from a root meaning to shine faintly, to glimmer. Even the word carried starlight. It was as if every tent he raised echoed heaven's canopy, a human reflection of divine dwelling.

And at each altar, he called on the name of God; the same voice that had once called him out of Ur. These altars became resting places for revelation, markers in the landscape of faith. Each one whispered the same rhythm: *"Rest first, then promise unfolds."*

The Land and the Dust: The Reversal of the Curse

When God brought Abram into the land, He did not hand him gold or stone; He gave him dust.

> *"Lift up your eyes and look from the place where you are...*
> *for all the land which you see I will give to you and to your seed forever.*
> *And I will make your seed as the dust of the earth." Genesis 13:14–16*

It is no accident that God chose the dust. Dust was the first material He ever touched, the first canvas for His breath. It was also the first thing cursed: *"Cursed is the ground for your sake."*

In Adam, dust became a reminder of failure. In Abraham, dust became a measure of promise. The same ground that once bore the sentence of toil now carried the blessing of rest. God was not merely giving Abraham a region of soil; He was redeeming the very element that had groaned since Eden.

The earth itself was being anointed with purpose. Every step Abraham took pressed covenant into the ground. His footprints turned curse to blessing. His journey traced the outline of Eden restored not enclosed behind gates but spread wide beneath stars.

The promise, *"I will make your seed as the dust of the earth,"* was not about number alone; it was about substance. His offspring would carry the same material as creation's beginning, divine breath moving through redeemed dust.

Rest, once lost to sweat, now multiplied through faith. The dust would no longer remind man of death but of inheritance.

Even the land itself began to rest under Abraham's obedience, waiting for the day when the seed of that same covenant would breathe again over its soil.

The Stars and the Sand: The Multiplication of Rest

Night fell on the desert, and silence stretched wider than the horizon. Abram stood outside his tent, dust still clinging to his feet. He looked up, and for the first time since leaving Ur, the voice came again gentle, almost smiling.

"Look now toward heaven, and count the stars if you are able to number them."
"So shall your seed be." Genesis 15:5

The *Hebrew* word for star is כּוֹכָב (*kokhav*), from a root that means to blaze, to roll like a sphere. Every star was a wheel of light, a spark of the same wisdom that had first ordered the cosmos. When God told Abram to count them, He was not testing his arithmetic; He was teaching him how to see the infinite through the finite and how to rest his eyes on what could not be held.

Abram's heart steadied.

The same Voice that once said, *"Let there be light"* was now saying, *"Let there be faith."* And the Scripture says, *"Abram believed the LORD, and it was counted to him for righteousness." Genesis 15:6*

The Hebrew word for believed, הֶאֱמִן (*he'emin*), is built on the root אָמַן (*aman*) and means to support, to make firm, to rest one's weight. Faith, in the Hebrew sense, is not mental agreement; it is leaning the full weight of yourself on the character of God. Abraham's belief was not striving but rest embodied. He looked down at the sand; the same dust God had blessed.

In Hebrew, sand is חוֹל (*chol*), from a root that also means to dance, to whirl, to move in rhythm. Heaven and earth were now speaking the same language: the stars rolled in their courses; the grains swirled beneath his feet. Two witnesses, light and dust, joined to testify that rest would multiply.

When God said, *"Your seed shall be as the stars of heaven and as the sand on the seashore,"* He was not contrasting two realms but marrying them. Heaven's fire and earth's clay, wisdom and rest, would unite in one lineage. The covenant was cosmic: a bridge between the invisible and the tangible.

Abraham stood between both, a living connection, dust beneath, stars above, and a promise within. The night became a cathedral, the galaxies a canopy of covenant. He did not need to see the land fulfilled; he was the fulfillment standing in seed form. Faith had turned the wilderness into sanctuary.

From that night onward, the rhythm of heaven and earth pulsed through his walk. Every footstep pressed promise into soil, every glance upward rehearsed eternity. The stars became his ceiling of rest, the sand his floor of faith. Between them, he learned to dwell in peace.

The Cutting of the Covenant: God Walks Alone

"And when the sun was going down, a deep sleep fell upon Abram; and, behold, horror and great darkness fell upon him." Genesis 15:12

The Hebrew word for deep sleep is תַּרְדֵּמָה (*tardemah*) and is the same word used in Genesis 2 when God caused a deep sleep to fall upon Adam. It is not the sleep of exhaustion, but of holy suspension; the moment when human striving ceases so divine creation can begin.

In Eden, God drew woman from Adam's side. In Hebron's field, God would draw a nation from Abram's rest. Both acts began with stillness, and both needed trust beyond sight.

God had told Abram, *"Bring Me a heifer, a goat, a ram, a turtledove, and a pigeon."* He divided them and laid them opposite each other, and as darkness fell, Abram waited.

It was an ancient covenant that was cut rather than signed. Normally, two parties would walk between the pieces together, each pledging: If I break this covenant, let me be as these.

But this night, Abram was not invited to walk. He was invited to rest.

While Abram slept, God Himself passed through a smoking furnace and a flaming torch moving between the halves. Fire and smoke: the same elements that would later rest on Sinai and in Solomon's temple. The covenant's Author walked alone.

"On that day the LORD made a covenant with Abram." Genesis 15:18

The Hebrew word made is כָּרַת (*karath*), means to cut. But something deeper happened: God did not just cut a covenant, He carved a promise into rest.

In that moment, the story of Adam found its mirror image. Where the first man slept and awoke to see life drawn from his side, Abram slept and awoke to see life drawn from his lineage. Both moments birthed relationship through rest.

This is the divine pattern of creation and covenant alike: God works while man rests. Wisdom builds: rest receives. In Eden, He formed a bride. In Hebron, He formed a people.

Both were the fruit of *tardemah*, holy rest that opens the way for new creation. And when Abram awoke, he carried more than a promise, he carried presence. The same fire that walked between the pieces would one day dwell in the tabernacle, and later, in hearts that trust as he trusted.

The Name and the Breath: The Covenant Sealed in Rest

"Neither shall your name anymore be called Abram, but your name shall be Abraham; for a father of many nations have I made you." Genesis 17:5

When God spoke, the wind shifted.

The same breath that hovered over the waters in the beginning, the same breath that once entered Adam's nostrils, now entered a man's name. *Abram* (אַבְרָם) meant *"exalted father"*: a title carrying promise, but not yet fulfillment.

Then God spoke again.

He did not discard the name; He completed it. He placed a single letter within it: ה (*hey*).

Abram became *Abraham* (אַבְרָהָם).

That letter, *hey*, is breath. It is the sound released from God's own Name, YHWH (יהוה). When God placed it into Abraham's name, He did not merely rename him. He breathed Himself into him. Identity was no longer something Abram carried; it became something God inhabited. An *"exalted father"* became a *"father of many nations,"* not by effort, but by inhalation.

This was not a change of calling. It was the fulfillment of one.

God did not alter who Abram was. He added His own breath to Abram's frame. Grace quietly and irrevocably entered the name the way breath enters lungs.

The same breath was given to Sarai.

Sarai (שָׂרַי), meaning "my princess," in Hebrew was renamed *Sarah* (שָׂרָה), "princess to nations." The promise expanded, not because of striving, but because God placed His breath within her identity as well. Together, Abraham and Sarah became a living testimony of what happens when divine breath meets human obedience.

A private promise became a public inheritance.

When the Hebrew letter *hey* entered their names, rest entered their destiny. They no longer wandered but began to carry covenant in their very sound. Eternity began to breathe through time, heaven resting within flesh.

Even the shape of the letter *hey* tells the story. It is formed like an open window (ה), an opening through which breath passes freely. In Hebrew thought, *hey* carries the sound of breath itself, the moment His presence moves from hidden to heard. When God breathed it into their names, He opened a window between heaven and earth.

Wisdom found her doorway again.

And rest became the place where promise could finally live.

Just as Adam had received breath in the garden, and Noah had received covenant on the waters, Abraham now received both breath and covenant united. He became the living bridge between creation and promise, the one through whom all nations would rediscover what rest truly meant: trust that breathes even in waiting.

In that moment, Abraham and Sarah stood as the new Adam and Eve, not in a garden of fruit, but in a wilderness of faith. Rest was reborn not through perfection but through belief. And the Spirit marked them with His breath as the first couple of the new creation story.

The Promise and the Laughter: Isaac, the Child of Rest

"I will bless her, and she shall be a mother of nations; kings of peoples shall be from her. Then Abraham fell upon his face, and laughed." Genesis 17:16–17

There, in the sand and starlight, the covenant came full circle. Abraham had learned to trust through silence and waiting. Now God announced the impossible: Sarah who was barren, aged, long past striving would carry life.

Abraham's laughter was not disbelief; it was release. Decades of wondering folded into a single exhale. It was the sound of rest finally realizing what faith had been holding all along. Later, Sarah laughed too, first in disbelief, then in delight. *"God has made me to laugh, so that all who hear will laugh with me." Genesis 21:6*

Their son's name, Isaac יִצְחָק (*Yitshaq*), in Hebrew means "he laughs." But its root, צָחַק (*tsahaq*), also carries the idea of radiant joy, of shining. It is laughter that illuminates and the reflection of divine delight in human time. Isaac was not just a child; he was the echo of Eden's joy, the sound of wisdom and rest rejoicing together again. His birth proved that covenant rest produces what striving never could. He was grace made visible, laughter wrapped in promise.

Abraham and Sarah had attempted to secure the promise by their own means once before. Ishmael was the result, a work shaped by effort

29

rather than rest. But God waited until all self-effort had died, until the womb was as barren as the ground before creation. Only then did He breathe again and say, *"At the appointed time, I will return to you, and Sarah shall have a son." Genesis 18:14*

The appointed time in Hebrew, מוֹעֵד (*mo'ed*), means a set feast, a divine appointment. Rest has its own calendar. It does not rush; it fulfills. And when the season of wisdom's timing arrived, the promise moved from word to flesh, from unseen to seen.

In Isaac's laughter, all of creation heard a familiar song. It was the sound of the Creator's delight when He first called the world *"good"* and the exhale of the Spirit after the storm had passed. Eden's joy had returned in a child's cry.

From Faith to Inheritance

When the laughter of promise echoed through Abraham's tent, heaven smiled. Faith had done its work; rest had taken root. The covenant that began with a whisper beneath the stars now had a heartbeat. Isaac was the first child born not of striving but of spoken rest; the visible proof that wisdom builds what surrender believes.

Where Abraham's story was movement, Isaac's would be stillness. Where Abraham followed a Voice into the unknown, Isaac would dwell in the land of promise and learn how to live from what grace had already given. If Abraham's faith opened the door, Isaac's life would teach the rhythm of staying within it.

He would inherit not only land and covenant, but the posture that sustains them both: quiet trust.

The story of rest was not finished; it was multiplying. The same breath that renamed Abraham now hovered over his son, waiting to be recognized. And in Isaac, the child of laughter, rest would take on a gentler sound: not the storm stilled, but the peace that remains after.

Selah Meditation: The Sound of Rest

Let your shoulders soften. Let the noise of your day settle. You do not need to solve anything here.

Abraham's story is not asking you to strive harder but inviting you to stop measuring what feels impossible. Notice where you have been holding your breath. Notice where you have been trying to make a promise happen instead of letting it unfold.

God does not rush fulfillment. He breathes it.

Sit with the sound of quiet laughter; the laughter that comes when control loosens and trust begins to rise.

This is what rest feels like: not empty stillness, but a gentle widening inside your chest where hope lives again.

You are not late. You are not behind. You are not forgotten. Let yourself rest in that knowing.

When you are ready, carry this with you: *God is still faithful while you are still becoming. And rest is not the pause before life begins; it is the place where new life is formed.* Remain here for a moment.

Breathe.

Notes:

5

ISAAC

The Laughter of Promise

**"And the LORD visited Sarah as He had said,
and the LORD did for Sarah as He had spoken.
For Sarah conceived and bore Abraham a son in his old age,
at the set time of which God had spoken to him."
Genesis 21:1–2**

The Child of Timing

The morning was quiet when Isaac's first cry broke the silence. It was not the cry of struggle, but of promise fulfilled. The tent filled with light that felt older than the sun itself, as though the laughter of Abraham and Sarah had gathered form and breathed. Isaac's birth did not come early or late; it came at the set time.

The Hebrew phrase, כָּעֵת הַזֹּאת (*ka-'et ha-zot*), means the appointed moment, the precise intersection of heaven's intention and earth's readiness. When wisdom completes her work, grace enters quietly. Sarah looked at the child and said, *"God has made me to laugh, so that all who hear will laugh with me."* And she called his name יִצְחָק (*Yitshaq*), which means "he laughs" in Hebrew.

In him, joy itself was sanctified. Laughter, once the sound of disbelief, became the sound of divine delight. Rest had taken human form: a baby sleeping in the arms of a woman who had once called herself barren.

The covenant had moved from promise to presence, from the realm of words to the rhythm of breath. Isaac's very existence carried the gospel of grace before the word was ever written; what flesh cannot achieve, rest welcomes.

Growing Beneath the Shadow of Promise

Isaac grew beneath the shadow of altars. Each stone Abraham had stacked still whispered of fire and surrender, but Isaac's life began not with sacrifice, but with security. He was the first child raised under a completed covenant; a son born into a world where rest had already been established. Abraham had carried faith through wilderness and waiting. Isaac carried faith through inheritance. He did not have to discover the covenant; he had to dwell in it.

And this is the deeper rhythm of rest: when faith stops building and starts abiding. Isaac's story is quieter because rest does not shout. He was the only patriarch who never left the promised land.

Even in famine, God told him, *"Do not go down to Egypt; dwell in the land which I shall tell you of." Genesis 26:2*

And Isaac obeyed. He stayed. He sowed in that land and reaped a hundredfold.

Where Abraham's journey began with *"Go,"* Isaac's calling began with *"Stay."* Both were obedience, but of different tempos. Abraham's was the obedience of movement; Isaac's, the obedience of maintenance, the stillness that guards what faith has already built.

The Wells of Rest

Isaac's greatest conflicts were not with armies or kings but with wells. Genesis says the Philistines stopped them, filling them with earth. Every well his father had dug was buried by envy. So, Isaac dug them again.

In Hebrew, the word for well is בְּאֵר (*be'er*), meaning to make clear, to explain, to reveal depth. Wells are symbols of revelation and the unveiling of what lies beneath the surface. Each time Isaac re-dug a well, he was re-opening the flow of what Abraham's faith had uncovered. He refused to strive for what was already his; he simply returned to what had been buried.

The first well he named *Esek* and means contention.

The second well was named *Sitnah*; Hebrew for opposition.

But the third he named *Rehoboth*, saying, *"For now the LORD has made room for us, and we shall be fruitful in the land." Genesis 26:22*

Rehoboth (רְחֹבוֹת) means spaciousness, wide places. It is the landscape of rest, the opposite of constriction. After the strife, came the space. After the digging, came the flow. Isaac did not conquer; he persisted in peace. He turned the labor of the ground into the joy of water.

The wells of Isaac became the pattern of every generation that would follow when the enemy buries the flow, rest does not fight but uncovers.

Wisdom does not strive; it re-opens.

Step Inside: Abimelech, Borrowed Authority

In Isaac's story, names carry weight. Abimelech (אֲבִימֶלֶךְ) is no exception.

The name is formed from two Hebrew words: *av* (אָב) which means father and *melech* (מֶלֶךְ) which means king. Abimelech means: "My father is king."

At first glance, it sounds like a strong, established, and legitimate name. But in Scripture, Abimelech consistently represents a borrowed authority: power rooted in position rather than promise, rule inherited through systems rather than intimacy.

This matters deeply in Isaac's account. Isaac does not arrive in Gerar as a conqueror or innovator. He comes as an heir. He is not digging new wells; he is reopening ancient ones, wells his father Abraham dug, wells that already carried covenant memory. Scripture says the Philistines had filled them with earth after Abraham's death (Genesis 26:15).

Gerar was a land of sojourners, fertile yet contested. A place where water existed beneath the surface, but inheritance was never secure. Isaac's fruitfulness there revealed the tension between promise and possession, and why rest must sometimes keep moving until it finds a place willing to receive it.

Earth buried water. This is not accidental imagery.

Water in Scripture speaks of life, Spirit, blessing, flow. Earth speaks of control, resistance, and containment. When Abimelech's people fill the wells, they are not merely claiming land; they are obstructing inheritance.

Abimelech's name, "my father is king," reveals the tension beneath the conflict. His authority is real, but it is not relational. It is political, generational, structural. Isaac's authority, however, flows from covenant. It does not dominate; it wells up.

This is why Isaac does not fight. He moves.

Each time a well is buried, Isaac re-digs. Each time it is contested, he names it and moves again. Striving never secures inheritance. Rest does.

Eventually, Isaac digs a well no one disputes. He names it *Rehoboth* "wide places." Not because the opposition disappeared, but because space opens naturally when inheritance is honored.

Only then does Abimelech come to Isaac, not to contend, but to make peace.

This is the quiet truth beneath the story: Borrowed authority eventually recognizes covenant rest. Systems that bury wells cannot sustain life. But those who carry inheritance will always find water again.

Isaac's wells could be filled with earth but not erased. Because what flows from promise cannot be permanently buried.

Beersheba: The Well of Seven, the Covenant of Witness

"And he said, "You will take these seven ewe lambs from my hand, that they may be my witness that I have dug this well." Therefore he called that place Beersheba, because the two of them swore an oath there." Genesis 21:30-31

The Hebrew name *Be'er Sheva* (בְּאֵר שָׁבַע) holds two meanings at once:
- The Well of Seven
- The Well of the Oath

Both are true and both reveal heaven's pattern hidden in plain sight.

When Abraham and Abimelech made peace at that well, it was not a treaty of convenience but a prophetic act. Seven ewe lambs, gentle, spotless, peaceful creatures, became living symbols of covenant rest. No war spoils, no weapons, no altar of blood, only seven lambs beside a well of water.

In Scripture, seven (שָׁבַע / *sheva*) is the number of completion, fullness, and Sabbath. It carries the sound of *shalom* made tangible. It is no accident that *sheva* shares its Hebrew root with *shavah* (שָׁבַע), to swear an oath. To swear covenant and to rest are, in Hebrew thought, inseparable realities.

To "*seven oneself*" is literally to enter covenant rest.

Thus, Beersheba is more than a boundary line; it is a revelation in physical form:
- Peace sealed by rest.
- Rest witnessed by water.
- Covenant marked by seven lambs of grace.

The number, the creatures, the water: each carries the memory of

Eden. In the beginning, creation was crowned by the seventh day; the day God rested.

At Beersheba, creation's rhythm repeats through covenant: Seven lambs beside a well declare that the ground can hold peace again. Abraham's well had been contended for. The servants of Abimelech had seized it; the flow had been blocked. But when covenant was spoken and the lambs were set apart, water became the witness. The earth yielded again. The well reopened.

It was as if the deep beneath recognized the sound of oath and responded, just as the waters of creation had once answered God's Word. The Spirit that hovered in Genesis 1 hovered again over Beersheba's waters, this time not to form the world, but to restore its rest.

When Isaac later returned to this same place and God appeared to him, the cycle completed itself: *"Fear not, for I am with you... and I will bless you." And there, Isaac built an altar, pitched his tent, and dug again the well. (Genesis 26:23–25)*

Abraham's covenant had left an imprint on the land; Isaac's obedience reopened its flow. The seven ewe lambs had spoken once, but the water kept speaking, testifying generation after generation that the Spirit's covenant of rest was still alive beneath the soil.

The Revelation of Beersheba

Beersheba is where the ground itself learned to keep covenant. In Eden, the curse had fallen on the ground *"for Adam's sake."* At Beersheba, grace flowed through it again, for Abraham's sake. The first garden lost its peace; this well recovered it. Water rose, lambs stood, covenant was sworn. Heaven, earth, and man were momentarily aligned again.

It was a foreshadowing of the greater Lamb and the living water to come, but it was already a restoration in miniature: the sound of Eden breathing again beneath desert sand. Beersheba was, in every sense, the first Sabbath well.

A resting place for God's promise, a witness in the land that the curse was being undone, one oath, one flow, and one covenant at a time.

The Blessing and the Continuation: Rest Passed Down

"And Isaac called Jacob, and blessed him, and charged him...
"May God Almighty bless you, and make you fruitful and multiply you,
That you may be an assembly of peoples.'" Genesis 28:1,3

The story of rest is always generational. It never ends with the one who receives it; it multiplies through the one who believes it. The covenant at Beersheba, the well of seven lambs, the oath of peace, was not meant to remain a monument; it was meant to become an inheritance. Isaac, whose hands had dug wells and whose life had flowed in quiet obedience, now laid those same hands upon his son.

The same Spirit that had hovered over the waters of creation, the same breath that filled Abraham's tent with laughter, now moved again in blessing. The God of Abraham had become the God of Isaac and soon, He would reveal Himself as the God of Jacob. This progression is not hierarchy; it is continuity.

Each generation receives the same rest in a new form. Abraham taught the world that rest begins by believing. Isaac taught that rest continues by dwelling. Jacob will teach that rest is recovered through surrender. Isaac's blessing was not a ritual; it was a transfer of rhythm. He was handing down the cadence of covenant, the pulse that beats beneath every act of trust.

And this is what the wells had been teaching all along: that rest is not found once but reopened again and again. Each generation must uncover its flow. Each must learn that wisdom still builds beneath the surface, and that when the ground is opened in peace, water always rises.

Isaac's story ends not with conquest, but with continuity. His greatest legacy is not what he built, but what he kept flowing. The covenant remained alive in him like an underground spring, and when he blessed Jacob, he simply pointed downstream.

The wells of Abraham had become the wells of Isaac, and soon, the God of Isaac would become the God of Jacob. Rest would keep traveling through bloodlines and nations until it found its final dwelling in a heart, not a land.

Selah Meditation: Uncovering the Hidden Well

Pause in this moment. Notice the weight of your body, the way you are already being held by the Holy Spirit. He is present.

Reflect for a moment in how Isaac did not go looking for water. He stayed long enough for the ground to give it back.

As you breath, allow your breath to relax. Not upward into the busy thoughts of your mind, but downward into the center of your being, into the place where patience lives.

There is a well inside of you. It is not dramatic. It does not rush to the surface.

It waits in silence, gathering itself.

You do not need to dig for it. It has always been present deep within. You only need to stop moving long enough for what is already there to be uncovered.

Stay here in this place for a moment.

Let the noise settle around you like dust. Allow the soil inside you to soften. Trust that what God placed within you has not dried up.

The water knows when it is safe to rise.

Notes:

_____

_____

_____

_____

_____

_____

_____

_____

_____

_____

_____

_____

_____

_____

_____

_____

_____

_____

_____

_____

_____

_____

_____

6
JACOB
The Wrestle and the Rest

**"And Jacob was left alone;
and there wrestled a man with him
until the breaking of the day."
Genesis 32:24**

The Night of Striving

The river ran dark beneath the moonlight. On one side lay everything Jacob had built; on the other, everything he feared to face. He had sent his family and possessions ahead, and now, at the edge of the *Jabbok*, he stood stripped of strategy. The man who had always grasped now had nothing left to hold. He had lived by cleverness, by calculation, by his own will. He had outmaneuvered his brother, outlasted his uncle, and outtalked almost everyone in between.

But the blessing he sought, the one promised to Abraham and Isaac, remained just beyond reach, because it could not be taken by striving. It could only be received by rest. And so, in the silence before dawn, the One who had chosen him came close.

The God Who Wrestles

Scripture says, *"a man wrestled with him until the breaking of the day."* The Hebrew word for wrestle is אָבַק (*'abaq*), from a root meaning to entwine, to cling like dust. It is the same word-picture as soil stirred into movement, a man made of dust caught up in the touch of the divine. All night they struggled, Jacob refusing to let go, not knowing that the One he fought was the only One who could make him whole.

This was not punishment; it was mercy. God does not wrestle to win, He wrestles to weaken what resists grace. At last, the stranger touched the hollow of Jacob's thigh, and his strength gave way.

In the moment of collapse, striving ended. Jacob's limp became his revelation. What he could not yield by will, he would now carry as reminder: rest begins where self-reliance ends.

The dust rose around them like a cloud of remembrance: an echo of Eden, an echo of the ground once cursed. But here, that dust became holy, a testimony that even the soil of struggle can host blessing. Then came the Voice:

"Let Me go, for the day breaks."
And Jacob answered,
"I will not let You go unless You bless me."
Genesis 32:26

The Name Exchange

The blessing Jacob demanded was not a gift but an unveiling. God asked, *"What is your name?" And Jacob said, "Jacob."* (יַעֲקֹב / *Ya'akov*) in Hebrew means the one who grasps, the supplanter. (Genesis 32:27)

Then the Man replied, *"Your name shall no longer be Jacob, but Israel* (יִשְׂרָאֵל), *for you have wrestled with God and with men, and have prevailed."* *(Genesis 32:28)*

The Hebrew name *Israel* means God prevails. It is not the triumph of flesh, but of grace. In that single exchange, the story of mankind shifted: Adam reached for divinity and fell; Jacob clung to divinity and was lifted.

The fight was never about dominance but identity. Jacob thought he was wrestling for a blessing, but heaven was wrestling to reveal one. The grip of fear became the grasp of faith. The man who once stole blessings now received one he could never earn.

Peniel: The Face of God and the Dawn of Rest

The dust of Jabbok hung in the air like incense, shimmering in the half-light of dawn. Jacob could still feel the hand that had touched him, the wound that had unmade him. His hip burned, but his heart burned brighter. He had been emptied but, in the emptiness, he was finally filled.

The river's name said it all: *Jabbok* (יַבֹּק) which means to pour out, to be emptied. He did not know it yet, but his crossing was a prophecy. To carry covenant, he had to be poured out of self.

All that was "Jacob," the planner, the grasper, the survivor, had been drained into that river. And as the water flowed, something divine was flowing back into him.

Rest always begins with emptying. It is the space created when self finally surrenders its claim to control.

At Jabbok, the Spirit hovered once more over the waters, just as in the beginning, and from that hovering a new creation rose.

> *"And Jacob called the name of the place Peniel,*
> *for I have seen God face to face, and yet my life is preserved." Genesis 32:30*

Peniel (פְּנִיאֵל) in Hebrew means the Face of God. It was the revelation Adam lost in the garden when fear hid him from that same face. Now, dust met glory again without shame. The man who once deceived his father to steal a blessing now stood before his Father, blessed by grace alone. The curse of separation had cracked open; heaven and earth met again, but this time not in Eden but a man.

Then, Scripture adds quietly: *"The sun rose upon him as he passed over Peniel, and he limped upon his thigh." Genesis 32:31*

The sun had always risen, but never like this. This dawn was not the beginning of a day; it was the beginning of rest. Jacob limped forward, every step a reminder. The limp was not defeat but design. A reminder that power and peace now moved in different rhythms: strength yielded, grace carried.

Just like in his new name: *Israel*, יִשְׂרָאֵל, God prevails.

And that is the secret of Peniel: man's striving may exhaust, but God's touch completes. The One who wounded him also healed him with a new name. The wound became witness; the limp became legacy.

Step Inside: Jabbok, The River of Emptying

Hebrew: יַבֹּק (*Yabbōq*)

Root: בָּקַק (*baqaq*), to pour out, to empty, to be drained.

Every time the Jabbok appears in Scripture it marks a threshold. It divides Gilead from the Jordan valley; it is the line between what was and what will be. When Jacob crossed it, he literally stepped into the word emptied.

"And he rose up that night, and took his two wives… and passed over the ford of Jabbok." Genesis 32:22

Rest always begins with pouring out. The self-made man must be emptied so the covenant man can breathe. Paul later echoes this in Philippians 2:7 when he writes of Christ, *"He emptied Himself (ekenōsen)."* Jabbok is Jacob's kenosis, his Gethsemane before dawn. Only the poured-out vessel can receive the flow of wisdom. So, the name of the river becomes prophecy:

You will cross over when you are emptied.

The name *Jabbok* comes from the Hebrew root *baqaq* and means to pour out which holds the secret of this transformation. Jacob's crossing was a baptism of sorts, the same movement the Spirit would one day repeat in every surrendered life.

Every true crossing into covenant rest requires this emptying. At Jabbok, humanity's compulsion to grasp was finally poured out, making room for divine rest to fill the hollow. Jacob's limp would forever say what words could not: *"I have been emptied, and therefore, I am whole."*

Bethel Revisited: The Ladder Remembered

Years before this night, Jacob had seen a ladder at *Bethel* (בֵּית־אֵל) which is Hebrew for "the House of God." He dreamed of angels ascending and descending upon it, a vision of movement between heaven and earth. The Hebrew word for ladder, סֻלָּם (*sullam*), comes from the Hebrew root *salal* and means to raise up, to build a highway. Jacob saw the original blueprint of creation's communion: rest as connection, not inertia.

When he wrestled at Jabbok, that same ladder appeared again, not in dream, but in flesh. The One who ascended and descended now stood before him, clothed in dust, touching dust, redeeming dust. Centuries later, Yeshua would say,

"You will see heaven open, and angels ascending and descending upon the Son of Man." John 1:51

He was naming Himself as the living *sullam*: the true *Bethel*. He is the ladder, the bridge, the meeting point between realms. What Jacob saw in sleep, the world would one day see in flesh.

Bethel and *Jabbok* are two sides of the same revelation: heaven opens when man empties.

Wisdom builds: rest receives. The Spirit moves up and down the rungs of surrender.

The Prophecy of the Limp: From Striving to Leaning

Jacob's limp was not erased; it became identity. The Scripture says Israel's children would remember it, even refusing to eat the sinew that shrank, so that every generation might know that strength is not the sign of covenant, dependence is. Israel would carry that limp through its history.

Every exile, every return, every failure and forgiveness was a nation walking with the memory of Jabbok. They were chosen not because they were unbroken, but because they learned to lean.

And so, when the Song of Songs asks, *"Who is this coming up from the wilderness, leaning upon her Beloved?"* Song of Solomon 8:5 it is the echo of Jacob in bridal form.

The wrestling nation becomes the resting bride. The limp becomes the lean. What was once struggle becomes intimacy. Rest has matured into love. The Hebrew for leaning carries the idea of resting one's full weight upon another. It is the physical picture of trust; the same trust Jacob found when his strength gave way. What began as *"I will not let You go"* ends as *"I will lean upon You forever."* The hand that once grasped now clings in worship. The limp that once hindered now harmonizes with grace. This is the full circle of rest: from wrestle to walk, from dust to face, from striving to leaning.

The Dawn of Rest

As Jacob limped into sunrise, the river still whispered behind him. The waters of Jabbok shimmered with first light, and the air itself felt like Sabbath. Every covenant up to this point had been made with altars and animals, but this one was carved into a walk. The altar was Jacob's body. The sacrifice was self-reliance. The sign was a limp that would outlive him. He didn't know it, but his story had become the template of redemption itself: a God who descends, a man who wrestles, a touch that wounds to heal, a sunrise that follows surrender.

And that morning, as he stepped toward Esau, the first rays of light rested on his face; the same face that had just seen God and lived. The world had changed in one night of emptying. And rest had a new name: *Israel.*

The Meeting with Esau: Reconciliation as Rest

"And Jacob lifted up his eyes, and looked, and behold,
Esau came, and with him four hundred men.
And Jacob passed over before them,

and bowed himself to the ground seven times,
until he came near to his brother."
Genesis 33:1,3

The desert morning was still wet with dew when Jacob saw the dust rising. Esau was coming, the brother he had deceived, the one he had feared for twenty years, the shadow that had followed him through every mile of exile.

But the man who watched the horizon that day was not the same one who had crossed Jabbok the night before. He walked differently now, literally and spiritually. Every step Jacob took was slower and more deliberate. His limp had become a language: I no longer stand on my own strength.

Jacob bowed seven times before Esau. Seven, the number of completion and the echo of Sabbath. Each bow was an unspoken confession; each lowering of his head was a loosening of his past. He had once grasped at his brother's heel; now he bent his knees. Where he had stolen, he now offered. Where he had schemed, he now surrendered. It was not fear; it was reverence. He was walking rest into relationship.

Then something happened that no one expected:

"And Esau ran to meet him, and embraced him, and fell on his neck, and kissed him, and they wept." Genesis 33:4

The tension of decades dissolved in a single embrace. No speeches, no negotiations, just tears. Jacob had wrestled with God and prevailed, and now that same grace prevailed in his brother. The reconciliation was not manufactured; it was heaven-made. When rest rules within, peace flows without.

The Hebrew text says Esau "fell on his neck": a phrase used nowhere else except for Joseph falling on Jacob's neck years later (Genesis 46:29). It is the posture of reunion, of grief and grace mingled. Both moments frame the story of rest between generations: Jacob reconciled to Esau; Joseph reconciled to Jacob: each one a picture of how mercy heals what striving broke.

The Seven Bows: Rest Made Visible

Why seven times? The Hebrew word *sheva'* (שֶׁבַע) means both seven and oath. Every bow was a covenant gesture. Jacob was not just apologizing; he was consecrating. He was sealing rest into his relationships. In bowing seven times, Jacob enacted what the ground at Beersheba had already reflected through seven lambs: peace sealed by covenant rest. It was as if the Sabbath itself was unfolding between brothers: the seventh step not into rest from labor, but rest from hostility.

The Spirit that hovered over Jabbok's waters now hovered over this reconciliation. The same *Ruach* that brought order to chaos was ordering their hearts. And in that embrace, Eden's lost harmony breathed again for a moment: brother to brother, flesh to flesh, dust to dust, held together by mercy.

The Face of Esau and The Echo of Peniel

When Esau raised Jacob up, Jacob said something stunning:

"I have seen your face, as though I had seen the face of God, and you were pleased with me." Genesis 33:10

The Hebrew word for face is *panim* (פָּנִים) and is plural, implying layers, reflections, and depths. Jacob recognized in Esau's forgiving face the same grace he had seen in Peniel. The two encounters mirrored each other:

Peniel	Esau
Alone in the dark	Surrounded by light
Wrestled with God	Embraced by man
Touched and renamed	Lifted and reconciled
"I have seen God's face"	"Your face is like God's"

Reconciliation is the final proof of revelation. You cannot truly see God's face and still see your brother as your enemy. *Peniel* prepared Jacob's soul; Esau confirmed it in flesh and blood.

This is the deeper rhythm of rest: when inner peace manifests as outer peace, and what is healed in secret becomes visible in love.

The Rest Between Brothers

Jacob and Esau parted soon after, each walking his own way beneath the same sun. But the air between them was clean again. No bitterness. No vengeance. No striving. It was as if the ground itself had exhaled.

For the first time since Eden, brothers stood face to face, and the curse of Cain's envy was momentarily undone. Rest had done what human reasoning never could: it had made peace without debt, reconciliation without revenge.

Jacob's limp remained, but it no longer slowed him; it reminded him. Every step forward was a reminder to his sons: *"Peace is the harvest of those who have wrestled into rest."*

Bethel Revisited: From Face to Dwelling

The road that wound away from the Jabbok followed the same rhythm as creation itself. Behind Jacob was Peniel: the place where dust met divinity, where he saw the Face of God and lived.

Ahead lay *Succoth*, the Hebrew word that means booths, shelters, and tabernacles. And between them stretched the nameless ground where Jacob and Esau met, where the vertical revelation of Peniel became the horizontal reconciliation of peace. It was a threshold between heaven and earth; the same pattern God had written since Eden: from Presence to peace, and peace to dwelling.

Jacob was walking through that rhythm in real time. What began as a wrestle was now becoming a home. When the embrace ended and the brothers parted, Jacob journeyed eastward and came to the open plain beyond the Jordan. There he stopped.

Scripture says quietly:

"And Jacob came to Succoth, and built him a house, and made booths for his cattle; therefore the name of the place is called Succoth." Genesis 33:17

The Hebrew word סֻכּוֹת (*Sukkoth*) comes from the root *sakhak* and means to weave, to entwine, or to cover. It speaks of shade, protection, and intimacy. It is the same root that would later name the *Feast of Sukkot*, the final feast of Israel's calendar: the celebration of dwelling with God in joy after deliverance. What Israel would later practice every year, living in small woven shelters under the open sky, began here with one man who limped his way into peace.

Succoth was the prototype of tabernacles, the first human echo of Eden restored. A man reconciled, resting under a handmade covering, his flocks at peace, the river whispering nearby. For the first time since the garden, dust dwelt in harmony beneath God's presence again. *Succoth* stood halfway between wilderness and promise; a threshold of temporary rest that pointed to something permanent. It was as if God was teaching Jacob the language of dwelling: you build booths now, but one day I will build a dwelling within you.

The Pattern Hidden in the Journey

Jacob's path reads like a map of redemption:

Step	Place	Meaning	Prophetic Fulfillment
Peniel	"Face of God"	Revelation and identity restored	The personal encounter and seeing His glory
Unnamed Ground	Meeting with Esau	Reconciliation, peace	The horizontal proof of vertical grace
Succoth	"Booths / Tabernacles"	Dwelling, rest, protection	The foreshadowing of Sukkot, God tabernacling with man
Bethel	"House of God"	Worship, abiding presence	The maturing of dwelling into habitation

Succoth became a living parable of rest: temporary shelters under eternal grace. It was the pause between revelation and habitation, the same space every heart must pass through before it can become a true Bethel and the house where God dwells.

When God later said to Jacob, *"Arise, go up to Bethel, and dwell there, and make there an altar unto God…" Genesis 35:1*

He was calling him from temporary rest into permanent presence. From booths to a house. From covered to indwelling. From Sukkoth to Bethel.

The Dwelling of Joy

Every future Sukkot feast would remember this: the joy of having passed through striving into shelter. *Israel* would sit beneath woven roofs, look up at the stars through palm branches, and remember: *"We once lived in temporary booths, and God was our covering."*

But the joy was not nostalgia but prophecy. Each booth pointed forward to the greater Tabernacle, the day when God would no longer dwell around His people, but within them. When the Word would become flesh and tabernacle among us (John 1:14).

Succoth is that whisper before the Word: *I will dwell with you. I will cover you. Rest beneath My shade.*

So, Jacob's journey becomes ours: from wrestling to walking, from face to embrace, from sheltering under mercy to becoming the very tent of His presence. The limp, the embrace, the booth, each a brushstroke in the same picture of rest becoming habitation.

Rest's Legacy: The Pillar, the Oil, and the Covenant of Peace

"And God went up from him in the place where He talked with him. And Jacob set up a pillar in the place where He talked with Him, even a pillar of stone: and he poured a drink offering thereon, and he poured oil thereon." Genesis 35:13–14

When the voice of God lifted from Bethel, silence filled the air like completion. The conversation was over, but God's presence remained. Jacob moved slowly, as though every motion carried the weight of remembrance. He picked up a stone, heavy and uncut, and raised it upright.

Scripture calls it a pillar, *matzevah* (מַצֵּבָה), not a heap, not an altar, but in Hebrew is a single standing witness. It was not built for sacrifice; it was raised for memory. The altar had spoken of surrender; the pillar now spoke of fulfillment. This was not the first time Jacob had done this.

Years before, fleeing from Esau with nothing but a staff and fear, he had placed a stone beneath his head and dreamed of a ladder reaching heavenward. When he awoke, he poured oil on that stone and said, *"This shall be God's house." (Genesis 28:22)*

Now, decades later, he stood in the same act, but everything had changed. The first pillar was promise; the second was proof. The first was the cry of a wanderer; the second, the song of a worshiper. The man who once bargained with God now simply bore witness to Him. What began with striving had ended in standing.

The pillar rose straight and silent, a reminder that rest always builds something upright in the end. Jacob had bowed seven times before Esau, seven arcs of humility, seven hues of reconciliation. Now one vertical stone completed the covenant geometry, heaven bending in mercy and earth standing in response. It was as if the rainbow's arc found its reflection in the land: a covenant of color turned into covenant of stone.

Then Jacob did what no patriarch before him had done. He poured oil and wine upon the pillar not on an altar of sacrifice, but on a witness of presence.

Oil (*shemen*, שֶׁמֶן) in Hebrew was the symbol of the Spirit: the invisible made tangible, the fragrance of divine nearness. Wine (*yayin*, יַיִן) in Hebrew was joy, communion, the fellowship of peace. Together they formed the language of the kingdom before the kingdom existed: anointing and rejoicing, His Spirit and gladness, rest and revelation. This act marked a shift.

Earlier in his life, Jacob had poured oil on a stone to mark a promise. Now he poured it to seal habitation. The Spirit was no longer visiting;

He was dwelling. The ground that had once borne curse was now consecrated by joy.

The patriarch who had wrestled with God now anointed the earth with peace. The covenant had moved from tents to territory, from encounter to establishment. Jacob's pillar stood as the first monument of fulfilled rest; a silent prophecy that one day another anointed stone would rise, not carved by human hands, and upon it the Spirit would descend and remain.

When Jacob left Bethel that day, he walked beneath the same sky that had once seen a rainbow after the flood. But this time, the sign was not above him but within him. The colors of mercy had become the posture of his soul: humility bowing below, wisdom standing within, and the oil of gladness resting upon everything he touched.

Ruling from Rest

The oil poured upon Jacob's stone would soon flow through his sons. Among them was one in whom that anointing would rise visibly: a dreamer clothed in wisdom, tested by waters and prisons, and raised as a pillar among nations.

The covenant of rest was not finished; it was about to govern. Through Joseph, the wisdom that once hovered over chaos would learn to feed the world.

Selah Meditation: Face to Face

Let the light dim for a moment. Not fearfully but the way night gathers when all running has ended. Maybe you have reached a place where explanations have stopped working. Where your effort has loosened its grip. And you are at a place where you can no longer carry yourself forward. This is Peniel. You are not here to wrestle. You are here because you stayed.

Feel His nearness, not above or ahead of you, but close enough to be unavoidable. You do not need the right words. You do not need to understand what is happening. You only need to remain. Notice what softens when you stop resisting. Notice where strength gives way to surrender. This is not loss but contact.

Let yourself remain here. Not doing. Not asking. Not reaching. But just being present. Notice how close He is. Close enough that you do not need to search for His face. Close enough that your breath settles without effort. He sees you. You are not being assessed or corrected. You are known.

Stay for a few slow breaths. Let the space become quiet. Let the silence hold you. There is nothing to take. Nothing to prove. Nothing to carry away. Know that He is here with you and that it is enough. He is enough.

Notes:

_____

_____

_____

_____

_____

_____

_____

_____

_____

_____

_____

_____

_____

_____

_____

_____

_____

_____

7

JOSEPH
The Rest that Rules

**"Now Joseph had a dream, and he told it to his brothers;
and they hated him even more.
There we were, binding sheaves in the field.
Then behold, my sheaf arose and also stood upright;
and indeed your sheaves stood all around
and bowed down to my sheaf." Genesis 37:5,7**

The Dreamer of Rest

Morning came soft and golden over Hebron's hills. The fields glistened with morning light as if an unseen hand had brushed each stalk with oil. Joseph lingered at the edge of the field, hands open, face tilted to the wind. The dream still burned behind his eyes as he remembered sheaves bowing, stars bending; and though he didn't yet have language for it, his spirit already knew something divine was rearranging itself through him.

He was only seventeen, still learning the difference between favor and understanding. His brothers saw only a coat; a woven thing of many colors, stitched from his father's affection. But Joseph felt something deeper in its threads, a fragrance familiar and ancient, the same oil that

53

Jacob had poured upon the pillar at Bethel. He didn't know it, but he was wearing a visible sign of invisible rest. He was clothed in prophecy.

That night's dream came in two movements, like the two breaths of creation. First came the earthly vision: sheaves of grain in a field, bowing before his own sheaf. Then came the heavenly vision: the sun, moon, and eleven stars bowing before him. He had not earned either vision; both were given.

That was the mark of true authority: rest that receives instead of strives. Joseph's calling was not to seize dominion but to carry alignment. What bowed to him was not people but creation itself responding to wisdom's rest.

- The sheaves bowed, declaring that provision would one day submit to divine order: earthly resources governed by heaven's timing.
- The stars bowed, declaring that understanding itself, wisdom and counsel, would one day find rest in him.

Together they spoke of two realms, matter and meaning, soil and spirit, brought into harmony under the governance of peace. The dream was not about hierarchy; it was about rest restoring rhythm. He told the dream simply, unguarded, unaware that purity often provokes jealousy. His brothers' eyes hardened; even Jacob rebuked him, though he kept the matter in his heart.

Dreams that come from rest are often misunderstood by those still living from striving. Yet heaven always hides its rulers this way, anointing them early, unveiling them slowly. Joseph walked back toward his brothers, the sheaves whispering against his legs.

The field itself seemed to bow as he passed, not to a boy, but to the Word that had been spoken. He did not know it yet, but the same God who had painted a rainbow in Noah's sky and stood with Abraham under oaks and stars was now sketching another covenant in motion: rest enthroned in wisdom, wisdom ruling through rest.

Step Inside: Dreams as Ladders

The Hebrew word for dream, חֲלוֹם (*chalom*), comes from the root חָלַם (*chalam*), meaning to bind firmly, to make whole, to recover strength. In Hebrew thought, dreams were not illusions of sleep but points of divine connection, rungs where heaven and earth touched. Jacob had once seen a ladder in a dream, angels ascending and descending upon it, revealing that rest always carries motion between realms.

Joseph's life would become that dream fulfilled. He would not just see the ladder, but he would walk it. Each ascent and descent as favored son, slave, steward, prisoner, ruler would become another rung of divine rhythm. What Jacob saw at Bethel in a vision, Joseph would live in Egypt as wisdom.

In that sense, Joseph is not merely the interpreter of dreams; he became the embodiment of one. He is the dream walking.

Joseph: The Dream Walking

In Eden, God dreamed of a world ruled from rest: a man and woman tending creation not by force but by fellowship, governing through trust, not toil. That was the first dream, divine order flowing through human harmony. But when Adam and Eve grasped at wisdom instead of receiving it, that dream was buried, not destroyed, just hidden like a seed in the soil of time. The whole story of Scripture since then has been the slow awakening of God's dream within humanity again.

When Joseph stands in the field wearing a coat brushed with many colors, he is not just Jacob's son but the continuation of Eden's intent. He is the first man in Scripture to rule the world's resources by the rhythm of wisdom, to steward creation's abundance through discernment born of rest.

Through Joseph, Egypt is not conquered but ordered. Men are not dominated but feed. Joseph embodies and governs with peace. He becomes Adam restored: man, once again governing the earth from the inside out and authority flowing not from hierarchy but from harmony with heaven. *"Joseph is the dream walking,"* means: the divine imagination that began in Eden now walks the earth clothed in a son who will display rest in wisdom.

But every dream must first descend before it rules. Before rest can govern, it must be tested in the depths and dry places where the promise seems buried, and wisdom works unseen beneath the surface.

The Pit: Rest Tested by Emptiness

"And they took him, and cast him into a pit: and the pit was empty, there was no water in it." Genesis 37:24

The sun had climbed high when they threw him in. The air down in the pit was cool, the light fractured. Above him, the circle of sky was small, like a single, watching eye. Joseph lay still on the dust and listened to his brothers' laughter fade as they sat down to eat.

Only hours before, he had stood in open fields beneath the wide blue sky, his father's robe on his shoulders and his future burning inside him. Now the robe was gone, torn from him, and his dream felt far away, like a voice shouted from another lifetime.

The pit smelled of iron and damp clay. He pressed his palm to the wall, it was dry. Scripture says, *"There was no water in it."* It was not a well, not a cistern that could refresh. It was a *bor*, a hole dug for keeping, not giving. This was the opposite of everything he had known. The boy who had dreamed of bowing sheaves now lay beneath the ground that once fed them.

But the pit is never the end in God's arithmetic. It is the place where wisdom begins to shape rest from within. Down there, stripped of color and noise, Joseph learned the first rule of rulership: rest is not proven in authority; it is proven in emptiness. When every voice is taken from you: favor, family, future; what remains reveals whether you were built on striving or on trust.

There, between silence and dust, the dream still pulsed quietly. Unseen, uncelebrated, but alive. He could not see it, but heaven had not withdrawn; it had only drawn close in another form. Every covenant has a descent. The ark had one. Abraham had one. Jacob had one. Now it was Joseph's turn to learn that rest rules from the inside out.

And though he did not know it yet, the same Spirit who had hovered over waters before creation was now hovering over this emptiness, waiting again for the command: Let *there be.*

Step Inside: *Bor*, The Pit and the Well

The Hebrew text is precise. It says, *"The pit was empty; there was no water in it."* The Hebrew word for pit is בּוֹר (*bor*), from a root meaning to hollow out, to make empty. In contrast, the Hebrew word for a living well is בְּאֵר (*be'er*), from *ba'ar* and means to make clear, to flow, to declare.

The *bor* is the shadow of the *be'er*. One holds stillness; the other, flow. One is the silence of testing; the other, the song of revelation. Between them lies the mystery of rest. Before wisdom can flow through you, it must first hollow you. Before you can speak clearly, you must learn to listen in the dark. Throughout Scripture, God works through both:

Isaac's wells: the flowing of provision and joy.

Joseph's pit: the hollowing that makes room for both.

When Scripture says, *"there was no water,"* it is not only describing geography but prophesying formation. Water represents the Spirit. In the pit, Joseph is not without the Spirit; he is learning what it means when the Spirit is quiet. He is becoming the cistern of wisdom; a vessel shaped by emptiness, so that when the time comes, he will hold what Egypt cannot.

Step Inside: The Geography of Dothan

"And the man said, 'They have departed from here; for I heard them say, Let us go to Dothan.' So Joseph went after his brothers, and found them in Dothan."
Genesis 37:17

The pit that swallowed Joseph's dream was in *Dothan*. A name that hides its own message.

In Hebrew, דֹּתָן (*Dothan*) is traced to *doth* or *dot*, and is related to דָּת (*dat*), and is a law, decree, or ordinance. Ancient traditions also remember it as "Two Wells" or "Twin Cisterns." Both readings are true at once: *Dothan* is the place of decrees between two wells.

Either way, it tells the same story; Dothan is where divine decree meets human testing, and the dreamer stands between emptiness and flow.

Two Wells: The Threshold of Choice

If Dothan means "Two Wells," the detail is astonishing. Joseph is thrown into a dry pit in a region whose name means wells. He is literally in a land of water but finds none. Everything about his environment says provision, yet his experience says privation. This is the geography of paradox and the spiritual threshold where God asks, *"Will you trust Me when My flow hides?"*

Isaac once re-dug his father's wells; Jacob once rolled the stone from a well to water flocks; but Joseph lies in a dry one. The covenantal line appears to have come to a standstill as rest is no longer flowing, only echoing. But what looks like stillness is actually gestation.

Dothan is the point where the inner well begins to form. The external supply disappears so that the internal spring can awaken. Dothan is the threshold of discernment: the place between visible and invisible water, where rest learns to drink from faith instead of circumstance.

Decree / Law: The Courtroom of Calling

If *Dothan* draws its meaning from the Hebrew word *dat* meaning law, decree; then this dry cistern becomes a courtroom, not a tomb. Heaven had issued a decree through Joseph's dreams, and now that decree is entering evidence in the earth.

The pit is the first ruling of Joseph's destiny; the legal proceeding where the promise is proven through process. Every word spoken from heaven must pass through the court of the earth. Decree demands demonstration.

At *Dothan*, the verdict is rendered: the dream will stand, but first it must descend. Rest must be refined before it can rule, and wisdom must be weighed before it can govern. *Dothan* is the courtroom of rest; the place where heaven's decree takes shape in human time.

The Echo of Dothan: Sight in the Unseen

Dothan appears again generations later, when Elisha the prophet is surrounded by a hostile army (2 Kings 6:13–17). His servant panics: Elisha prays, *"Lord, open his eyes that he may see."* And the servant's sight opens to chariots of fire encircling the city. The same geography, the same revelation: what looks surrounded is actually encircled by glory.

In Joseph's day, the pit hid purpose. In Elisha's day, the hills hid protection. Both times, Dothan revealed the same truth: rest sees what fear cannot.

Dothan is the geography of spiritual sight. It is where eyes open to armies of fire, where emptiness conceals fullness, where the unseen proves more real than the seen.

Symbol	Meaning	Revelation in Joseph's Story
Two Wells	Duality, testing, choice	Between emptiness and flow; learning trust in unseen provision
Law / Decree	Heaven's verdict	The promise entering process; decree made manifest
Elisha's Dothan	Unseen armies, open eyes	Sight restored; rest perceives protection
Joseph's Pit	Hollow without water	Formation of wisdom; Spirit hovering unseen

Dothan is the valley where decrees descend. The place between two wells; where old flow ceases so new flow can begin. Where God hides His dreamer in a dry cistern so that unseen waters can fill him from within. It is the courtroom of rest, the geography of divine sight. Heaven opens eyes there.

The caravan of Ishmaelites appeared on the horizon with traders carrying balm and myrrh. The decree had been issued; the next phase of formation was about to begin. The pit had done its work. Rest was ready to travel.

Potiphar's House: Rest as Stewardship

"And the LORD was with Joseph, and he was a prosperous man;
and he was in the house of his master the Egyptian."
Genesis 39:2

The caravan moved south, dust rising behind it like a fading memory. Chains bit into Joseph's wrists, but he did not resist. He watched the horizon with eyes that had seen both dream and darkness, and somehow the two had begun to feel like one story.

Egypt came into view, a land of order and excess, temples and silos, stone and sand. To Joseph, it must have felt like another world altogether: a civilization that worshiped the river but had never met its Maker. Here, in the house of Potiphar, captain of Pharaoh's guard, Joseph would learn what it means to govern rest within systems of striving.

Potiphar's estate was vast: courtyards, storehouses, servants in procession. Joseph entered it as property, but heaven entered it with him as presence. The text says simply: *"The LORD was with Joseph."* It is the same phrase used of Eden: *"And the LORD God was with them."* The fellowship that Adam forfeited had now followed a slave into Egypt.

Everywhere Joseph's hands touched began to flourish. The house breathed differently; its rhythm changed. Potiphar did not understand why, only that this young Hebrew carried order. The same wisdom that once measured the heavens now managed his household. Joseph did not rule through command but through calm. An authority so quiet it reordered chaos without raising a voice. He became overseer of everything yet still remained a servant.

That paradox was his anointing. Rest is never control, only flow. To steward rest is to allow things to prosper because they have found their right place.

Potiphar's house became a miniature Eden; a garden enclosed within stone walls. There was structure, fruitfulness, and peace. In every account ledger and storeroom, the echo of Genesis returned: *"and the LORD saw that it was good."* Joseph was learning to tend again; to keep and to cultivate, not through ownership but through wisdom. The dreamer was becoming the gardener.

Step Inside: The Garden Re-imagined

In Genesis 2:15, Adam is given the garden *"to work it and to keep it."* The Hebrew verbs are עָבַד (*avad*); to serve, to cultivate, and שָׁמַר (*shamar*); to guard, to preserve. Both appear again in Joseph's story.

When Joseph serves Potiphar, he *avads*; when he guards his master's trust, he *shamars*. He is reliving Adam's original mandate, but in captivity. The garden has moved to Egypt.

Notice the difference: Adam tended creation from abundance; Joseph tends it from bondage. Adam lost rest by grasping; Joseph keeps rest by yielding. Adam fell through curiosity; Joseph stands through restraint. One reached for what was forbidden; the other refused what was offered.

In Potiphar's house, the serpent returned, not with fruit, but with flattery. The test was the same: *Will wisdom wait?*

Joseph's *"No"* to Potiphar's wife was not repression but restoration. Eden choosing rightly at last. The garden reappears wherever a heart keeps fellowship intact. Joseph did not need trees or rivers to live in paradise; he needed obedience flowing from rest.

So, the LORD prospered everything he touched. Not because of luck or labor, but because the soil of his soul was still aligned with heaven's rhythm. Rest had become portable again. The sanctuary within a servant.

Rest that builds must also be proven under accusation. Wisdom must show that it can withstand falsehood without losing peace. The next test would strip Joseph of position just as the first stripped him of family; and once again, rest would descend before it rose.

The False Accusation: The Test of Integrity

"And it came to pass after these things, that his master's wife cast her eyes upon Joseph; and she said, Lie with me." Genesis 39:7

The house was quiet that day. Servants had gone about their errands, the sunlight falling in long, gold bands across the stone floor. Joseph was checking ledgers, inventorying grain, when he felt her presence before he heard her voice.

The air itself changed to heavy and watchful. *"Lie with me,"* she said. Three words, whispered like an invitation but echoing like a test. It was the garden all over again: the fruit pleasing to the eyes, desirable to make one wise.

For a moment, time folded. Adam's shadow flickered against the walls of Egypt. Would rest grasp again, or would wisdom wait? Joseph's answer was quiet but resolute:

"How then could I do this great wickedness, and sin against God?"

Not against Potiphar, not even against the woman, but against God. That is exactly how rest speaks, from an awareness of His Presence, not pressure. She reached for him; he turned and fled, the garment tearing from his body. The robe that symbolized his favor once again lay in another's hands.

In every season, Joseph's coat was taken; first by envy, now by accusation, but each stripping only revealed a deeper layer of anointing. Falsehood clings to garments; truth clings to the soul. He ran not from desire but from distortion, not from beauty but from bondage disguised as intimacy. He ran because he knew that rest cannot coexist with deceit.

Behind him, accusation gathered like thunder. The house that had flourished under his care now turned on him in suspicion. Potiphar's wife's words twisted truth into venom: *"See, he came in to mock me."* And Joseph, who had ruled as a steward, was bound again and cast into prison.

But the Scripture says, *"The LORD was with Joseph, and showed him mercy."* Mercy does not prevent the descent; it travels with you through it. Rest was still intact, though bruised and stripped; it was unbroken.

The serpent had whispered again, and this time humanity had answered correctly.

Step Inside: The Forbidden Tree Revisited

The temptation in Potiphar's house is the mirror of the one in Eden. The words of Genesis 3 hover behind the scenes: *"And when the woman saw that the tree was good for food, pleasant to the eyes, and desirable to make one wise…"* In both stories, the test revolves around seeing and seizing.

Potiphar's wife *"cast her eyes upon Joseph."* The same verb appears in Genesis 3; to see, to desire. The Hebrew word *ra'ah* means more than sight; it means to interpret, to define as good. In Eden, humanity sought to define good apart from God. In Egypt, Joseph redefined good by alignment with God.

There are always two trees:

- One promises knowledge through grasping.
- The other offers life through trust.

Joseph chose the second. In his refusal, the order of Eden was restored. He reestablished the lost equilibrium, *chokmah* (wisdom) governing through *nuach* (rest). He showed that true wisdom is not about knowing more; it is about staying aligned and in tune with God.

In Genesis 3, after Adam and Eve sinned, they made garments to cover their shame. In Genesis 39, Joseph loses his garment to preserve his purity. The reversal is deliberate. Where the first humans covered their guilt, Joseph's nakedness becomes his integrity. He does not hide; he flees. Rest has nothing to conceal.

The Prophetic Echo

Every act of restraint builds a future altar. Because Joseph refused this counterfeit intimacy, God would later trust him with the power to feed nations. He who denied himself momentary pleasure was granted eternal purpose. The forbidden fruit was traded for the grain of life.

In Eden, man reached for what was forbidden and lost the garden. In Egypt, Joseph released what was offered and became the garden. Rest had learned to rule itself.

The cell door closed, and the house of Potiphar faded into memory. But even here, in the lowest place, the same sentence followed him: *"The LORD was with Joseph."* He had lost everything external; position, favor, freedom; but gained what cannot be taken: the rhythm of divine companionship. In the darkness of the prison, the dream was not dead. It was incubating. Rest was now being perfected in confinement. And soon, dreams would return. Not his own this time, but those of others proving that wisdom's rest was ready to interpret, not just receive.

The Prison: Hidden Workshops of Wisdom

"But the LORD was with Joseph, and showed him mercy, and gave him favor in the sight of the keeper of the prison." Genesis 39:21

The sound of the door closing behind him was final; a slow scrape of wood and iron that seemed to seal him off from everything he had ever known. The air was damp. The walls, rough. The pit had been brief, but this confinement would stretch like unmeasured time. Yet somewhere in that narrow corridor of stone, Joseph began to sense something familiar. The same Spirit that had met him in dreams, that had followed him into slavery, was here, too. Quiet but nearby.

Mercy had a way of following him, even into injustice. At first, he waited. Days turned into weeks, and silence pressed against him like weight. The memory of his father's house faded; the colors of his coat faded too. He was stripped of every identity except one: the beloved of God.

When Scripture says, *"The LORD was with Joseph,"* it does not mean that circumstances improved. It means the air itself began to hum with order again. Even in prison, Joseph carried a portable Eden. He swept floors, tended tasks, listened to the breathing of those who had lost hope. In a place built for despair, he became a keeper of peace.

Over time, the keeper of the prison noticed: whatever Joseph touched ran smoother; whatever he oversaw prospered. The same invisible rhythm that had blessed Potiphar's house now flowed through cell blocks and corridors. Soon Joseph was given charge of the prisoners. He managed their meals, their needs, their moods. He learned the art of governing hearts.

The dreamer who once saw sheaves bowing was now learning how to serve them. The leader in waiting was being trained in compassion. Another facet of wisdom that only grows in dark places. Rest was being refined into rule. And wisdom, like a craftsman, was shaping him in secret.

Step Inside: Pressure and Formation

The Hebrew word for prison in this story is בֵּית הַסֹּהַר (*beit hasohar*), literally "the house of enclosure." Its Hebrew root, *sahar*, means to encircle, to surround, to press in. It is related to the noun *tsarah* meaning narrowness or distress which is the same root used in the Psalms when David says, *"You have enlarged me when I was in distress." (Psalm 4:1)*

The pattern is ancient: God uses narrow spaces to create wide souls. The pressure of confinement is never punitive; it is formative. The vessel must be compressed before it can pour. The olive must be crushed to release oil; the grape pressed to yield wine.

Joseph's prison was heaven's olive press, the place where his anointing was extracted drop by drop until wisdom replaced youth. Each limitation became a boundary of design. Rest learned to stay steady under weight. Silence became a tutor, patience, and a prophet.

The word *sahar* also carries the sense of orbit: to revolve, to circle, to turn. While Joseph felt stationary, heaven was orbiting him. The stars that had bowed in his dream were still circling above, their pattern unchanged, their timing precise.

The prison was not a pause; it was an orbit. Rest was revolving into rule. The pressure was shaping the vessel that would hold nations.

Then one morning, two new prisoners arrived, men of rank and reputation: Pharoah's cupbearer and his baker. Both had dreamed strangled dreams and woke unsettled. Joseph listened not with curiosity, but with compassion; and for the first time, he spoke interpretation into another's confusion.

The dreamer had become the interpreter. Rest had matured into discernment. Wisdom was now fluent in other people's mysteries.

The Cupbearer and the Baker: The Language of Dreams

"And they said to him, 'We each have had a dream,
and there is no interpreter of it.'
So Joseph said to them, 'Do not interpretations belong to God?
Tell them to me, please.'" Genesis 40:8

The morning light barely reached the lower chambers of Pharaoh's prison. Joseph was checking rations when he noticed two new faces: the cupbearer and the baker, servants of Pharaoh himself. Their clothes were torn, their faces anxious, and their eyes still clouded by sleep.

He greeted them quietly, his voice steady. *"Why do you look so sad today?"* They looked up, startled that anyone had asked. *"We have dreamed a dream,"* they said, *"and there is no interpreter of it."*

Joseph paused.

Those words carried weight. *We have dreamed a dream.* He remembered his own. It had been years since the field, years since the stars. But something inside him stirred again; the same Spirit that had spoken before.

"Do not interpretations belong to God?" he said. *"Tell me them, I pray you."*

That one sentence revealed what the years had done. The boy who once announced his dreams was now discerning others'. He no longer needed to be the center of revelation; he had become a conduit for it. Rest had shifted from receiving to releasing.

The cupbearer spoke first. A vine, three branches, grapes pressed into Pharaoh's cup.

Joseph listened, his spirit aligning. *"This is the interpretation,"* he said. *"In three days Pharaoh will lift up your head and restore you to your place."*

Then came the baker's dream. Three baskets of white bread on his head, and birds eating from them. The interpretation was darker; in three days, Pharaoh would lift his head from him.

Two dreams. Two fates. One interpreter who never claimed ownership of either outcome. Joseph did not manipulate or soften the truth. He did not use revelation to control. He simply served it. Because wisdom never interprets for advantage; it interprets for alignment.

Days later, both dreams unfolded exactly as spoken. The cupbearer was restored. The baker executed. And Joseph remained. Two lives turned, but the interpreter stayed still. He had done his part; the rest was heaven's timing. Rest does not rush results. It simply speaks what it hears and trusts the cadence that follows.

Step Inside: Dreams as the Vocabulary of Heaven

In Hebrew, the word for interpretation in this passage is פִּתְרוֹן (*petaron*), from the root פָּתַר (*pathar*), meaning to open, to loosen, to untie a knot. To interpret a dream is to open it; to loosen heaven's language so it can breathe in human understanding.

Dreams, in Hebrew thought, are the speech of the Spirit wrapped in symbol and story. They are not riddles meant to confuse; they are codes designed to invite relationship. Only those who walk in rest can interpret them, because only rest can hear without agenda.

Joseph says, *"Do not interpretations belong to God?"* He does not claim the gift as his own; he recognizes that true interpretation flows from union. It is not intellect but intimacy that opens the meaning of mystery.

The earlier Hebrew word for dream, חֲלוֹם (*chalom*), we have seen before: its root חָלַם (*chalam*) means to bind firmly, to make whole, to restore health. In other words, dreams are heaven's way of binding what is divided, of restoring coherence between soul and spirit. They are bridges of healing, and its interpretation is the crossing.

For Joseph, interpreting the cupbearer and baker's dreams was not just prophecy; it was participation in restoration. One man was restored to service; another returned to the earth. Both, in different ways, completed the cycle of heaven's order. Even judgment, when rightly discerned, is part of healing.

Dreams are the Spirit's grammar of grace; the syntax of rest written in symbol and silence. When rest listens, heaven speaks clearly.

Two dreams fulfilled. One word still waiting. Joseph's interpretations had rippled into Pharaoh's court, but his name was forgotten the moment the cup was lifted. He didn't protest. He had learned that delay is not denial; it is preparation for elevation.

When rest has finished its hidden work, wisdom calls for it by name. And soon, another dream would come, not to a prisoner, but to a king. And the world would change because a man of rest knew how to listen.

Pharaoh's Dream: Wisdom in Motion

"And Pharaoh dreamed: and, behold, he stood by the river." Genesis 41:1

The river that fed Egypt; the Nile, heartbeat of a nation gleamed in Pharaoh's sleep. He stood upon its bank, the morning mist curling like incense. From the waters rose seven sleek, strong cows. They grazed among the reeds, full and content. Then seven others followed: gaunt, hollow-eyed, and hungry. And the lean devoured the fat. Pharaoh awoke, trembling. He fell asleep again.

Now seven heads of grain rose from a single stalk, plump and golden. Then seven thin heads, scorched by the east wind, swallowed them whole. He woke a second time disturbed and bewildered. The magicians of Egypt could not read the dream. The symbols refused to open for those who did not know the voice behind them.

Then the cupbearer remembered. *"There is a young Hebrew, a servant of the captain of the guard; he interpreted our dreams, and they came to pass."* Pharaoh sent for him at once. Joseph was shaved, robed, and brought before the throne; to the very place his first dream had pointed toward years ago.

Pharaoh said, *"I have heard it said of thee, that thou canst understand a dream to interpret it."* Joseph answered, *"It is not in me: God shall give Pharaoh an answer of peace."* That sentence was the hinge of history. Joseph responded with not *"an answer of power,"* but peace.

In Hebrew, *shalom*, the word that means wholeness, completion, rest. Joseph stood before the world's most powerful man, not with strategy, not with spells, but with serenity.

He listened as Pharaoh described both dreams. Joseph's response came like light through a prism clear, steady, and ordered: *"The dream of Pharaoh is one. God has shown Pharaoh what He is about to do."* Seven years of plenty. Seven years of famine. Cycles written in divine arithmetic. Abundance followed by scarcity, not as punishment, but preparation.

Joseph did not merely interpret; he aligned. He saw the rhythm beneath the chaos and offered structure to match heaven's pattern. *"Let Pharaoh select a wise and discerning man, and set him over the land of Egypt. Let him gather one-fifth of the produce in the years of plenty, and store the grain under Pharaoh's authority, to be kept for the years of famine."*

He did not ask for the position; he described the function of wisdom.

Pharaoh, hearing truth that carried peace, answered, *"Can we find such a one as this, in whom the Spirit of God is?"*

And just like that, the boy from the pit stood in the palace. The dream had walked full circle. The ladder Jacob saw, the field Joseph dreamed, the pit he endured all converged here. Rest had ascended into rule. Joseph was clothed in linen, the sign of purity; given Pharaoh's ring, the symbol of delegated authority; and set over all Egypt, to govern with order and mercy.

The Spirit that hovered over chaos in Genesis 1 now hovered again through a man. Wisdom was no longer abstract; it had a face, a voice, a plan. The rest of God had entered the systems of men.

Step Inside: Numbers and Cycles of Rest

The structure of Pharaoh's dreams is mathematical poetry.

- Seven cows, seven heads of grain were symbols of completion, creation, and covenant.
- Fourteen totaled two sevens joined in tension symbolizing transition and doubling.

In Hebrew thought, numbers are never static; they pulse with meaning. Seven is שֶׁבַע (*sheva*), from a Hebrew root meaning to be full, satisfied, complete. It is also related to *shavua*, "oath" because seven marks divine commitment.

Every seventh day, seventh year, and seventh cycle carries rest and renewal. When Joseph interprets Pharaoh's dream, he is not performing numerology but recognizing the rhythm of God's faithfulness encoded in time. Creation itself operates in sevens: six movements of work, one breath of rest.

Egypt's dream mirrors the same law written into the cosmos. The seven years of plenty echo the abundance of Eden; the ease of walking with God, provision without toil. The seven years of famine echo the exile; humanity outside the garden, longing for restoration. And the whole fourteen-year cycle embodies redemption: the return of rest through wisdom that plans ahead.

Joseph becomes the embodiment of Sabbath strategy: he learns to store during overflow so that famine becomes not destruction, but discipline. This is not survival but stewardship. Heaven's rhythm moves through his administration.

In Egypt, seven no longer merely means a number. It becomes a governance principle: the architecture of rest applied to economy and time. Joseph's leadership turns sacred pattern into practical policy. Wisdom always builds from flow, not reaction. Rest does not fear famine; it prepares for it in peace. The number seven is not luck, but the language of order restored.

Through Joseph, the cycle of sevens returns creation to harmony. Even Egypt, the symbol of the world's striving, begins to breathe to heaven's tempo.

Years would pass. The Nile would rise and fall, fields swelling then withering, but the granaries of Egypt stayed full as vessels of foresight and faithfulness. People came from every land to buy grain, unaware that they were standing before a son of rest.

And one day, among those who came to bow, were faces Joseph had not seen in decades; faces that once looked down into a pit. The dream had finally reached its fulfillment: the sheaves were bowing, not in subjugation but in reconciliation.

The famine had done what family could not; it had gathered them again.

The Grain and the Brothers: The Reconciliation of Rest

"And Joseph's brothers came and bowed down themselves
before him with their faces to the earth." Genesis 42:6

The years of plenty had passed. The fields that once shimmered with abundance now lay bare under a sun that refused to yield. Famine spread like a shadow, and every road led to Egypt.

In Canaan, Jacob heard that there was grain in the land of the Nile and bread in the house of bondage. He sent ten of his sons to buy it, keeping Benjamin behind. So, they journeyed south, the same path their ancestors had walked, carrying empty sacks and an inheritance of guilt.

When they reached Egypt, the grain-houses towered like mountains. At their center sat a man robed in white linen, with a seal upon his hand, the governor of all the land. They bowed before him, not knowing. The dream from long ago rose in the air between them; sheaves bending toward a single sheaf, not in subjugation, but in fulfillment.

Joseph recognized them immediately. They were older, now weathered and cautious, and the fire of arrogance dimmed to ember. But memory lives in tone and gesture, and the way they bowed triggered the ache of every buried year.

He could have spoken, revealed, and accused. But wisdom held him still. Rest does not rush restoration; it lets truth unfold in time. He spoke to them through an interpreter, testing not their loyalty but their transformation.

"Where do you come from?" he asked. *"From the land of Canaan, to buy food."* He accused them of being spies, a mirror of their own past betrayal.

They protested, *"We are twelve brothers… one is no more."* The words pierced him like prophecy. One is no more. They did not know that the one they mourned stood breathing before them.

For three days, Joseph confined them, a symbolic Sabbath of reflection. Then he released all but Simeon.

Simeon, whose Hebrew name means hearing, was bound while the others were sent home with grain and a command to return with

Benjamin. Joseph was not acting in cruelty, but in wisdom: true reconciliation requires restored hearing, and hearing could not yet be released.

He filled their sacks with grain and secretly returned their silver. Mercy hid itself in the mundane. They carried home provision they had not paid for, the same way grace always travels.

When they returned a second time, Benjamin with them, Joseph's composure wavered. He prepared a feast and the brothers seated in order of birth, Benjamin's portion fivefold greater than the rest. They marveled, but Joseph's heart broke quietly. He left the room and wept. The kind of weeping that releases decades of delay.

Then, to finish the test, he hid his silver cup in Benjamin's sack. When they were accused, Judah stepped forward. He offered himself in Benjamin's place, saying, *"Let your servant remain as a slave… and let the lad go up with his brothers."*

It was the moment Joseph had waited for: not vengeance, but virtue; not confession born of fear, but love expressed through substitution. Then Joseph could no longer restrain himself. He dismissed the servants, and his voice broke across the hall: *"I am Joseph; does my father yet live?"*

Silence. Then trembling. Then weeping that filled Pharaoh's house. He drew them near. *"What you meant for evil,"* he said, *"God meant for good, to save many alive."*

It was the gospel before the Gospel, extending forgiveness as governance, and mercy as mastery. The boy who once dreamed of dominion now ruled through reconciliation. Rest had found its highest form and peace was expressed as pardon.

Step Inside: Why Joseph Chose Simeon to Stay Behind

Joseph's decision to keep Simeon was not arbitrary, nor was it punitive. It was surgical.

Simeon's name comes from the Hebrew *shama*, "to hear, to listen, to receive." In Scripture, hearing is never passive. To hear is to respond, to obey, to be changed. Broken hearing is always the first fracture in broken relationships with God, with others, and with oneself.

Joseph binds hearing because hearing is what must be restored before reunion is possible.

The brothers had spoken the truth with their mouths, *"we are guilty,"* but they had not yet fully heard it with their hearts. Words had surfaced, but repentance had not yet settled. By holding Simeon, Joseph creates a pause long enough for conscience to awaken and for memory to mature into responsibility.

This is wisdom at work beneath the visible story. Joseph does not confront them with his identity. He does not force confession. He does not demand apology. Instead, he creates a space where hearing can deepen.

By sending the brothers home with grain, Joseph meets their physical need. By keeping Simeon, he addresses the deeper famine; the famine of listening, of reckoning, of truth received rather than merely spoken.

Only when hearing is restored can Benjamin, son of the right hand, be safely brought near. Only when the brothers learn to listen again can the family be reunited without repeating the same violence under a different name.

Joseph is not delaying reconciliation. He is protecting it. He knows what wisdom always knows: union rushed is fragile, but union born from restored hearing can last.

Simeon remains bound not as punishment, but as a witness. A living reminder that something essential is still being formed beneath the surface.

And while the brothers walk away thinking the story has paused, wisdom is quietly arranging its return.

Step Inside: The Seven Bows Revisited

Genesis records that when Jacob met Esau, he bowed seven times before his brother. It was a choreography of humility where each bow became an echo of covenant, each movement a color in the rainbow of reconciliation. Seven, *sheva*, the number of fullness, oath, and rest.

When Joseph's brothers bowed before him, that pattern returned. Another family estrangement met its Sabbath. Seven bows in Canaan, seven sheaves in Egypt; each bow not about subservience but surrender to restoration.

In Hebrew thought, bowing שָׁחָה (*shachah*), means not only to kneel, but to align, to bring oneself into right order before another. It is the posture of worship, yes, but also the posture of peace.

When the brothers bowed, they were not losing dignity but re-entering harmony. Creation itself bends before rest. Jacob's seven bows healed Esau's rage. Joseph's brothers' bows healed history. Both scenes are rainbows of reconciliation; arches of humility that bridge what was broken.

In them, we see the hidden mathematics of mercy: humility multiplies restoration. When rest rules the heart, even old wounds become altars.

Seven bows equal seven hues of grace. Each movement bends pride into peace. Each lowering becomes a lifting. And beneath the surface, covenant is rewritten in love.

The family moved to Egypt and seventy souls were planted in the fertile land of Goshen. The famine waned, but the fruit of forgiveness endured. Joseph's household became a sanctuary: a living garden in a foreign empire. His wisdom fed nations, and his mercy preserved generations.

Years later, Jacob blessed his sons and passed the promise. But before he died, he said to Joseph, *"I had not thought to see your face; and, lo, God hath showed me also your seed."* Rest had ripened into generations.

Goshen: The Geography of Rest

"You shall dwell in the land of Goshen, and you shall be near to me…"
Genesis 45:10

When Joseph revealed himself to his brothers and sent for his father, he did not place them in Pharaoh's palace or in the center of the empire. He set them apart in *Goshen*. A fertile region on the eastern edge of the Nile delta, where the river branched into many channels and the soil remained lush even in drought.

In Hebrew, גֹּשֶׁן (*Goshen*) carries the sense of drawing near, approaching closely. Its root, *nagash*, means "to come near, to enter into proximity." That is what Goshen was: a geography of nearness. Not just to Joseph, but to God's presence that was with him since the pit.

Pharaoh said, *"You shall dwell in the best of the land."* Joseph understood that nearness was the best. Abundance without His presence is still famine.

So, the family that once fractured in envy now lived together in provision, planted by the same river that had sustained Egypt. But their sustenance came not from Pharaoh's system but from Joseph's favor, the overflow of rest turned into structure.

Goshen became a living Eden inside empire. A garden bordered by oppression but untouched by it. When the plagues later fell on Egypt, Goshen would remain in light while darkness covered the land (Exodus 8:22, 9:26). It was a protected ecosystem of covenant. The Spirit that hovered over the waters of creation now hovered again over a patch of soil in Egypt.

Goshen was Eden reborn in exile. A river-fed sanctuary where rest was cultivated under foreign rule. And that is the mystery of rest: God does not have to remove you from Egypt to give you Eden. He plants Eden within you until the land itself shifts around your presence.

Step Inside: Goshen and the Rivers of Eden

In Genesis 2, four rivers flow outward from Eden, Pishon, Gihon, Tigris, and Euphrates carried the essence of overflow and boundary. In Egypt, the Nile's branches mirrored that design where rivers flowed out of a central source, watering a land dependent on rhythm, not rain.

The Nile was the world's imitation of Eden's rivers, but in Goshen, Joseph turned imitation back into revelation. He stewarded the flow, aligning natural provision with divine pattern.

The grain-houses were like channels, and the storehouses were like tributaries of mercy. Joseph governed the Nile as Adam once governed Eden, not through dominance, but through design.

Goshen thus became a prophetic bridge between the two gardens:

- Eden, the first home of rest.
- Goshen, the restored home of rest-in-exile.

And eventually, Canaan which was the promised home of rest redeemed. Goshen was the seedbed of deliverance. From there Moses would rise, the Israelites would multiply, and the Exodus would begin; the next great movement of rest breaking through bondage.

Every awakening begins in a Goshen. A hidden place of nearness where the river still flows, and wisdom builds while the world burns.

Goshen's Promise

When Joseph told his family, *"You shall dwell near me,"* he was echoing God's first desire in Eden: *"Walk with Me."* Goshen was the continuation of that covenant conversation. Geography turned into intimacy; a reminder that rest always manifests as nearness.

The book of Genesis ends in Goshen showing that a river still flows and a people still multiply. And in the midst of an empire, rest holds its ground.

The Blessing of Jacob: The Crossed Hands of Grace

"Then Israel stretched out his right hand and laid it on Ephraim's head, who was the younger, and his left hand on Manasseh's head, guiding his hands knowingly, for Manasseh was the firstborn." Genesis 48:14

Jacob was old, his eyes dim. The light in his tent fell in soft patterns, flickering through the fabric. The same kind of light that once fell through branches in Eden, the same kind of glow that had danced on the waters of the flood, the same Spirit that had followed this family through famine and fullness alike.

Joseph entered with his two sons, Manasseh and Ephraim, boys born of Egypt but raised in covenant. They were the fruit of exile: one named for forgetting, the other for fruitfulness. Joseph positioned them carefully: *Manasseh*, the elder, toward Jacob's right hand, and *Ephraim*, the younger, toward his left. He had arranged everything properly, decently, in the expected order of blessing.

But the Spirit within Jacob had other plans. Slowly, deliberately, he crossed his hands. Right over left. Strength over sequence. Grace over law. Joseph noticed at once. He tried to correct him, his tone gentle but firm: *"Not so, my father, for this is the firstborn."* But Jacob refused. *"I know, my son, I know. He also shall become a people, and he also shall be great; but truly his younger brother shall be greater than he."*

The old man's voice trembled with the weight of eternity. He was not just blessing two boys; he was painting again the eternal pattern of divine reversal: the younger raised above the elder, the last made first, the humble exalted, the broken made whole.

In that crossing of arms, heaven whispered the language of redemption. It was the foreshadowing of a greater crossing yet to come, a Cross where divine favor would again defy human order, where blessing would pass through mercy rather than merit. Jacob's arms formed the sign of covenant grace, the same geometry that would one day mark Golgotha.

And the right hand of strength rested upon Ephraim, whose name means fruitfulness. Fruitfulness crowned the future, not forgetting. Grace defined the inheritance, not grief. He blessed them and said, *"By you shall Israel bless, saying, 'God make you as Ephraim and as Manasseh.'"* And thus, he set Ephraim before Manasseh.

The two sons stood silently, unaware of the magnitude of what was unfolding. In this small act, the order of all creation was being rewritten again. The first blessing after the famine, the first declaration of the next generation, the continuation of Eden's echo through covenant love.

Step Inside: The Crossing of Reversal and Grace

Every crossing in Scripture reorders the story:

- The ark rests reversed placing judgment beneath, mercy above.
- The Red Sea parts reversed, and death was held back as life

walked through.

- The Cross itself reversed everything, swallowing sin and revealing righteousness.

In Hebrew, the idea of crossing is bound to the verb עָבַר (*avar*), meaning to pass over, to traverse, to transition. It is the root of *Ivrim*, "Hebrews," the people defined not by where they dwell, but by what they cross. Jacob, the first man called *"Israel,"* had spent a lifetime crossing boundaries: from Canaan to Paddan-Aram, from deceit to dependence, from wrestling to resting.

Now, in his final act, he crossed his hands was a prophetic gesture saying, *"This is how God blesses."* Through reversal. Through grace. Through the unexpected hand of mercy.

Manasseh's name means to forget the pain of the past. *Ephraim's* name means fruitful in the land of affliction. When Jacob blesses Ephraim first, he is declaring:

Fruitfulness shall come before forgetting. The blessing of the future will heal the memory of the past. Overflow will define your identity, not pain.

That is the wisdom of rest in action. History is not erased but redeemed. Sorrow is not denied but transformed into seed. Grace does not cancel the story; it reorders it. What was meant for pain becomes the pattern of provision. What was meant to shame becomes the soil of fruitfulness. And when Jacob crosses his hands, he is showing that rest is always cruciform. It stretches across human striving and divine sovereignty, holding them in tension until grace prevails.

Reflection: The Bones That Prophesy

When Jacob dies, Joseph weeps. He buries his father in the land of promise, but his own bones remain in Egypt for a time. Before his death, he says to his brothers, *"God will surely visit you, and you shall carry my bones from here."* (Genesis 50:25)

Those bones are not relics; they are prophecy. They declare that rest is never confined to geography. Even in the grave, wisdom waits to move. Joseph's bones whisper through the centuries: *"Carry rest forward. Do not leave it buried where you found favor. Bring it into the next promise."*

And when the Exodus begins, the children of Israel carry his bones through the desert, a silent testimony that rest must travel. The man who once governed Egypt through peace still leads Israel through wilderness by promise. Even his remains are a roadmap. Rest that begins in Eden, is tested in the ark, refined in the covenant, enthroned in wisdom and now waits in the dust, knowing resurrection will finish the reversal.

The bones of rest still prophesy: Fruitfulness will rise again. The dream will walk again. Grace will cross every boundary until the promise rests at last.

Epilogue: The Rest that Remains

The years of Joseph's reign slipped by like the slow turning of a river. Children played in Goshen's fields; the river glimmered under Egyptian suns. The storehouses that once overflowed with grain now stood as quiet monuments to foresight and faith. Egypt, which had once bowed before famine, had learned to breathe in rhythm with heaven.

But Joseph knew the story was not over. He had seen too much to mistake prosperity for permanence. Even rest, when confined to one place, becomes an idol. The promise had never been Egypt: it had always been God's presence.

He lived to see Ephraim's children on his knees and Manasseh's descendants like young olive shoots. Each time he blessed them, he remembered his father's crossed hands: grace always passing through paradox.

In his last days, Joseph gathered his brothers. His voice, aged but unwavering, carried the same peace that had once steadied Pharaoh's court. *"God will surely visit you,"* he said, *"and bring you out of this land to the land He swore to Abraham, to Isaac, and to Jacob."* Then he added something strange, tender, deliberate: *"You shall carry up my bones from here."* He did not ask for a monument. He asked to move when God moved. Even in death, Joseph refused to settle. His bones became covenant anchors buried in Egypt, but aimed toward promise. They rested, but they also waited. Centuries later, when Israel marched through the parted sea, they carried more than spoils from Egypt.

They carried Joseph's bones of rest as a reminder that what God births in wisdom He will always finish in mercy. In that act, a truth was sealed for every generation after him: rest is not the end of the story; it is the beginning of everything new. It is the soil of overflow, the womb of re-creation, the pulse beneath every promise.

Rest began in Eden as breath. It rose on Ararat as mercy. It burned in Abraham's faith. It wrestled with Jacob in the night. It ruled through Joseph's peace. And now it waits in bones that will one day walk again.

The story pauses here not as a conclusion, but as a hush. The river slows, but it does not stop. Something greater is gathering downstream. In Goshen, the garden within empire, the children of promise multiply under the eyes of kings who have forgotten Joseph's name. But heaven has not forgotten. The same Spirit that once hovered over the waters of creation now hovers again over this people of rest-in-waiting.

Soon, another deliverer will rise, and through him, rest will move again. But this time not only for a family, but for a nation. For now, the land is quiet. The storehouses are full. The covenant breathes softly beneath the dust. Rest remains. And from that rest, overflow is about to begin.

Selah Meditation: When the House is Full

You do not need to move on yet. Let this chapter settle in you. Notice your breathing. You do not have to change it, just notice it. There is no urgency here.

Imagine a wide place where nothing is threatened. Where provision is already stored. Where tomorrow does not need to be negotiated.

This is your Goshen. It is not a spotlight or a throne.

Imagine this place within you beginning to flourish. A place where what was once scarce is now sufficient in Him. What was once guarded within you can finally rest.

Let your inner posture soften. The vigilance you learned in earlier seasons

can loosen its grip here. You do not have to watch the horizon. You do not have to interpret every sound.

Wisdom has already arranged the storehouses. Grace has already made room. Stay with the quiet fullness for a few breaths. The kind that does not rush toward the next thing, because it knows there will be enough when the time comes.

This is what mature rest feels like. Calm.

When you rise again, carry this with you: You are allowed to live from what has already been prepared. You are allowed to trust what has been stored. You are allowed to rest without explanation. Remain here a moment longer.

Your land within is at peace.

Notes:

INTERLUDE
The Overflow: Restoring Eden's Rhythm

**"And a river went out of Eden to water the garden,
and from there it divided and became four heads."
Genesis 2:10**

Before there was work, there was water. Before there was toil, there was flow. The garden was sustained not by rain or striving, but by overflow with rivers moving outward from the center where God walked. That is the first image of rest. Not motionless but moving. Not static, but steady.

Rest was never the absence of activity; it was the presence of alignment. Eden breathed because wisdom flowed freely. The four rivers; Pishon, Gihon, Hiddekel, and Euphrates carried life in a different direction, each bearing the same source.

That is what intimacy with the Father looks like: everything you touch flows from what He has already finished.

The Pattern of Overflow

The divine order was never meant to be scarcity and striving. It was meant to be saturation. In Eden, every living thing received without grasping, produced without exhaustion, gave without depletion.

Rest was not an interruption of work; it was the rhythm that made work fruitful. When sin fractured that rhythm, humanity began to labor

77

for what once flowed. We began to till ground that used to give freely and sweat for bread that once grew on trees.

But God never changed His design. He has been restoring that Edenic economy ever since through covenant, mercy, and wisdom that orders chaos back into peace.

Joseph lived in that restoration. In him, Eden's rivers flowed again, not through soil, but through structure, not through rainfall, but through revelation. His stewardship was not survival, but rhythm recovered. He stored during overflow and governed by peace.

That is the strategy of rest: the art of moving with heaven's timing until rest multiplies itself.

The Rhythm of Abundance

When we live in union with the Father, our lives stop leaking and start flowing. Everything we need begins to come to us because everything we are moves from Him. We no longer create from deficit but from fullness. We no longer work for peace; we work from peace. That is the secret of the seventh day.

The Sabbath is not a pause but pulse. It is the day when everything made flows in the frequency it was created for. Joseph became the embodiment of that pulse: his wisdom ordered resources, his rest became provision, and his peace governed nations. The abundance in his hands was not luck, but overflow from intimacy.

What Eden released through rivers, Joseph released through heaven's rhythm. Rest reproduces and multiplies life.

When the world calls for panic, rest calls for pattern. When the world measures success by accumulation, rest measures it by abiding. Overflow is not more of what we have but more of who He is flowing through us.

The Call to Become Eden Again

This is where the story turns toward us. Because the same river that once flowed through Eden, and the same Spirit that once moved through Joseph, now flows through those who live in union with Christ.

Rest is not a place you visit but His abiding presence that dwells. The overflow of Eden now moves through human hearts. You are the garden restored. You are the river released. When intimacy with the Father becomes your source, wisdom becomes your current. And when wisdom flows, everything grows in right order. Relationships heal, creativity blooms, and peace begins to govern where panic once ruled.

This is the overflow of rest, the Eden that cannot be lost, only lived.

It is the sound of rivers moving again through redeemed soil, carrying fruit for the healing of nations.

Stay here for a moment. Let the flow find its rhythm again. You were never designed to survive the famine; you were made to steward the overflow. Rest is rising in you like a river, and wisdom knows exactly where it's going.

Reflection: Pause Before Deliverance

The rivers have found their course again. Lean in and you can almost hear them beneath the silence. The soft movement under the surface, the quiet strength of a world preparing for its next breath. Overflow is never loud but rises like dawn, steady and sure. It does not announce itself with thunder; it simply fills every low place until all things are level again.

Let your heart rest in that vibration. Let the pulse of Eden settle back inside of you. The gentle assurance that what He starts, He sustains and what He fills, He keeps in motion. You never have to force what naturally flows by the Spirit or manufacture abundance.

When His river of rest moves through you, everything around you will automatically find its balance again. This is the holy hush before the next awakening, the stillness before deliverance, and the breath between promise and movement.

Listen closely. The current is shifting, and a nation is beginning to stir. And from within Goshen's quiet fields, the sound of mercy is gathering strength.

"Be still. The river within is about to part."

Notes:

_____

_____

_____

_____

_____

_____

_____

_____

_____

_____

_____

_____
_____
_____
_____
_____
_____
_____
_____
_____
_____
_____
_____
_____
_____

8

MOSES

Rest in Deliverance

**"And a man of the house of Levi went and took
as wife a daughter of Levi. So the woman conceived
and bore a son. And when she saw that he was
a beautiful child, she hid him three months."**
Exodus 2:1-2

The Cry and the Current

Egypt never slept. The hum of wheels and the rhythm of whip and
wail filled its mornings. Brick by brick, the empire built monuments to
its own strength, yet beneath the noise the ground pulsed with another
rhythm, the groaning of a people remembered by God.

Somewhere in Goshen, a mother rocked a newborn. Pharaoh's decree
thundered through the streets, but love is always louder than law. When
she looked upon the child, she saw that he was goodly; the Hebrew word
for *'tov.'* The same word that marked the first light of creation rose again
in her spirit.

God had once looked upon the dawn and said, *"It is good;"* and now a
mother in bondage looked on her son and heard heaven whisper the
same. What God had spoken over light, He was now speaking over life.

Something new was being formed in the shadow of empire. Creation was restarting in a cradle of reeds.

The writer of Exodus is not just telling a story about deliverance; he's using language of creation to announce that a new world is being formed. In Genesis, *"The earth was formless and void ... and God said, 'Let there be light.'"* In Exodus, *"Israel groaned ... and God said, 'I have come down.'"* Moses' birth is the dawn of a new creation.

The waters of chaos in the Nile echo the *tohu va-bohu* waters of Genesis 1. The *tevah* (ark) floats above them just as creation hovered above the deep. When Yocheved saw that the child was *tov* (good). It mirrored exactly what God saw in creation at the beginning. Light is appearing again and this time its not cosmic, but covenantal.

She hid him three months, but love can only hide for so long. When she could conceal him no more, she wove a small vessel of bulrushes, sealing it with pitch (*kaphar*), the Hebrew word of covering, and the language of mercy. It was the same substance that once sealed Noah's ark. Another *tevah* (ark) floated again, carrying rest above judgment.

The basket slid into the current. The Nile moved slow that morning, heavy and gold with sunrise. The same river that had swallowed Hebrew sons now bore one who would free them. Even the water remembered Eden's rhythm; creation drawn out of chaos. Pharaoh's daughter came to bathe, her attendants trailing like shadows. She saw the basket among the reeds and sent for it. The cry inside broke something open in her; compassion flooded her heart like the river itself.

She named him *Moses* which means "drawn out." He would live his name. The one drawn out of water would draw a nation through water. The one cradled in pitch and mercy would carry the covenant through fire and wilderness. The rhythm of reversal was already at work; rest rising again through redemption.

Step Inside: *Tevah,* The Ark of Atonement

The Hebrew word תֵּבָה (*tevah*) appears only twice in the Torah: Noah's ark and Moses' basket. Both float above chaos; both carry the seed of a new beginning. Both are coated in *kaphar* (כָּפַר), pitch, the substance of covering. The same Hebrew root that will later become *kippur*, atonement. It is the grace that keeps rest afloat when the world floods with fear.

Each *tevah* is a womb of covenant:

- Noah's *tevah* carries creation through judgment.
- Moses' *tevah* carries deliverance through death.

- The Ark of the Covenant, the third *tevah* carries glory through the wilderness.

All three are containers of God's presence. Each hold what cannot drown: the breath of God, the word of promise, and the mercy of His covering. In Hebrew thought, what floats is what is surrendered. Rest always begins with release. You cannot steer a *tevah*; it has no oars, no rudder, and no control. It moves only by the current of grace. Just as Noah and Moses were carried by His grace so it will be with every soul carried by covenant waters.

Egypt's river was meant to destroy Hebrew sons, but it became the cradle of deliverance instead. The same current that carried death became the pathway of mercy. And when Pharaoh's daughter drew Moses out, she completed the pattern: The one drawn out will draw others out. Moses' very name became prophecy and a reminder that everything born of rest eventually becomes a vessel of rescue.

The Hidden River: Rest Concealed

"And he fled from the face of Pharaoh, and dwelt in the land of Midian; and he sat down by a well." Exodus 2:15

Moses grew within marble walls, his cradle now a palace, and his lullaby the language of empire. He learned Egypt's wisdom: the maps, the magic, and the mathematics of mastery but something restless stirred beneath the gilded surface.

He belonged to another frequency, a song older than pyramids, a memory of reeds and river-water still pulsing in his veins. When he saw an Egyptian strike a Hebrew, justice leapt ahead of wisdom. He struck down the oppressor and hid the body in the sand. But deliverance born from striving cannot endure; it burns out before it begins.

The next day, when his act was exposed, he fled not just from Pharaoh, but from the version of himself that still believed freedom could be forced. He crossed the wilderness into Midian. The Hebrew name Midian means place of judgment or strife, and it lived up to its meaning. Midian is where passion meets purification, where a calling is stripped of self, and where zeal learns silence.

He sat down by a well which was the ancient meeting place between heaven and earth. It was by a well that Hagar first saw the God who sees, and by a well that Rebekah's kindness was tested. Now another well waited to become witness.

There he met Zipporah, whose name in Hebrew means bird. Rest found wings in the wilderness. For forty years he tended sheep. Every morning the desert opened like a blank scroll, and wisdom began to write its letters on him. The silence was not empty; it was forming him. The rhythm of Eden returned walking, watching, naming, and listening. Every breath became a conversation with the unseen Spirit that hovered.

The prince who had once commanded builders now learned to follow bleating lambs, and in their gentle obedience, he learned something sacred: authority born from attentiveness, and leadership shaped by listening. Midian became his hidden river.

While the Nile had carried him from death into destiny, this river of solitude carried him from self-reliance into rest. The world saw a fugitive. Heaven saw a man being re-formed from dust again.

Step Inside: The Wilderness as Womb

In Hebrew, the word for wilderness, *midbar* (מִדְבָּר) shares its root with *davar* (דָּבָר), word. The wilderness is not empty space; it is space cleared for speech. It is where noise falls away and God's voice can finally be heard without competition.

This is where Moses lived. *Midian* did not test him. It quieted him.

For forty years, his life narrowed to the essentials: sheep, stone, wind, and sky. No crowds. No urgency. No proving. Just long days where nothing dramatic happened, and that was the work. Wisdom was forming something that could not survive the pace of Egypt.

Forty, in Scripture, marks this kind of interval. Not punishment, but gestation. A span long enough for identity to be reshaped, but short enough to preserve hope.

Moses' forty years in Midian echo a pattern already woven through Scripture:

- the flood's forty days, where creation returned briefly to mercy's waters
- Israel's forty years, where a nation learned to trust daily bread
- Yeshua's forty days, where obedience matured in hiddenness

In each case, forty measures the space between promise and manifestation, where God works beneath the surface. Moses' life itself unfolds in three such movements:

- forty years in Egypt, where strength was learned
- forty years in Midian, where strength was surrendered
- forty years leading Israel, where strength was entrusted

This was not delay but preparation.

The rabbis speak of the womb as the place of mercy, noting that the

Hebrew word *rechem* (רֶחֶם), womb, shares its root with *rachamim*, compassion. Formation happens where mercy encloses what cannot yet stand on its own.

Midian was that enclosure.

Scripture often hides its most important work in stretches that look like nothingness. Waters cover the earth. Wombs carry unseen life. Wilderness holds men who will one day carry nations. What appears empty is often where wisdom is arranging what rest will later reveal.

Moses did not know what was being formed in him. He only knew that Egypt's noise had faded and something quieter had taken its place. His pace slowed. His listening deepened. His attention learned how to stay.

And when the time was full; without warning, and without spectacle the fire appeared. Not in a palace. Not in a crowd. But in the ordinary place where Moses had finally learned to pause.

And there, in flame that did not consume, rest took form and spoke.

The Flame That Rests: Eden's Fire Rekindled

"And the Angel of the LORD appeared to him in a flame of fire from the midst of a bush. So he looked, and behold, the bush was burning with fire, but the bush was not consumed." Exodus 3:2

Moses had seen fire before.

The desert knew flame well, lightning striking dry brush, wind scattering sparks across the hills, brief brilliance flaring and vanishing as quickly as it came. Fire in Midian was familiar. It consumed and moved on.

But this fire stayed.

It clung to the bush without devouring it. Branches did not blacken. Leaves did not curl or fall. Nothing collapsed into ash. The flame rested, alive, steady, contained, as though glory itself had chosen to dwell rather than pass through.

Something in Moses slowed. His feet stopped before his thoughts did. And he turned. Then Moses said, "I will now turn aside and see this great sight, why the bush does not burn." Exodus 3:3

The fire had already been burning long before Moses altered his pace. The Angel of God had appeared before attention shifted, before dust settled beneath slowing feet. God did not arrive because Moses noticed Him. Heaven had already leaned toward the earth.

But revelation waited.

Moses could have kept walking. The desert had trained him to endure, to survive, to pass by what could not be carried or controlled. Shepherding had shaped his vision to scan the horizon, not linger over wonder. The path ahead was practical, predictable. Nothing demanded he stop.

And yet he did.

He turned aside, not in fear, not yet in obedience, not even in understanding. He paused from his forward motion and allowed his attention to bend toward the flame. It was not repentance or resolve. It was availability.

Nothing about the fire changed when Moses turned. The bush did not blaze brighter. The glory did not intensify. God did not draw nearer. What shifted was Moses himself, his posture and willingness to remain.

The glory had been present all along. Now it had found someone willing to stay.

And only then did the voice speak.

"Moses. Moses."

The world seemed to hold its breath as he stepped closer, as if creation remembered something ancient in that moment. Where once there had been trees heavy with fruit, now stood a thorned bush crowned with fire in different soil, but the same Spirit. Life was burning without exhaustion.

This was the mystery Eden had always carried: strength without strain, power without violence, fire held in communion. Rest was not the absence of flame; it was flame received without resistance.

The bush was not holy because it burned. It burned because God was near. But the ground became holy when Moses stayed.

God was revealing what had always been true: I *still dwell with the ordinary. I still speak where attention yields. I still reveal Myself where someone is willing to pause.*

In Hebrew, the word for bush סְנֶה (*seneh*), means thorny bramble. Even here, in the terrain of the curse where thorns once crowned the Fall, the presence of God descended. The fire did not erase the thorns. It inhabited them.

Moses was standing where the residue of the curse had become a dwelling place for glory and where resistance now held His Spirit. Thorns, still thorns, filled with life that did not consume them. Redemption was taking shape before his eyes.

"Remove your sandals," God said.

It was more than reverence. It was remembrance. Skin meeting soil again. Dust no longer avoided but welcomed. Moments before, the ground had been ordinary. Now it carried weight, warmth, awareness. Holiness was not descending from above; it was rising through contact.

Eden's ground had closed beneath disobedience. Horeb's ground opened through a simple yielding.

Everything felt strangely familiar, though Moses had never stood here before. A tree bearing life. A voice calling a man by name. Earth made sacred by encounter rather than distance.

It was as if the story had not moved forward at all but folded back on itself with God walking with dust again, not in evening cool, but in fire gentle enough to approach. Not hidden among leaves but revealed in a flame.

The Father had returned to walk with man.

And Moses, barefoot and trembling, stood in the place where the world remembers what it was made for.

Step Inside: The Fire That Rests

The bush is more than spectacle. It reveals divine rest in paradox, energy that does not exhaust and passion that does not destroy. Here, the essence of God's presence meets the frailty of creation, and instead of annihilation, there is habitation.

In Hebrew, the word for dwell is שָׁכַן (*shakan*), meaning to settle, to abide, to rest within. From it comes שְׁכִינָה (*Shekinah*), the indwelling glory.

What Moses witnesses in the desert is not random fire; it is *Shekinah* finding its resting place again on earth. This is Eden's flame returning to visibility. The bush becomes a preview of what will later be built in gold and acacia wood, the *Mishkan*, the Tabernacle, where God's presence will descend and rest between cherubim. The bush is the prototype of the dwelling place, a portable Eden, a mountain in miniature. The flame that rests within the bush will soon rest upon a nation.

The message of the bush is not, "*I Am fire.*" It is, "*I Am with you.*" And wherever He abides, fire becomes rest and dust becomes holy.

The Exodus: Rest Confronts Chaos

*Afterward Moses and Aaron went in and told Pharaoh,
"Thus says the LORD God of Israel: 'Let My people go,
that they may hold a feast to Me in the wilderness.'" Exodus 5:1*

The bush's fire still burned behind Moses' eyes when he returned to

Egypt. The same flame that rested in the thorn now burned quietly in the heart of a man who had learned stillness. He carried no weapon, no army, only a name.

Ehyeh Asher Ehyeh. "I AM."

The self-existent stillness that holds all creation together. Before Pharaoh's throne, two worlds faced each other: empire built on endless motion, and eternity built on rest. Pharaoh's gods promised power through labor, but God spoke of a feast in the wilderness, a return to divine rhythm marked by joy, movement, and song. It was not rebellion He demanded, but rhythm restored.

The Hebrew phrase for "Let My people go" (*shalach et ami*) does not only mean release; it also means send forth, set in motion toward purpose. God was not removing His people from work, but restoring them to worship. *"That they may hold a feast unto Me…"*

The word for feast, חַג (*chag*), comes from a root meaning to move in a circle, to dance. So, the first command to Pharaoh was not to toil harder, but to enter the circle of celebration. Eden's vibration was returning through invitation.

The Signs of Rest

Moses lifted his staff, and the plagues began. In heaven's eyes, they were not punishments. They were reversals, acts of divine reordering. Every sign dismantled an idol of Egypt's striving.

Sign	Hebrew Term	What It Reveals
Nile to blood	*dam (blood, life)*	Egypt's false lifeblood exposed, and control turns to corruption.
Frogs	*tsefardeim*	The voice of chaos multiplied, and Pharaoh's noise made visible.
Lice	*kinim*	The dust itself rebelling and creation unmade by pride.
Flies	*arov*	Swarming confusion causing no rest without order.
Pestilence	*dever*	Death among beasts and laboring strength failing.
Boils	*shechin*	Flesh reacting to internal unrest.
Hail and fire	*barad*	Heaven and earth colliding creating judgment through imbalance.
Locusts	*arbeh*	Consumption devouring production.

| Darkness | *choshekh* | The absence of light with no sight, and no rhythm. |
| Death of the firstborn | *bekor* | Striving's ultimate loss: the fruit of self-effort dies. |

Each plague was a mirror. Egypt was seeing itself. Striving always leads to chaos; rest always leads to renewal. Pharaoh's heart grew '*kaved*', heavy. That's the same Hebrew word used when God's glory "filled" the tabernacle (*kavod*). But here the weight became resistance. The same glory that softens those at rest hardens those who strive. The difference is not in God but in the heart that meets Him.

Step Inside: I AM, The Stillness That Speaks

When God spoke His name to Moses from the fire, He did not give a title.

He offered a state of being.

Ehyeh Asher Ehyeh, אֶהְיֶה אֲשֶׁר אֶהְיֶה

Most often translated "I AM WHO I AM," the phrase is more fluid than English allows. It can also be heard as:

"*I will be what I will be,*"

"*I am the One who is,*"

or even, "*I am becoming what I am becoming.*"

But none of this mean changeability.

The Hebrew verb *hayah* does not describe instability. It describes His living presence: being that continues, endures, and remains faithful to itself. It is existence without effort. Being without urgency. Life that does not need to prove itself.

God was not defining Himself for Moses. He was revealing the ground Moses was standing on.

Pharaoh ruled by pressure. His kingdom was built on forced production, endless output, and the fear of not being enough. Egypt was a world where value came from labor and identity came from performance.

Against that roar, God did not shout. He spoke from still fire and said, *Ehyeh.*

"I AM."

Not I will overpower.

Not I will compete.

Not I will hurry.

Just being present, sufficient, unthreatened.

This is why the first miracle of the Exodus was not a plague.

It was Moses standing calmly before Pharaoh, carrying a Name that did not rush. Rest stood where striving ruled. Presence confronted power without imitating it.

Ehyeh is the God who does not react.

Asher is the spaciousness that allows Him to remain Himself.

Ehyeh again, the One who remains.

"I am who I am."

"I will be with you as I am."

"I remain."

The stillness at the bush was not weakness. It was the deepest authority in the universe.

And Moses was being invited, not to wield power, but to stand inside that stillness and let it speak through him.

The Threshold of Passover

Then came the night of reversal. Judgment would pass through the land, but mercy moved ahead of it in the form of blood.

"When I see the blood, I will pass over you." Exodus 12:13

The word *pesach* means to hover, to guard, to pass over in protection. It's the same motion as the Spirit in Genesis 1: hovering over the face of the waters, shielding creation in mercy. The blood on the doorposts marked a home as covered rest.

The destroyer could not enter what mercy had enclosed. Each home became a miniature Eden. God's presence dwelling again with life inside, death passing by outside. That night, the world turned. What Egypt called slaves, God called sons. The people who once labored to build Pharaoh's monuments now left carrying gold and the wages of rest restored.

Reflection: The Strength of Stillness

Deliverance did not begin with a sword but a whisper. The greatest act of war in history was an invitation to a feast.

Centuries later when Yeshua came, He did not draw weapons or armored angels. Only breath. A man tormented by a legion of spirits fell at His feet and Yeshua did not shout. He spoke. Softly. A whisper that carried the weight of worlds. The demons heard the same Voice that once said, *"Let My people go,"* and they fled before it. Heaven has never needed noise to break chains, not even a word from the One who is Rest Himself. His very presence is enough.

Every sign, every plague, every drop of blood declared one truth: God's rest is stronger than any empire's striving. When you face your own Pharaohs with voices demanding more bricks, more proof, and more control, remember this: The bush still burns. The Name still speaks. And rest still confronts chaos by simply being present.

The Sea: Rest Parts the Deep

"Then Moses stretched out his hand over the sea; and the LORD caused the sea to go back by a strong east wind all that night, and made the sea into dry land, and the waters were divided."
Exodus 14:21

Darkness, wind, and water: the same elements that began the world now gathered again on the edge of deliverance. Behind them, Egypt thundered with chariots. Before them, the sea heaved like a living wall. Between them, the breath of God began to move.

Scripture says a *"ruach kadim,"* an east wind, blew all night. The same *Ruach* that hovered over the waters in Genesis 1:2 now hovered again, dividing chaos from covenant. Creation was happening again, not in a garden this time, but in the dark corridor of deliverance.

The Womb of Waters

The Red Sea was not a battlefield; it was a birth canal. The waters stood up on both sides, and Israel passed through on dry ground, the language of *yabashah*, the same word used in Genesis 1:9 when God said, *"Let the dry land appear."* It was the moment the earth came out of hiding and the moment creation emerged from the womb of water.

This is why the early rabbis called the crossing *"the birth of the nation."* The womb opened, the waters broke, and life came forth. Egypt's cries echoed the labor pangs of judgment; Israel's first breaths were those of freedom.

"The waters were a wall to them on their right hand and on their left."
Exodus 14:22

Those walls were not barriers but boundaries of mercy. The same force that held chaos at bay during creation now held it apart long enough for new life to emerge. It was the membrane of forty all over again, the protective enclosure between the unformed and the revealed. Every step through the sea was a step through the womb of redemption.

Step Inside: The Reeds and the Rest

The Hebrew name for the sea is '*Yam Suf,*' the Sea of Reeds. The word *suf* literally means reed or papyrus which is the very same material that formed Moses' basket.

Do you see it?

The pattern has come full circle. What once carried one child through the waters now carries an entire nation. Moses' personal exodus becomes Israel's collective rebirth. Both stories are *tevah* stories, arks floating above chaos, sealed with mercy, and moved by breath. Both emerge into new covenant ground. The ark, the basket, the sea are manifestations of God's same rhythm: rest enclosed, then released.

Pharaoh's Pursuit: Striving Drowns in Stillness

Egypt followed them into the sea, chariots grinding into the same path grace had opened. But what was womb to Israel was tomb to Egypt. Striving cannot survive where rest reigns. The waters that cradle surrender crush resistance.

When the morning light rose, the waters returned to their strength, *lashuv l'eitano*, literally, "to their eternal order." Even the sea knew how to rest again. Creation exhaled, and what was chaos became completion.

The Crossing as Covenant

In Jewish liturgy, the Red Sea is called *Kriyat Yam Suf* and means, "the cutting of the sea." The word *kriyat* comes from the same root as covenant cutting (*karat berit*). God was not just making a path; He was cutting covenant with His people. The sea was the knife, the path was the scar, and the other side was the promise. When Israel stepped onto dry ground, they were no longer slaves, but sons. The covenant that began with one man named rest (*Noah*) was now sealed in the birth of a nation called to live in it.

The Sound of Stillness

For a long moment, the world stood silent. Only the wind moved. Then, from the far side of the shore, a cry of wonder rose. It was the sound of creation hearing its own heartbeat again. Water had given way to land. Death had given way to life. Chaos had yielded to rest. The sea had finished its song; now Israel would begin theirs.

The Song of the Sea: The Sound of Creation Remembered

"Then Moses and the children of Israel sang this song to the LORD, and spoke,

saying: "I will sing to the LORD, For He has triumphed gloriously!
The horse and its rider He has thrown into the sea! Exodus 15:1

When Israel's feet touched the solid earth, the first thing they did was sing. Because when creation stands on dry ground after the storm, its natural response is worship.

This is not just a song of victory; its creation finding its voice again. The same Spirit that hovered over the waters at the beginning now moved through a people made new. Every note was a return to Eden's breath, sound and stillness woven together into praise.

The First Music of Rest

The Hebrew song begins:

"אָשִׁירָה לַיהֹוָה," *Ashirah l'Adonai,* "I will sing to the LORD."

The word *ashirah* is from the root *shar*, meaning to go straight, to flow, to be level. At the Red Sea, Israel does not sing to feel better. They sing because something has already been completed, and the body must exhale truth.

Singing is what happens when breath agrees with what God has done. The body gives voice to completed deliverance, and the soul agrees aloud with reality restored.

So, this was not entertainment. It was recognition. The waters had already parted. The threat had already fallen silent. What remained was breath finding its way back into order.

Israel sang because chaos had lost its hold. Their voices did not summon freedom; they named it.

In Scripture, creation begins with speech. Here, re-creation is sealed with song. Voice becomes the witness and breath becomes testimony. Rest is restored not as silence, but as harmony.

Each movement of the song echoes the first ordering of the world: separation, triumph over the deep, emergence, and praise. Not because music recreates the cosmos, but because the people have finally stepped back into it.

Each phrase of the song mirrors a day of creation:

Creation	Song of the Sea
Light from darkness	*"The LORD is my strength and my song."*
Waters divided	*"At the blast of Your nostrils, the waters piled up."*
Dry land appears	*"The floods stood upright like a wall."*
Sun and moon set in place	*"Your right hand, O LORD, has become glorious in power."*

Life fills the earth	*"You stretched out Your right hand, and the earth swallowed them."*
Humanity formed	*"You in Your mercy have led forth the people You have redeemed."*
God rests	*"You will bring them in and plant them in the mountain of Your inheritance."*

The song itself becomes the seventh day; the sound of rest settling over creation.

Miriam's Dance: The Rhythm of Eden

"Then Miriam the prophetess… took a tambourine in her hand, and all the women went out after her with tambourines and dances." Exodus 15:20

Miriam, the first woman in Scripture called a prophetess, becomes the embodiment of Eden's joy restored. Her tambourine (*tof*) comes from the same Hebrew root as *taphaph* which means "to strike rhythmically, to beat with the heart." The heartbeat of God is being heard again in human hands.

She leads the women in circles, *chag*, the same word God used when He told Pharaoh, "*Let My people go, that they may hold a feast (chag) unto Me.*" The dance Moses prophesied in Pharaoh's court now moves in desert dust. The circle has come full. Eden's harmony that was broken by striving now moves again in unity and rhythm. Worship becomes motion, and motion becomes rest.

Step Inside: The Structure of the Song

Hebrew poetry is not linear but architectural. The *Shirat HaYam* (Song of the Sea) is built like a sanctuary or a lyrical tabernacle. It begins with a call to praise (*the outer court*), moves through God's mighty acts (*the holy place*), and ends with His dwelling among His people (*the holy of holies*).

"You will bring them in and plant them in the mountain of Your inheritance, in the place, O LORD, which You have made for You to dwell in."
Exodus 15:17

The word plant here, *nata'*, is the same word used in Genesis 2:8, *"And the LORD God planted a garden in Eden."* The song ends with dwelling as Eden is being planted again, not in soil, but in sound.

The Theology of Sound

In Hebrew thought, sound is creative. When God said, *"Let there be light,"* the sound itself shaped reality. Now, through Israel's singing, creation participates in its own redemption. The silence of slavery is broken; breath becomes praise; rest becomes resonance again.

This is why the song begins in *"I will sing"* and ends in *"The LORD shall reign forever and ever."* It starts with human response and ends in divine permanence: the full circle of relationship restored. Worship is remembrance; the echo of creation recognizing its Maker again.

The Breath Between Notes

After the last word faded across the sea, there was a stillness deeper than silence. The people stood, hearts racing, eyes wet. They had been born through water, and now, for the first time, they simply rested. No one commanded them to move. No task awaited. Only God's presence. Only His deep abiding shalom and the hum of a world reborn.

Reflection: The Song That Never Ends

If you listen closely, you can still hear it, the sound creation makes when it remembers who it belongs to. Every wave, every wind, every whisper of prayer is a note in that same song. It began in Eden, echoed through the ark, rose again from the sea, and will one day fill every corner of creation when rest finally reigns.

"The LORD shall reign forever and ever." Exodus 15:18

The Wilderness and the Manna: Rest Tested, Rest Taught

"Then the LORD said to Moses, "Behold, I will rain bread from heaven for you. And the people shall go out and gather a certain quota every day, that I may test them, whether they will walk in My law or not." Exodus 16:4

After the song, silence. The sea behind them, the desert before. No walls of water now, only endless horizon. The first days of freedom feel more like emptiness than arrival. But God leads them here deliberately into the landscape where striving cannot survive. Here, there are no markets, no fields, no storehouses. Only dependence. Only daily breath. The wilderness is not punishment but a detox of the soul. Here, the habits and striving of Pharaoh and Egypt are unlearned and deconstructed. The heart must relearn the art of rest.

Bread from Breath

When the people cried out for food, God did not answer with fields or harvests. There were no seeds to plant, no tools to sharpen, no cycles to manage. Instead, bread appeared.

It fell quietly, thin as frost and light as dew, resting on the ground before the sun could claim it. And the people asked the only question they had words for:

> *"When the Israelites saw it, they said to one another, 'man hu'?*
> *for they did not know what it was." Exodus 16:15*

"Man hu?" In Hebrew means "What is it?" The Hebrew word *manna* was formed by their question. It is not a definition, but a confession: What is this?

Even God's provision arrived as mystery, bread that could be eaten but not explained, received but not possessed.

Scripture did not correct their question.

It preserved it.

Manna was named not for what it was, but for what it evoked. Provision arrived before comprehension. Sustenance came wrapped in wonder. Even daily bread refused to be mastered by definition.

This was not food that could be stored, strategized, or controlled. It could not be hoarded without spoiling. It could not be gathered for tomorrow without trust. It trained the body to wake into dependence and the soul to receive without grasping.

Every morning, Israel stepped out into mystery and ate. Not explanation. Not certainty. But enough.

Manna taught them that rest precedes understanding. That wisdom does not always arrive with clarity, but with faithfulness. And that the God who feeds His people does not always explain Himself, He sustains them first.

Their nourishment began as a question because covenant life begins the same way: not with answers, but with daily trust in what is given.

From Toil to Trust: The Reversal of the Ground

When Adam stepped out of Eden, the first sound he heard was not thunder; it was the earth groaning.

> *"Cursed is the ground for your sake; in toil you shall eat of it all the days of your*
> *life. By the sweat of your face you shall eat bread..." Genesis 3:17–19*

The bread of labor became the sign of lost rest. Every crumb was a reminder of distance; the ground resisting what once grew freely. But here, in the wilderness, something astonishing happens. Bread no longer rises from the cursed soil; it falls from heaven. No sweat, no plow, no seed, only surrender.

What Adam reached for in striving, Israel receives through stillness. The curse is being reversed in plain sight: dust no longer earns its food; it opens its hands to receive it. The ground remains silent, but heaven speaks again, and its language is provision without price.

Manna is more than nourishment. It is redemption made edible. Every morning whispered, *"You will eat bread again, but this time not by sweat, only by trust."*

Step Inside: The Test of the Seventh Day

God commanded them to gather just enough for each day, except on the sixth. Then, they were to gather double. On the seventh, nothing would fall. The rhythm was deliberate: six for labor, one for love; six for motion, one for meaning.

The Hebrew word for 'test' in Exodus 16:4 is *'nasa'* meaning to lift up, or to prove through carrying. This was not a trap; it was a tenderness. God was lifting their hearts into a higher frequency. Manna rotted when hoarded. What was meant for daily trust turned sour under anxiety.

The same miracle that sustained them in rest spoiled in striving. It was the lesson of Eden retaught: Do not grasp; just receive. Do not seize, just savor. Each sunrise suddenly became communion; a chance to relearn that life flows from abiding in His Presence, not performance.

The Mystery of the Omer

Each family gathered an omer per person: about two quarts. When they measured it, those who gathered much had nothing over, and those who gathered little had no lack. Every heart was full, and every need was met, not by equality of effort, but by equity of grace. This was divine economy. Rest does not compete; it completes.

The Hebrew word *'omer'* (עֹמֶר) shares a root with *'amar'* which means to speak. Provision was linked to His voice with heaven feeding those who listened.

The First Sabbath

"See! For the LORD has given you the Sabbath;
therefore He gives you on the sixth day bread for two days.
Let every man remain in his place;

97

let no man go out of his place on the seventh day." Exodus 16:29

The Sabbath was not a demand; it was a gift. It arrived before Sinai, before law, woven into manna like breath into bread. The Hebrew *Shabbat* means to cease, to settle, and to celebrate completion. The wilderness became the first rehearsal of Eden's rest. Every seventh sunrise whispered the vibration of creation: *"Enough."* That single word was worship. No work, no gathering, no proving; just being. Each Sabbath, heaven's sound synchronized with human hearts again. The desert became a sanctuary of stillness.

Step Inside: The Manna and Wisdom

In ancient Hebrew symbolism, manna and *'chokmah'* (wisdom) share a spiritual parallel. Both descend from heaven. Both nourish the inner life. Both can only be received with humility.

Proverbs 9:5 echoes this pattern: *"Come, eat of my bread, and drink of the wine I have mixed."*

Wisdom feeds in the same way manna falls, daily and fresh, received rather than possessed. When it is gathered for control, it spoils into knowledge without life. But when it is received in rest, it becomes revelation that sustains the soul.

The Jar of Memory

"And Moses said to Aaron, "Take a pot and put an omer of manna in it, and lay it up before the LORD, to be kept for your generations." Exodus 16:33

One jar of manna was placed in the Ark of the Covenant. It was the tangible reminder that rest feeds what labor cannot. Inside the ark rested:

- Word (the tablets of law),
- Life (Aaron's rod that budded),
- Provision (the jar of manna).

The same triad that existed in Eden; voice, fruit, and fellowship now dwelt again in a vessel of covenant. The wilderness had become womb again holding the DNA of divine frequency.

The Tabernacle: Eden Restored in Structure

"And let them make Me a sanctuary, that I may dwell among them." Exodus 25:8

When God spoke those words to Moses, they carried the same

creative force as "*Let there be light.*" A world was about to be built again, not from chaos, but covenant. The God who once walked among trees would now dwell among tents. Eden's blueprint was being reissued with man building in partnership with wisdom.

The Architecture of Rest

The instructions for the tabernacle fill thirteen chapters which is the same number of verses that form Genesis 1's creation account.

Coincidence? Never.

It is the echo of re-creation. The wilderness had become the new creation space, and the tabernacle was its beating heart; a microcosm where heaven and earth would breathe together again. Every loop, socket, curtain, and cubit was divine geometry: rest translated into architecture.

Creation	Tabernacle
Light divided from darkness	Golden lampstand illuminating the holy place
Waters separated	Bronze laver reflecting heaven's image
Land appears with seed	Table of showbread was daily provision renewed
Luminaries placed in heavens	Priests robed in glory and beauty
Creatures filled the earth	Altar receiving offerings of life
Humanity formed in God's image	High priest bearing His name before the people
God rests	Glory filling the tent and God's presence dwelling in stillness

What began as creation spoken into being now returns as creation invited to dwell: form prepared, life sustained, communion restored, and rest finally given a place to remain.

Step Inside: The Word Shakan and the Glory of Rest

The Hebrew for "dwell" is שָׁכַן (*shakan*) and means to rest, to abide, and to settle down. From it comes שְׁכִינָה (*Shekinah*), the indwelling glory and the felt weight of God's presence. When the last stitch was tied and the final peg driven,

"The cloud covered the Tent of Meeting,

and the glory of the LORD filled the tabernacle." Exodus 40:34

The Hebrew word for 'filled' (*male*) is to complete, to fulfill, to satisfy. Creation's seventh day was happening again. Fire and fragrance, weight and warmth, and rest enthroned in form. This was marriage in matter: infinite dwelling within finite frame, God's presence '*shakan*' (dwelling) among His people.

The Ark: Rest Between the Wings

At the center stood the Ark of the Covenant, a chest of acacia wood overlaid with gold. Inside it rested manna, Word, and rod: symbols of provision, voice, and resurrection. Its lid, the '*kapporet*' ("covering"), was the meeting of blood and glory.

From *kaphar*, "to cover, to atone," God was now clothing humanity with mercy. Cherubim faced one another, wings touching. They mirrored the guardians of Eden's gate, but this time, no sword flashed between them. Fire no longer barred; it blessed. The doorway to communion stood open again.

> *"And there I will meet with you," said the LORD, and I will*
> *commune with you from above the mercy seat." Exodus 25:22*

The verb '*ya'ad*' ("meet") also means to appoint, to betroth. The ark was not a courtroom; it was a bridal chamber. Eden's union was being renewed.

Step Inside: Wood and Gold: Humanity Overlaid with Glory

> *"And they shall make an ark of acacia wood;*
> *two and a half cubits shall be its length,*
> *a cubit and a half its width, and a cubit and a half its height.*
> *And you shall overlay it with pure gold, inside and out you shall overlay it,*
> *and shall make on it a molding of gold all around..." Exodus 25:10–11*

The Ark was made of acacia wood and is '*atzei shittah* (עֲצֵי שִׁטָּה) in Hebrew. The word '*etz* again means tree, reminding us that this vessel of covenant is still rooted in creation's language. But this is no ordinary tree. Acacia wood was chosen for its incorruptibility. It is a desert tree: thorned, gnarled, and enduring. It thrives in arid, hostile soil where other trees cannot live. It resists decay, termites, and rot.

In other words, it is a resurrection tree. It grows in barren ground yet remains incorruptible. Even its thorns echo redemption's pattern; the curse's emblem transformed into covenant's vessel. Acacia is the only tree strong enough to endure the wilderness and flexible enough to be shaped for glory.

In the Tabernacle, God did not choose cedar of Lebanon (*royal, fragrant*), but acacia of the desert (*humble, enduring*). Glory always rests on what can withstand wilderness.

The Gold: Divinity Clothing Humanity

Once the ark's frame was built, it was overlaid in pure gold, inside and out. The Hebrew word '*tsaphah*' means to cover, to plate, to sheathe completely. Gold in Scripture represents divine nature, purity, and incorruption. When Moses covered the acacia wood in gold, it became a physical prophecy: *humanity clothed in divinity.*

The ark is therefore the first visible union of these two realities: flesh and glory, earth and heaven, tree and light. It is, in essence, a Tree of Life restored in form. The incorruptible wood (*humanity redeemed*) overlaid in radiant gold (*divine glory indwelling*).

This is the mystery of covenant: *God dwelling within what He has redeemed, and glory resting upon what grace has purified.*

The Echo of Eden and the Prophecy of Christ

When the first Adam fell, the Tree of Life was veiled behind cherubim. Now, in the wilderness, God instructs another '*etz*' to be fashioned, not as a forbidden object, but as a dwelling place. The ark becomes Eden's tree reborn which is rooted in desert soil, crowned with gold light, and guarded by cherubim once again. The sword burns above it in welcome.

Later, this same pattern finds its final fulfillment in the Cross, another tree of plain and humble wood, overlaid not with gold, but with glory. The incorruptible life of the Son will inhabit the corruptible frame of humanity, and the Tree of Death will become the Tree of Life again.

Acacia wood and gold are covenant in code: mortality wrapped in immortality, earth carrying eternity.

Symbol	Meaning	Fulfillment
Acacia Wood	Humanity, incorruptibility through endurance	The body of Christ, unbroken in the wilderness of sin
Gold Overlay	Divinity, purity, eternal glory	The Spirit resting upon redeemed creation

Ark of Covenant	Dwelling place of Presence	Christ in us, the hope of glory
Cherubim Above	Guardians of Eden's way	Witnesses of restored access
Mercy Seat	Place of covering	Atonement becomes union through grace

The Ark of the Covenant told a silent story: *God does not abandon the dust, He adorns it with beauty.*

Reflection: Trees of the Tabernacle

Every beam, every board of that desert dwelling came from trees that once stood in the heat, scarred by wind, rooted in unyielding ground. When God told Moses to build His house, He did not import cedar from foreign lands. He used what the wilderness already held. Rest never looks for perfection before it dwells; it inhabits what is available and makes it holy.

So too with us. We are acacia; thorned, weathered, and ordinary. But in the hands of Wisdom, we are overlaid in gold, filled with glory, and called His dwelling place.

"You are the temple of the living God," Paul would later write, as God has said: *'I will dwell in them and walk among them'."* 2 Corinthians 6:16

We are the ark now: wood covered with glory, dust alive with His presence, and the Tree of Life walking once more among creation.

The Tabernacle as Moving Eden

The tabernacle was not static; it moved. When the cloud lifted, the camp lifted. When the cloud settled, they settled. God's presence dictated their pace. It was the vibration of rest turned into movement. Everywhere the people went, a piece of Eden walked with them, gold for the glory, wood for humanity, linen for purity, oil for anointing, and fragrance for communion. The desert that once devoured became a dwelling place for delight.

This is the mystery of rest: it can bloom even in barren places when wisdom builds a home for glory.

Step Inside: The Tabernacle and the Human Heart

In later Hebrew thought, the tabernacle was seen as a reflection of the human body.

- The outer court: the body, visible and temporal.

102

- The holy place: the soul, scented with worship.
- The most holy place: the spirit, where His Spirit dwells.

The ark corresponded to the heart; the seat of covenant, where God speaks not from distance but from within. The tabernacle, then, was not simply a structure; it was humanity redeemed as God's resting place. The story was moving from Eden's garden to Sinai's mountain, and into Israel's heart. The dwelling was always meant to become internal again.

Selah Meditation: Held in the Midst

Let the pace of your body slow here. You do not need to finish anything, and you do not need to understand what comes next. Allow yourself to be in this space without urgency: without solving, without proving, without carrying what can be set down for a moment.

Imagine a place where nothing is demanded of you, where the noise settles without effort and the tension in your shoulders loosens on its own. Outside, the wilderness may still stretch wide, but inside there is shelter. There is a stillness inside your heart that does not come from escape, but from being covered by His wings.

Bring your attention to your breath for a moment. Trust is like the breath. It arrives and leaves on its own, steady and unforced. There is no rush here, only His presence. Provision, too, comes this way: not all at once, not ahead of time, but daily, quietly, faithfully. Just enough for today. It does not need to be stored, hoarded, or controlled. It simply meets you where you are.

Let the fear of scarcity soften. Let the need to manage tomorrow loosen its grip. You are not sustained by what you gather, but by what is given. There is a care already surrounding you, holding you steady even as the world beyond this moment continues to move.

Remain here for a few slow breaths. Allow the racing thoughts to settle. In this space there is no striving, no proving, or reaching ahead. Just rest inside the One who is already keeping you. He loves you deeply.

When you arise, carry this knowing within you: you are being held, even now. And where you are held, you are in rest.

Stay here a moment longer.

Notes:

9

JOSHUA

The Rest that Takes Territory

"Moses My servant is dead; now therefore arise."
Joshua 1:2

The Jordan Still Breathes

Before dawn, the Jordan lay silent as a ribbon of bronze beneath a paling sky. Joshua stood on its bank with the ark glinting behind him, its golden cherubim half-veiled in mist. He had seen water like this before; the Red Sea rising in fury, the river of Egypt swallowing a generation. Now, again, the same element waited before him not as barrier, but as invitation.

The air was heavy with dew and memory. Behind him, tents shuddered softly under the wind, each one carrying the breath of a promise older than the desert itself. The wilderness had been a womb; now the womb was opening. The time for wandering was over, but the time for striving had not yet begun. Rest was waiting on the other side, but it would not come through battle but with trust in motion.

Joshua's hands trembled. He remembered the day Moses laid hands upon him; the fire that passed, and the silence that followed. He had been trained to fight, to serve, to wait but not to lead through stillness. That was new. That was holy.

The Commission and the Weight of Continuity

When God spoke, it was not with thunder. It came like the breath that moved across Eden's first dawn: *"Moses My servant is dead; now therefore arise."* The word settled on Joshua's shoulders with the weight of eternity. He had heard commands before, orders, decrees, and instructions, but this one vibrated with the memory of creation itself.

"Arise."

In Hebrew, the word is קוּם (*qum*), to stand, to be established, to be confirmed. It is not a word of motion; it is a word of resurrection. When God says '*qum*,' He is not simply telling a man to get up; He is awakening what He Himself has already formed.

Joshua felt that word in his bones. It was as if the ground beneath his feet remembered Genesis: the first sunrise breaking over waters, the world standing upright out of chaos.

Step Inside: קוּם (*Qum*), The Word That Stands

The Hebrew verb '*qum*' means to rise, to stand, to be established, to be confirmed. But in its earliest pictographic form when Hebrew was still written with symbols, it paints an even richer image.

Qof (ק): a circle with a line descending from that represents the sun on the horizon, a moment of dawning, or transition from darkness to light.

Vav (ו): a nail or hook is something that joins or secures.

Mem (ם): water is chaos, a womb, or flow.

So, in its ancient essence, קוּם (*qum*) carries this picture: *"The dawning that secures order over the waters."* It is resurrection language written into creation itself. Every time God says '*qum*,' something dormant is invited to stand upright again in His order. It is the echo of the first sunrise over Eden's chaos and the call that wakes the world.

The Pattern of *Qum* in Scripture

The word *qum* moves like a hidden current through the story of rest, rising again and again at the moments where God invites humanity to arise.

In the beginning, the earth rises from the waters and light rises over darkness. Though *qum* is not spoken in Genesis 1, its movement is already present. Creation itself stands up out of formlessness. This is *qum* in its first song, the posture of creation answering its Maker.

Later, after Lot chooses his portion, Yahweh speaks directly to

Abram: *"Arise, walk through the land."* Rest now takes on motion. Promise is not grasped but walked into. *Qum* inaugurates covenant as obedience that trusts the ground beneath each step. Abram does not rush to possess; he rises to receive.

Years pass, and the word comes again to Jacob. *"Arise, go up to Bethel."* The call arrives after exile, fear, and fracture. *Qum* becomes the bridge back to communion. It gathers what has wandered and lifts it toward altar and remembrance. Here, rising is not triumph but return.

When Moses hears the word, it carries weight. *"Arise, go to Pharaoh."* *Qum* now stands upright in the face of oppression. Rest does not retreat from power; it confronts it. The word that once lifted creation now stands before empire, steady and unyielding.

After Moses dies, Yahweh speaks again but this time to Joshua: *"Now therefore, arise."* The moment marks transition. Instruction gives way to inheritance. *Qum* becomes the hinge between what has been taught and what must now be lived. Nothing is discarded; everything is carried forward through transformation.

Through the prophets, the word widens. *"Arise, shine, for your light has come."* Here *qum* becomes *qumi*, spoken in the feminine to Zion, to the Bride. What was once addressed to individuals is now spoken over a people. The call is no longer merely to stand, but to awaken together into glory.

And finally, the word reaches its most intimate expression. Yeshua enters a room of mourning and says, *"The child is not dead, but sleeping."* Then He speaks in Aramaic, *"Talitha, qumi."* He reawakens what already belongs to it. *Qum* completes its circle from the rising of creation to the rising of the dead. What began at dawn now answers resurrection morning.

Rest That Stands

When God says *'qum'* to Joshua, He is not merely telling him to get up and move. He is re-establishing the order of divine rest within creation's story. He is saying: *"As light stood over darkness, now you will stand over promise. As the earth rose from the waters, now you will rise from wilderness."*

The Hebrew does not only mean "rise," but it also means be established, confirm, or make valid. So, God's words could be read: *"Moses is complete; now therefore, be established."* That subtle shift changes everything. Joshua's leadership is not about succession; it's about stability. The command is not to move forward in haste, but to stand firm in fulfillment.

Qum and Wisdom's Rhythm

In the language of *chokmah* (wisdom), '*qum*' is what happens when structure becomes presence and governance. It is the moment when the blueprint of wisdom's labor receives the breath of rest's indwelling. Eden "stood up" in the same cadence; the ark "stood" in the Jordan; and the temple "stood" when glory filled it. Each standing place is a new manifestation of '*qum.*'

Every time rest becomes visible, something rises and remains. '*Qum*' is the word that wakes the stillness into strength.

Application to Joshua's Call

So when God says, *"Now therefore arise,"* He is awakening Joshua as the embodiment of everything that has gone before. He is saying: *"Stand as Adam should have stood. Rise as Noah's ark rose above the waters. Be established as Abraham was. I am raising in you the order that once stood in Eden."*

This single word becomes the hinge between the lost rest of Adam and the fulfilled rest that Christ will later bring. Joshua's '*qum*' is the prototype of resurrection rest and the same command that one day will call,

"Arise, shine, for your light has come." Isaiah 60:1

The Hebrew phrase that followed, '*chazaq ve'ematz,*' "be strong and courageous," was not a summons to aggression, but to rootedness. '*Chazaq*' means to take hold, or to fasten. '*Ematz*' in Hebrew means to stand firm. Together, they form the frequency of '*qum*' itself: strength anchored in stillness.

Joshua closed his eyes and let the word settle into his soul. He was no longer a servant under Moses; he was a vessel through which God would keep building. He was not taking over but standing up in what God had already begun.

And what God began was not with a sword, but with a heart. Before Israel crossed a single boundary, God crossed one. Before walls fell, a woman's soul had opened. Rest was already moving ahead of the people and flowing into unexpected places, softening impossible ground by finding one house in a city built to resist Him.

Rahab's Window: Mercy in the Wall

The city of Jericho did not sleep. Its gates were shut, its torches burned all night. Beyond the walls, the Jordan shimmered like a blade, and rumors rippled through every alleyway where Israel had crossed.

Inside those walls lived a woman named *Rahab*, a name that in Hebrew, '*Rahav*,' means spaciousness, wide place.

Yet her life was the opposite, confined and narrow, hidden behind stone and reputation. The irony itself was prophetic: within a city hemmed by fear, God had planted room for mercy. Rahab's house was built into the wall itself, the very structure meant for separation. But heaven delights in paradox. What humanity builds to divide, God uses to deliver.

The night the spies came, the wind off the plains carried the scent of dust and expectation. They slipped through the gate as merchants, but their eyes betrayed them as they watched looking for something more than lodging.

When Rahab saw them, she recognized something ancient in their gaze, a fire that did not belong to slaves or wanderers. She hid them beneath flax stalks on her roof, the same flax used for linen, the fabric of priests, the covering of the tabernacle, a symbol of purity.

Even in secrecy, a priestly act was unfolding: the house of shame becoming a sanctuary of His presence. Outside, soldiers pounded on doors, searching, shouting, cursing. Inside, Rahab whispered a confession that rewrote history:

> *"I know that the LORD has given you the land…*
> *For the LORD your God, He is God in heaven above and on earth beneath."*
> *Joshua 2:9–11*

Her declaration broke the curse of Canaan before a trumpet ever sounded. Faith spoke where fear lived, and that word carved an opening in the wall before the stones ever fell.

When the soldiers left, Rahab took the scarlet cord and tied it to her window. The word cord in Hebrew is תִּקְוָה (*tiqvah*) also means hope and expectation. It is the same word used later in Proverbs:

> *"The hope (tiqvah) of the righteous will be gladness." (Prov. 10:28)*

Hope, in the language of heaven, is always a thread; something thin but unbreakable, connecting heaven's promise to earth's frailty. As the cord unfurled in the torchlight, its color shimmered deep red, the same hue that once stained Eden's soil with Adam's breath, the same color brushed on Hebrew doorposts at Passover, the same lifeblood sealing every covenant since Noah. That scarlet thread was not decoration; it was prophecy woven into fabric.

Step Inside: The Rest Hidden in the Wall

The wall of Jericho represents more than defense; it is the architecture of fear and humanity's attempt to secure itself apart from God. Every stone whispered, *"We will protect ourselves."* But within that wall, in a single home, rest is learning to breathe again. Rahab does not escape the city by running; she remains still. She does not fight for her survival; she waits. And that waiting, trusting the unseen promise, is the purest form of *nuach* (rest).

Faith is always rest in motion. Even the way her salvation unfolds is Edenic: a woman, a word, a covering, a seed. Through Rahab, the lineage of the Messiah will one day come, uniting scarlet with gold, faith with fulfillment. Her story becomes a living proverb: *Wisdom hides in humility; rest hides in trust.*

As dawn crept over Jericho's wall, Rahab stood at her window, the scarlet cord fluttering against stone like a heartbeat. She could feel the stillness before the storm, the peace before the trumpet. And though her city trembled, her heart did not. She had already entered her promised land.

Crossing the Jordan: Creation Replayed

Morning came like a held breath. Mist curled above the river, the same color as the linen that wrapped the ark. Joshua stood before the priests, his voice steady though his heart beat like thunder.

"When you see the ark of the covenant of the LORD your God carried by the priests, then you shall set out from your place and go after it." Joshua 3:3

This was no ordinary crossing. This was Genesis again. The river flowed heavy this time of year; snowmelt from the Hermon heights swelling its banks. The people gathered, two million souls pressed together, their eyes fixed on the priests bearing the ark of God's presence.

The air glistened, full of silence and expectancy. Then it happened. The moment the soles of their feet touched the edge, the Jordan remembered.

The Hebrew word for Jordan, '*Yarden,*' comes from *yarad,* "to descend." It is the river that falls, that humbles itself between two lands. But when the ark stepped in, the descent reversed. The water rose upward and became a wall standing far off at the city called Adam.

Adam.

The first name in the first garden. Even the geography bore witness. The river that had flowed downward since Eden now lifted upward in reverence, as though creation itself remembered its Maker. The waters that once carried death now carried memory, and as they rose, the ground emerged.

Joshua walked beside the priests, watching the water heap in the distance, the earth dry and gleaming where chaos had been. He whispered a word he had heard from Moses long ago:

"The LORD will fight for you; and you shall hold your peace." Exodus 14:14

The ark stood in the center, golden wings hovering, silent over the dry riverbed. It did not move, or rush but rested. That stillness held back an entire river. It was wisdom's rhythm made visible: rest halting chaos, structure holding space for life.

As the people passed, some stared in awe, some wept, some ran, but all of them crossed over beneath the gaze of rest. Each footstep pressed into fresh clay that once lay hidden under water, and behind every step, heaven whispered, *"This is how I build, by stillness before strength."*

When the last sandal touched Canaan's soil, Joshua turned back and saw it; the priests still standing, and the ark unmoved. They had not hurried the miracle. The crossing was not powered by effort but anchored by His Spirit.

Joshua called twelve men forward, one from each tribe. *"Lift a stone,"* he said, *"and carry it upon your shoulder from the place where the priests' feet stand firm."* The men obeyed, heaving river stones slick with silt and silence. They carried them to the far shore, to build a memory that would outlast emotion.

"That this may be a sign among you, that when your children ask,
'What do these stones mean?' you shall tell them..."
Joshua 4:6

Even in victory, God was teaching them how to remember. The stones were not to burden them, but to anchor the moment in their bodies. Memory, when untethered from touch, drifts. Each stone became a witness: *rest is not seized in triumph but carried forward in trust.*

When they reached the western bank, they set the stones at Gilgal, a circle of testimony built from the bed of chaos. And when the last priest stepped out, the Jordan sighed. Its waters fell forward again, rushing past as if nothing had happened, yet everything had.

Revelation: The Stillness that Holds Chaos

Every crossing in Scripture carries the same quiet truth: *chaos yields not to force, but to His Spirit.*

At the Red Sea, the waters fled as deliverance rushed forward. At the Jordan, the waters paused as inheritance took its first breath. One crossing was escape. The other was arrival. In both, rest stood at the center.

Eden knew it first as God walked without urgency. Noah knew it next as God rested upon the waters that could not overwhelm. Israel touched it again when God stood firm where the river strained to move. And in time, rest would no longer move around humanity at all; it would dwell among them, and then within them, and finally offer itself completely in Yeshua.

That night at Gilgal, the people slept with the sound of the river behind them and dry ground beneath them. Children laughed. Elders wept. They had crossed into promise but something quieter had crossed into them.

Joshua looked back toward the Jordan, and it was as if the river itself whispered what the day had taught them all along:

Rest does not wait for peace.

Rest makes peace.

Gilgal: The Place of Rolling

Before them stretched the plains of Jericho, but God's gaze was not on the city. It was on the people themselves. They had come out of Egypt, but Egypt still lived in their memory. So, He spoke to Joshua again softly, but with the weight of promise:

"Make for yourself flint knives, and circumcise the sons of Israel a second time."
Joshua 5:2

It was not punishment but preparation. Before they could possess the land, they had to reclaim their name. Joshua obeyed, and Scripture says,

"He circumcised the sons of Israel at Gibeath-haaraloth." And the LORD said to Joshua, "This day I have rolled away the reproach of Egypt from you." Therefore the name of the place is Gilgal.
Joshua 5:9

In Hebrew, *Gilgal* (גִּלְגָּל) comes from *galal* (גלל) and means to roll, to turn, or to uncover. It is the same root used when David writes, *"Roll your burden upon the LORD, and He will sustain you." Psalm 55:22*

Gilgal is not only a place of removal, but of renewal. Something is rolled away so something truer can be revealed. This moment was not about physical circumcision alone, but about the unveiling of the heart. As Deuteronomy says, *"Circumcise the foreskin of your heart, and be stiff-necked no longer."*

The wilderness had been a long baptism. Gilgal was rebirth. The old cycle of striving and shame was being cut away, and the mark of covenant returned Israel to who they truly were: sons and daughters of rest. This is how the Bride finds her stature again: not by advancing, but by returning. This is how the Bride finds her stature again: not by advancing, but by returning to the place where striving rolls away and belonging is restored.

That night they camped at Gilgal, just east of Jericho. The smell of wet earth lingered in the air, and the stones carried from the Jordan rested nearby as silent witnesses to a crossing that had changed everything.

That same night, they ate from the land for the first time.

Grain roasted over new fire. Bread baked from soil they had not tilled.

The taste was different, heavier, fuller, and formed through touch rather than waiting.

And then, without announcement, without warning, the manna ceased.

No trumpet marked its ending. No farewell fell from heaven. Morning came and the ground was bare. For forty years grace had arrived daily without effort. Now the silence itself was the sign.

Heaven had not withdrawn. It had entrusted.

What once fell freely would now rise through partnership in walking, tending, and receiving. The rhythm of Eden began again: God present, people responsive, and the land alive beneath their hands.

Joshua stood beneath the moonlight, its silver washing over the stones lifted from the Jordan. Something had quietly closed. Something else had opened. The wilderness was behind them. Rest had taken root as inheritance.

Step Inside: The Hebrew Echo of Identity

The Hebrew word for "reproach" in Joshua 5:9 is חֶרְפָּה (*cherpah*), meaning disgrace, insult, shame. It shares its root with '*harap*,' meaning to strip or expose. Here God uses it in reversal: He strips away the shame that stripped them. He exposes to heal, not to humiliate. The place of exposure becomes the place of restoration. In Hebrew thought, identity is not static but unfolds through covenant. Each name, each cut, each altar is a revelation of relationship. When God says, *"I have rolled away your reproach,"* He is restoring belonging, not modifying behavior.

The First Meal of the Land

"They ate of the produce of the land of Canaan that year.
And the manna ceased on the next day." Joshua 5:11–12

That same night after the cutting and stillness, the manna stopping was not loss; it was maturity. Heaven was saying, *"You can now harvest what you once only received."* Grace had not ended but evolved. For forty years, bread had fallen like mercy. Now, bread would rise from trust. It was the restoration of Eden's rhythm: to tend what grows rather than beg what falls.

The Commander of the Lord's Host

And then when the people rested, when identity was restored, and when trust was complete, God's presence appeared again. Joshua lifted his eyes and saw a man standing opposite him with a drawn sword in his hand.

"And it came to pass, when Joshua was by Jericho, that he lifted his eyes and looked, and behold, a Man stood opposite him with His sword drawn in His hand.
And Joshua went to Him and said to Him,
"Are You for us or for our adversaries?"
So He said, "No, but as Commander of the army of the LORD I have now come."
And Joshua fell on his face to the earth and worshiped, and said to Him,
"What does my Lord say to His servant?" Joshua 5:13-14

The voice that spoke from the bush now stood before him as fire in flesh. The same Spirit that rested over the ark now embodied before him. He was not for or against: He was. In Hebrew, Joshua's name, *Yehoshua*, shares the same root as *Yeshua*. At Gilgal, heaven was already foreshadowing the day when another Joshua would roll away reproach, not from one nation, but from all creation.

Jericho: The Silence Before Sound

The morning after Gilgal, the air was still thick with the scent of new bread. Across the plain, Jericho gleamed in the sun, a ring of stone and pride rising from the dust. It was said to be impenetrable, built on generations of fear. But Joshua stood quietly, watching the light move across its walls. He did not see a fortress. He saw an ending. God's presence had already gone before him. The Commander of the Lord's Host had appeared with a sword drawn, and that was all the assurance that Joshua needed. This was not a conquest by strategy; it was the fulfillment of it through stillness.

The Instructions of the Impossible

"You shall march around the city, all you men of war;
you shall go all around the city once. This you shall do six days.
And seven priests shall bear seven trumpets of rams' horns before the ark.
But the seventh day you shall march around the city seven times,
and the priests shall blow the trumpets." Joshua 6:3–4

It was a command that sounded foolish to human reason but in heaven's mathematics, seven is never about repetition. It is about completion. Each circuit was a day of creation retold, each silent step another echo of *"Let there be."*

The number seven (שֶׁבַע, *sheva*) shares its root with *shava* and means to be complete, to swear an oath.

So, the seven days around Jericho were not about strategy; they were an oath in motion; a covenant performed in stillness.

The Silence that Speaks

Joshua commanded the people:

"You shall not shout or make any noise with your voice, nor shall a word proceed out of your mouth, until the day I say to you, 'Shout!' Then you shall shout."
Joshua 6:10

Silence became their weapon. Not suppression, but surrender. For six days, they walked with only the sound of feet and wind. The Ark led, the priests followed, and the people, the once-grumblers of wilderness, said nothing. It was a miracle of its own kind: *a nation learning to trust without proof, to move without explanation.*

Step Inside: The Sound of Seven

Every sound in Hebrew thought carries spiritual weight. The word for "sound," קוֹל (*qol*), also means voice. The *'qol'* of the shofar on the seventh day mirrors the voice that shook Sinai. At creation, *'qol'* Elohim, the voice of God, formed light. At Jericho, the *'qol'* of obedience will collapse walls. The same Word that builds worlds can unmake strongholds. In wisdom's order, sound always follows silence. Silence builds the chamber where sound gains authority. The six days of quiet were not wasted, they were womb days. Creation itself held its breath again, waiting for a seventh-day exhale.

115

The Seventh Day: The Rest That Roars

The dawn of the seventh day rose red over the plains. No one spoke. The priests lifted their trumpets, shofars made from the curved horns of rams, the same animal once caught in a thicket to save Isaac. Each horn was a memory of substitution; each note a proclamation: *"Mercy reigns here."* Seven circuits. Seven blasts. Seven seals of silence broken.

Then Joshua cried,

"Shout! For the LORD has given you the city!"

The sound erupted with harmony. It was creation's first sound replayed: light bursting forth, order rising from vibration. Walls did not simply fall; they folded. The Hebrew verb נָפַל (*naphal*) means to collapse in surrender. Even the stones obeyed rest and yielded.

Rahab's Scarlet Thread

In the middle of the ruin stood one section of wall unbroken, a window washed in the soft light of scarlet glistening. The same *'tiqvah'*, thread of hope, that once marked Rahab's house now became the dividing line between judgment and mercy. She and her family were drawn out, and the city of fear became a doorway of grace. From her line would come kings and prophets, and, generations later, the Messiah Himself. Even in destruction, rest protected the promise.

Revelation: Stillness as Warfare

Jericho was never about walls. It was about trust. Every battle of the spirit is first a battle of flow: the choice between reaction and rest. God did not need soldiers; He needed silence that obeyed. The enemy is not conquered by striving but by alignment; by standing still long enough for His Spirit to move through you.

This is the wisdom of rest: that what is established in stillness cannot be shaken by sound. Rest does not resist; it reveals. And when it reveals, creation yields.

When the dust settled and the city lay open, Joshua fell to his knees. He knew this victory was not won by men's might. It was born in the same silence that once birthed the world. He closed his eyes, the roar fading behind him, and in that sacred stillness, he heard the whisper again; the same word that had started it all:

"Arise."

Selah Meditation: The Rest That Wins Without Noise

Pause here. Just let the momentum of the page slow down within you.

Let your shoulders relax.

Notice your breath as it enters… and leaves… without being pushed. Imagine the space around you filled with peace. The dust has settled and all is calm. The ground is steady beneath your feet. Nothing is rushing you forward. Nothing is asking you to explain yourself.

This is the stillness that follows trust. Feel how firm the ground is beneath you. Not tense. Not braced. Simply held.

This is what rest feels like when it has done its work. Not loud or triumphant. Certain.

Let your breathing ease into that certainty. The same calm that stood in the river. The same hush that surrounded the city.

The same Spirit that moved without force is already here within you.

You do not need to push down the walls in front of you. You do not need to raise your voice or strive. Just remain. Rest is not retreat. It is the place where your heart stops proving and begins trusting. Where you are no longer striving to overcome, but willing to stand.

Stay for a few quiet breaths. When you rise, carry this knowing with you:

What you yield to God does not need a shout to fall.

Notes:

_____

_____

_____

_____

_____

_____

_____

_____

_____

_____

_____

_____

_____

_____

_____

_____

_____

_____

_____

_____

_____

_____

_____

_____

_____

_____

_____

_____

10
DAVID
The Heart of Rest

**"Here's the one thing I crave from God, the one thing I seek
above all else: I want to live with Him every moment in His
house, beholding the marvelous beauty of God, filled with awe,
delighting in His glory and grace.
I want to contemplate in His temple."**
Psalms 27:4 TPT

The Shepherd of Stillness

The morning light spilled over the hills of Bethlehem, soft and golden, touching each blade of grass until the fields glittered as though heaven itself had bent down to kiss the earth.

A boy sat on a stone worn smooth by his own sitting, harp across his knees. The flock moved slowly around him, the white of their coats catching the dawn. He plucked at the strings, half singing, half breathing a song that seemed to rise out of the soil itself.

The melody began as a whisper of love; simple and wordless but the longer he played, the more it filled the valley. The sheep lifted their heads; some drifted closer, hooves silent in the wet grass. The sound was not command; it was invitation. Even the wind seemed to join in, weaving through the notes, carrying them toward the hills. A lark answered, then another, until the air quivered with a quiet joy.

He sang of the One he could not see but deeply loved and somehow knew. He sang of kindness that watched and never slept, of hands that shaped the hills and knew the names of lambs and stars alike. Every phrase was both question and answer...*You are my song, and I am Yours.*

When his eyes lifted, the horizon was gold and trembling. The breeze brushed through his hair like a blessing. He laughed softly, as his heart gazed toward the One he loved, aware heaven was listening. He felt the pleasure of the Creator moving through creation again.

The earth swayed gently under the rhythm of that song. Grasses bent, light danced, sheep pressed close. For the first time since Eden, love had a voice in the open air, and the land remembered the sound.

The Beloved: A Union Restored

He was only a boy, nameless to the world, yet heaven already called him beloved. The name that would one day crown him, דָּוִד (*Dāwīd*), meant beloved, friend, darling. The Hebrew letters of David's very name tells the story of his life: a door opened toward God, a life joined in intimacy, and a door that never closed again. He did not contain God's presence but carried it through. Even before a prophet's oil found him, the Father had whispered it into the soil of his heart: *You are loved, and you will love Me in return.*

In Eden, love and rule had never been separated; the tending of the garden was the act of worship itself. Now, on Bethlehem's hillside, that song of union stirred again. God's presence that had once walked with Adam found a resting place in a shepherd's melody.

Every note David played was communion. The space between his breath and the wind became holy ground. He did not reach for God; he responded to the One who was already near. And the more he sang, the more the world around him aligned to the ancient cadence: love as dominion, worship as rest. Heaven leaned close to listen. The same Voice that had once said, "*Let there be light,*" now whispered in the quiet: "*Let there be love.*" And the heart of a shepherd became the dwelling place of a King.

Bethlehem: The House of Bread and the Portal of Provision

The song of love that rose from the hills did not rise from just anywhere. It came from Bethlehem, בֵּית לֶחֶם (*Beit Lechem*), a name that means House of Bread. Every syllable was a prophecy waiting to unfold.

In the beginning, the first Adam reached for food outside of trust; he took what was not his to take. Here, in this little village, the second pattern began: *bread born not from grasping, but from giving.*

The ground that had once been cursed for Adam's sake now listened to a shepherd's song and began to heal. The boy's worship was not only praise; it was cultivation. Every melody watered the soil of covenant. Every breath turned labor back into delight. In Bethlehem, rest began to knead creation again: slow, rhythmic, and holy.

Beit (house) in Hebrew speaks of dwelling; intimacy, belonging, the structure of home. *Lechem* (bread) comes from the root לחם (*lacham*), meaning to eat, to share, even to fight or contend. It is paradoxical: the same root can mean to feed or to wage war.

Bethlehem therefore carries a secret: it is the house where sustenance and struggle meet, the place where provision overcomes the curse of toil. To tend the flocks in Bethlehem was to stand between hunger and satisfaction, to guard the boundary where the Creator would one day feed the world again.

The boy did not know it, but his fields were the cradle of the Bread of Life. The same hills that echoed his harp would one day hear the cry of the infant Christ. So, when David played, he was not merely worshiping but prophesying. His song tilled the soil that would bear redemption. The sound of his harp was the heartbeat of heaven saying,

> *"…man shall not live by bread alone;*
> *but man lives by every word that proceeds from the mouth of the LORD."*
> *Deuteronomy 8:3*

Bethlehem's name became its destiny. From its earth would rise a vibration of mercy, the grain of heaven broken for the world's hunger. And all of it began here with a boy, a harp, and a song that fed creation.

Israel's Cry and Heaven's Answer

By the time David's song drifted over the hills, Israel had forgotten the sound of rest. They wanted a king; someone visible, someone they could measure by stature and strategy. They were tired of waiting on the invisible guidance of God. So, they cried out to Samuel, *"Give us a king to judge us like all the nations."* It was not rebellion so much as exhaustion; they mistook human control for divine care. Heaven's answer was patient.

God allowed Saul to rise, a man tall and impressive, the image of what Israel thought strength should look like. But Saul's heart was loud with pride and striving. He led by fear, fought to maintain appearance, and sought approval more than God's presence. Under his rule, the people had a king, but they lost their song.

The throne they wanted became the mirror of their own anxiety. Israel had traded His presence for performance. Yet even while Saul built monuments to his strength, heaven's search never stopped. God was listening for another sound; one not born of ambition but of adoration. Somewhere, in the quiet hills of Bethlehem, that sound was rising on the strings of a harp. It was the sound of union.

The Heart of Union

When David sang, he was not performing; he was communing. Every psalm was an act of covenant, where sound met breath, and love met His presence. He did not sing to reach God; he sang because God had already reached him. It was not ambition that made him a king; it was the posture of his heart. God could entrust him with rule because his heart already ruled from rest. Leadership rooted in intimacy always returns people to intimacy.

Where Adam once broke fellowship through desire, David restored it through devotion. His reign would teach Israel what rule looks like when it flows not from fear, but from rest. He led not as one who controlled, but as one who was carried.

Step Inside: The Hebrew Texture of Love

The root דוד (*dod*), from which David's name comes, is woven throughout the Song of Songs where it means beloved, lover, intimate companion. It is not the language of duty, but of delight, a reciprocal love that rejoices simply in nearness. David's very name, then, is a prophecy: *the Beloved through whom divine affection returns to earth.*

When his psalms cry, *"My soul follows close behind You; Your right hand upholds me." (Psalm 63:8)* a voice long buried rises again, the sound of Eden remembered. *I heard You walking in the garden, and I ran toward You.* The harp in his hands becomes the sound of Eden restored.

The Secret Place

Scripture calls David *"the sweet psalmist of Israel,"* but that sweetness was learned in solitude. He built a sanctuary before any temple was ever raised; an inner holy of holies where silence and song met face to face. In the quiet hills, his worship was not ceremony, but conversation. He was rediscovering what Adam once knew: that dominion is born of delight, and government of communion.

> *"One thing I have desired of the LORD, That will I seek:*
> *That I may dwell in the house of the LORD All the days of my life,*
> *To behold the beauty of the LORD,*
> *And to inquire in His temple." Psalm 27:4*

That is the language of union. He wanted not the throne, but the gaze. And that is why God called him a man after My own heart.

Step Inside: The Hebrew Heart

When God said, *"Man looks at the outward appearance, but the LORD looks at the heart,"* He was not speaking of emotion but of essence.

The Hebrew word for heart is לֵב (*lev*) and sometimes *levav*. It means more than feeling; it is the seat of inner thought, will, desire, and consciousness; the center of a person's being. In ancient Hebrew, the *lev* is the place where spirit and flesh meet, where decisions are birthed and intentions are weighed.

Unlike the modern view that divides head and heart, Hebrew language sees no such split, only perfect heart brain coherence. The *lev* thinks, discerns, remembers, loves, and obeys. It is the engine of wisdom, the womb of worship, and the throne of rest. To have *"a heart after God's own heart" (lev kelevavi)* means more than to love what He loves; it means to be tuned to His inner rhythm, to think and feel and move in the same cadence as Heaven.

It is union not by proximity, but by pulse. David's *lev* was shaped in stillness. While Saul built monuments to control, David built quiet altars of trust. His strength was not in sword or strategy but in this inner sanctuary; a heart resting where God rests, burning where God burns, and yielding where God yields.

So, when God whispered to Samuel, *"Rise and anoint him; for this is the one,"* He used the word קוּם (*qum*): to arise, to stand up into calling. It is the same word spoken generations earlier to Joshua:

> *"Moses My servant is dead; now therefore arise (qum) and cross this Jordan."*
> *Joshua 1:2*

Each '*qum*' is a resurrection word with rest awakening into motion. Heaven never commands rise to begin striving; it calls one to rise when the heart is already still. That is why God could trust David with His people: the call to arise came to a heart already resting in union.

To '*qum*' is not to scramble upward; it is to stand into divine breath;

the same breath that hovered over waters, and the same that filled Adam's lungs. When Samuel rose to anoint, creation itself seemed to stand taller. A new heart had been found and in it, the flow of God's rest was alive again.

"Man looks at the outward appearance, but the LORD looks at the 'lev' (heart)."

In that single verse, the blueprint of Eden pulses again: The Creator walking with one whose heart beats with His own.

Samuel's Visit and the Anointing

The day Samuel arrived in Bethlehem, the air itself seemed to pause. For years, the prophet had carried the grief of Saul's downfall like a stone in his chest. He came to Jesse's house still trembling from that loss, not knowing that heaven was already breathing through the doorway. *"Bring your sons before me,"* he said.

One by one they came; Eliab with his soldier's stance, Abinadab with the calm of discipline, and Shammah with eyes that had already seen battle. Each looked the part of a king. But God's voice was clear in the prophet's heart:

"Do not look on his appearance or on the height of his stature…
for the LORD does not see as man sees. Man looks at the outward appearance,
but the LORD looks at the lev (heart)." 1 Samuel 16:7

So, Jesse sent for the youngest. No one thought to include him before; he was unseen like the seed beneath the soil that the world assumes is still dead. He came in from the fields, dust on his sandals, sunlight in his hair, and the faint scent of sheep clinging to his tunic. But within his eyes carried the stillness of a boy who had been alone with God.

Samuel felt the shift before God spoke. It was the same hush that fell when the Spirit first hovered over the waters: creation waiting for a new word. Then came the whisper:

"Rise (qum) and anoint him, for this is the one." 1 Samuel 16:12

Oil met skin, and time seemed to fold. The horn tipped, and the golden river ran down David's head, tracing his brow, his cheek, his heart. The scent of it filled the house; the same fragrance that once rose from Eden when man walked with God. The Spirit of God rushed upon him from that day forward, not as a momentary visitation, but as habitation.

In that anointing, heaven had chosen not a warrior, but a worshiper. Not the tallest, but the tenderest. Not the one most fit for command, but the one most ready for communion. This was not the crowning of a king; it was the coronation of intimacy. The oil did not signify power but authority. And the boy anointed in secret would one day bring the Ark, the symbol of His very presence, back to the heart of a nation that had forgotten its song.

The Ark and the Dance

The years after Saul's fall were heavy with silence. The Ark, the heartbeat of Israel's worship, had been forgotten for a generation. It rested in a house on the edge of memory, while the people carried on with religion without God's presence. They had order, but not intimacy; motion, but not rest. David's first desire as king was not conquest or crown but communion. He could not bear to rule from a throne while God's presence still dwelled in exile.

"and let us bring the ark of our God back to us,
for we have not inquired at it since the days of Saul."
1 Chronicles 13:3

It was not nostalgia but genuine ache. The shepherd who once sang to an invisible God now longed to bring His presence fully home.

The Ark as Echo of Noah's Ark

The Hebrew word for ark is אָרוֹן (*aron*) and is a chest, a container, or a vessel for what cannot die. It is the same word used for Noah's ark and for the basket that carried Moses. Each '*aron*' was built for one purpose: to preserve life through judgment. In Noah's day, it floated above floodwaters. In Moses' infancy, it drifted across Egypt's Nile of death.

And now, under David's reign, it traveled the dust roads of Israel. It carried not animals or infants, but the covenant itself, life's law written in stone and mercy's blood soon to cover it. Every '*aron*' tells the same story: *When chaos rises, God makes a place for life to rest.* Inside the '*aron*,' mercy waits for manifestation.

Even the atonement lid is called the '*kapporet*,' from the root כָּפַר (*kaphar*) and means to cover, or to atone. It is the same word used when Noah sealed his ark with pitch, so the waters could not enter. Both arks are "covered" in grace; both carry covenant through chaos.

When David led the procession, he was doing more than moving furniture; he was reenacting creation's story of deliverance. Wood overlaid in gold moved once again toward its resting place.

The Six Steps and the Sacrifice

The procession began with drums, trumpets, and hearts pounding in cadence. But every six steps, they stopped.

Not because six was flawed, but because six was full. Six is the measure of creation's movement, the cadence by which God shaped earth and sky, and body and breath. In Hebrew, the sixth letter is *vav* which is the joining stroke, the connective thread between heaven and earth, motion and meaning. Six steps carried the ark forward in the same pattern that once carried light into darkness and land out of the waters.

And then they paused.

David insisted that the seventh movement must belong to God.

Six steps of motion, one pause of offering.

Six carried by human breath, one returned to divine breath.

In that pattern, Sabbath did not wait for stillness but moved through the streets of Jerusalem. Each pause became an altar and a heartbeat. The people began to recognize what creation had always known: *rest is not the absence of movement, but the yielding of movement back to its Source.*

The ark advanced, and so did their hearts, learning again the ancient order written into the world from the beginning: life unfolding through motion, sustained by worship; work carried by mercy, creation moving forward because it knows where to stop.

In Hebrew, this rest is called מְנוּחָה (*menuchah*), the settled center where life comes into order. It is the stillness of Eden restored, the gentle hush that fills the air when His presence draws near. As the ark advanced, *menuchah* moved through the people like light returning to a long-darkened room.

The Dance of David

When the ark entered the city's gates, David did something no king had done before. He danced. Not as a monarch, but as a child returning home. He cast off the robe of rank and moved with abandon before the Lord, clothed only in linen and awe. Each motion was a psalm made visible; each turn, a pulse of love.

The harp had become his body with strings of muscle and sinew vibrating with heaven's own music. That day the city heard a frequency creation recognized. The same sound that once moved through Eden's leaves now moved through a man.

It was not rhythm alone but resonance: the joining of heaven's tone and human flesh until the two became one sound. David was not dancing for God; he was dancing with Him. This is what Eden always meant: a people who are the song, whose lives become the music of divine rest moving through creation.

The prophets would later call this the '*kol mayim rabbim*,' "*the voice of many waters.*"

It is not a choir of performers, but the vibration of hearts in union, every life echoing the frequency of the river that once flowed through paradise. David's dance was the first measure of that melody returning to earth.

Michal, Saul's daughter, watched from her window and despised him in her heart. Striving cannot recognize surrender; pride cannot comprehend purity. Where she saw disgrace, heaven saw restoration.

David's dance was not disorder but communion finding expression in the body. The king of Israel was modeling the forgotten truth: authority in rest looks like love unashamed.

Step Inside: David's Dance and "*Kol Mayim Rabbim*"

When Scripture uses the phrase '*kol mayim rabbim*,' "the voice of many waters," it is always describing moments when God's presence moves with overwhelming fullness (Ezekiel 43:2; Revelation 1:15). And although the phrase itself does not appear in the story of David's dance, the pattern behind it is woven through David's own writings and Israel's experience with the Ark.

David is the one who first describes God's voice as waters:

"The voice of the LORD is over the waters; The God of glory thunders; The LORD is over many waters." Psalms 29:3

He repeats the imagery again in his later years as he describes God's presence breaking in like floodwaters and storms (2 Samuel 22:14–17). The Ark had already parted the Jordan River (Joshua 3–4), teaching Israel that waters respond to God's nearness, that the movement of the Ark is the movement of His voice. By the time the Ark enters Jerusalem, David's theology and Israel's memory both carry this association: where God's presence moves, creation responds like water stirred by wind.

So, when David danced, stripped of status and full of surrender, it was not merely celebration. It was the human heart in utter surrender resonating with the same Spirit the prophets would later describe as "*the voice of many waters.*" Revelation joins these images again with harps, worship, and the sound of many waters (Revelation 14:2). David held a harp. David wrote the psalms. David used water language for God's voice long before Ezekiel or John heard it.

This is the connection: not a mystical claim, but biblical continuity.

David's dance is the earliest moment in Scripture when worship and Spirit flowed together through a human body in unbroken union, so whole and aligned, that later prophets would name its resonance *kol mayim rabbim*, the sound of many waters. This is not the sound of music; it is the sound of a life whose inner chambers vibrate with God's fullness.

It is the same place Yeshua spoke of in John 7:38: "*out of his belly will flow rivers of living water.*"

The belly in Hebrew is *beten*, the seat of desire, or the womb of longing and is the very realm the serpent was cursed beneath in Eden (Genesis 3:14). Where the enemy was sentenced to dust and unfulfilled hunger, humanity becomes the place of overflowing satisfaction. Yeshua fills the seat of desire with the fullness of Himself. The region once associated with the serpent's humiliation becomes the chamber of the Spirit's river.

David embodied this reversal long before the language existed. His dance was not emotional display, it was the first human echo of *kol mayim rabbim*: heaven's river moving through human desire, desire aligned again with Eden's Tree of Life, desire filled, not starving; desire restored, not shamed.

And what David carried in seed, the prophets would later behold in fullness. The sound that moved through his body becomes the very phrase by which they describe the presence of God.

A Lovesick Bride Echoes the Sound of Many Waters

The prophets who came after David, Ezekiel and John, describe God's presence with this same phrase:

kol mayim rabbim: קול מים רבים ("the sound of many waters.")

For Ezekiel, it was the sound of God's glory returning to the temple (Ezekiel 43:2). For John, it was the voice of the risen Messiah Himself as he shared, "*His voice as the sound of many waters.*" (Revelation 1:15)

But then something stunning happens.

In Revelation 14:2 and 19:6, the same sound is no longer coming only from God; it is coming from the Bride.

"And I heard a voice from heaven, like the voice of many waters, and like the voice of loud thunder. And I heard the sound of harpists playing their harps."
Revelation 14:2

"And I heard, as it were, the voice of a great multitude, as the sound of many waters and as the sound of mighty thunderings, saying,
"Alleluia! For the Lord God Omnipotent reigns!" Revelation 19:6

The sound of many waters becomes the sound of a multitude. The voice of the Lamb becomes the voice of the Bride, not because she replaces Him, but because she shares in His very vibration. This is the fulfillment of what David embodied in a single moment: a human life resonating in Oneness with the presence of God. David's belly became the chamber of bridal longing, and his body answered heaven like a harp touched by the Bridegroom's hand.

Revelation shows the end of that story: What David tasted alone, the Bride will embody in *Echad* (oneness) with God. A whole people not striving, not performing, not shining from themselves, but in sweet union with the One who dwells within them. The Lamb sings. The Bride echoes as she embodies the Lamb. Two voices, one sound: the sound of many waters.

This is not metaphor; it is *Echad*. The waters that once parted at the Ark, that thundered in David's psalms, that roared in Ezekiel's visions, that poured from the side of Messiah, that John heard in the voice of the risen Lamb: His waters will dwell in and burst out of the Bride.

And when she awakens to that truth, her worship will cease to be separate sound; it will become a vibrational expression, the echo of the Lamb's own voice moving through His people. This is the culmination of *kol mayim rabbim*: not noise, but oneness. Not multitude, but union. Not chaos, but the harmony of rest restored.

The Ark Finds Its Rest

The dance slowed, and with the final swell of the shofar, the ark crossed the threshold. The trumpets faded, the dust settled, and the golden chest gleamed beneath the sun like a promise fulfilled.

Then stillness.

No sound but the breath of the people and the quiet of God's presence returning home. For the first time since Eden, the Ark of Covenant and the heart of man rested in the same place.

The Scripture says the ark '*nuach*' (נוח), meaning "to settle, or to rest." The same word describes Noah's ark coming to rest on Ararat, and the same essence as '*menuchah*:' rest after the storm, peace after pursuit. The Spirit that once hovered above chaos now dwelt within praise. David lifted his hands and whispered the song that would forever define his reign:

"Arise, O LORD, to Your resting place, You and the ark of Your strength."
Psalm 132:8

And as the Ark rested, so did creation. For His presence had found a home not only in the tent of the king, but in the heart that danced without shame.

Step Inside: '*Qum*' Returned

In Scripture, קוּם (*qum*) always implies more than standing up. It means to stand into destiny, to establish, and to set upright what has fallen. When God told Samuel, "*Arise, anoint him,*" He was raising rest upright inside of history. When David later sings, "*Arise, O LORD,*" he is offering that word back; inviting God to stand upright within him, within the nation, within creation itself.

David's '*qum*' is not command but communion. It is the sound of heart answering heart. The one who once rose into anointing now calls God to rise into indwelling. Every syllable is love returning to its source.

In Hebrew poetry, verbs are relational; they pulse. So, when David says '*qum*,' he is not moving God from absence to presence. He is acknowledging that rest is reciprocal. The One who caused him to stand now finds standing place in him. The ark does not just rest with David; it rests in him. This is covenant in its purest form: mutual arising, mutual abiding.

The Pulse of Response

Eden began with God's voice and man's breath answering it. David recovers that sound. The Father speaks "*Rise*" to the son, the son replies "*Rise*" to the Father. It is worship as dialogue, creation as duet. Every act of true praise carries this pulse: the upward movement of the human spirit meeting the downward movement of divine love, until both ascend and descend together. This is the motion of Jacob's ladder embodied in sound and flesh.

This is what David knew by instinct: communion is not a ceremony; it is shared motion. Heaven and earth breathe in unison. That is why his psalms are filled with verbs of ascent with rise, lift, exalt, stand; each one echoing that same ancient '*qum*,' each one a resurrection word.

In that song, "*Arise, O LORD, to Your resting place,*" David gives voice to the deepest truth of all creation: Rest is where God and man rise into each other. The invitation is not upward escape but inward habitation. As David's body once danced the sound of Eden, now his words open its gate.

The Desire to Build a House

The song faded, but the echo of '*qum*,' "Arise," did not. It lingered in David's chest like a heartbeat that would not slow. The ark had found its tent, His Spirit had returned, yet something in him still ached. He wanted the '*qum*' to become '*shakan*' where God's rising presence would become the indwelling presence.

Night fell over Jerusalem. The city was quiet, the new tent glowing faintly with oil-light. David sat before the Lord and whispered what had grown inside him since the fields of Bethlehem: "*See now, I dwell in a house of cedar, but the ark of God dwells within curtains.*" It was not guilt but longing. He wanted Eden rebuilt, the garden-walk restored. He wanted the world to wake each morning under the same nearness he had known in the hills.

But God answered with tenderness, not correction:

*"Would you build Me a house to dwell in?
I have not dwelt in a house since the day I brought Israel up from Egypt...
The LORD will make you a house." 2 Samuel 7:5, 11*

The reversal was the revelation. David dreamed of stone and cedar; God dreamed of heart and lineage. The Father was saying, "You cannot build Me what you already are."

Step Inside: The Words of Dwelling

The Hebrew word for house is בַּיִת (*bayit*) and is a home, a household, the place where lineage continues. And the word for dwell is שָׁכַן (*shakan*), the root of Shekinah, the indwelling glory. God's answer to David was not a denial but an unveiling: the true '*bayit*' He desired was not a temple of hands but a heart of rest.

The *Shekinah* would one day fill that heart completely, not in a single man only, but in a people made of living stones, each one breathing the same song of union.

The Covenant of Rest

Then Nathan brought the promise:

*"Your house and your kingdom shall be established forever before you;
your throne shall be established forever." 2 Samuel 7:16*

In that moment the covenant turned inward. God would take the pulse of David's worship and let it beat through generations, until one day a Son would rise from his line; the ultimate '*Qum*,' the Living Ark, the Word made flesh and resting among us.

David bowed low. He did not argue or strive. He simply sat before God, the boy-shepherd again, his heart full and still.

"Who am I, O Lord God, and what is my house,
that You have brought me this far?"
2 Samuel 7:18

In that quiet humility, the pattern of Eden pulsed once more: God walking with man, man resting in God. The builder became the dwelling. The heart became the house.

Selah Meditation: Heart as Dwelling

Pause here. You do not need to continue reading for a moment. Just settle into this moment and breath. Let your shoulders drop. Let your jaw soften. Notice how much effort you have been carrying without realizing it. You are not being asked to offer anything. You are being invited to receive.

Stay with your breath, not controlling it, just noticing it. Feel the quiet strength beneath your ribs, the steady pulse that has been faithful even when you were tired. This is the place Yeshua chooses to dwell. Not after you improve. Not when you are louder or more certain. But now, where striving loosens and your heart yields to His Spirit.

You do not need to build a house for Him. You are already the place where He rests. Remain here for a few slow breaths. Let Him settle into the places where you have been holding tension. Let Him inhabit the places you usually rush past. The dwelling He desires has always been within you. And it has never required effort, only your openness.

Stay a moment longer.

Notes:

11

SOLOMON
The Wisdom of Rest

**"The Lord laid the earth's foundations with wisdom's blueprints.
By His living-understanding all the universe came into being.
By His divine revelation He broke open
the hidden fountains of the deep, bringing secret springs
to the surface as the mist of the night
dripped down from heaven."
Proverbs 3:19-20 TPT**

The Dawn of Peace

The morning air over Jerusalem carried the scent of cedar and dust. Solomon stood on the height of Moriah, where the city's heart opened toward heaven. The sun had not yet cleared the ridge, and all around him the mountain waited, still and golden in silence. This was the same mountain where Abraham once lifted the knife, where covenant breath first mingled with sacrifice.

Now, generations later, another son stood in that place, not to offer death, but to build dwelling. Where one father had laid wood upon the altar, this son would lay wood into walls. The pattern of Eden was still unfolding. Solomon inhaled deeply, the air cool and thin. His name,

Shlomo, meant peace, but not peace as the world names it.

In Hebrew, *shalom* means wholeness, completion, harmony restored. It is the sound of nothing missing, nothing broken. That was what his father longed for: God resting among a reconciled creation. And now, that dream had been handed to him like an unfinished song.

> *"My son, the LORD be with you," David had said, voice trembling with age,*
> *"and may He give you wisdom and understanding,*
> *that you may build a house for the LORD."*
> *1 Chronicles 22:11–12*

Solomon could still hear his father's blessing that carried life like a seed in his spirit. The man after God's heart had left him one inheritance: rest. Now, from that rest, he must build the house of wisdom.

The wind moved softly through the cedars, whispering like breath between verses. Solomon closed his eyes. He felt the pulse of the mountain beneath his feet: steady, ancient, alive. It was the same rhythm that had hummed beneath the waters of creation. He understood then what his father had meant: Eden was not lost. It was waiting to be built again.

The Name of Peace: Solomon's Identity

Names in Hebrew are never mere labels; they are blueprints. They reveal assignment, essence, and prophecy. Solomon's name, שְׁלֹמֹה (*Shlomo*), is rooted in שָׁלוֹם (*shalom*), a word far deeper than peace as the world defines it. *Shalom* means wholeness, soundness, completion, harmony between opposites. It is when all the fragments return to their center and nothing is missing, nothing is broken. To speak *shalom* is to call chaos back into order, to rejoin what was divided in Eden. That is who Solomon was born to be: the living reconciliation between David's longing and God's dwelling, between '*nuach*' (rest) and '*chokmah*' (wisdom).

Even the letters of his name tell his story:

- שׁ (*shin*): flame, divine presence.
- ל (*lamed*): shepherd's staff, authority in teaching.
- מ (*mem*): water, the flow of revelation.
- ה (*hey*): breath, spirit, grace.

Solomon's name echoes this truth: the transforming fire of His presence leads His people out of chaos and flows gently with the breath of His Spirit. The fire of David's worship becomes the water of Solomon's wisdom. The staff of leadership is held by the breath of grace.

Every stroke of his name whispers the same truth: He is peace made flesh.

Solomon's reign begins with silence: no wars, no enemies, no striving. It is the first time in generations that Israel breathes easy. And it is from this stillness that the voice of God will soon break forth again.

"Now Solomon the son of David was strengthened in his kingdom, and the LORD his God was with him and exalted him exceedingly." 2 Chronicles 1:1

Solomon's first act as king is not to conquer, but to worship. He ascends to *Gibeon*, where the ancient tent of meeting still stands, the echo of Moses' tabernacle. There, surrounded by the smell of burning offerings and the hum of night insects, Solomon kneels; a king in linen before the One that once filled David's harp. He does not speak quickly. He listens. And in the silence, God draws near as He always does when rest becomes reverence.

Wisdom as the Architect of Rest

Before Solomon built walls, he built stillness. Before he gathered stone and cedar, he gathered understanding. He knew what his father had taught him beneath the stars of Bethlehem: nothing that lasts is born from noise. Every divine structure begins with a whisper.

The Hebrew word for wisdom, חָכְמָה (*chokmah*), means far more than intellect or knowledge. It speaks of divine skill, creative intelligence, the very artistry of God's mind at work. It is the invisible blueprint by which creation itself was ordered.

The LORD by wisdom (chokmah) founded the earth;
By understanding He established the heavens;"
Proverbs 3:19

In that single verse, heaven reveals its secret formula: wisdom gives foundation; understanding gives structure; knowledge fills it with light.

It is the architecture of Eden: divine order flowing outward from divine rest.

Step Inside: The Hebrew Pattern of Chokmah

The letters of *chokmah* (חָכְמָה) themselves hold its mystery:

- ח (*chet*) is a doorway or fence, symbol of covenant enclosure and life preserved.
- כ (*kaf*) is the open palm, symbol of capacity and stewardship.
- מ (*mem*) is water, the flow of revelation and hidden depths.

- ה (*hey*) is breath, spirit, divine presence.

Together, '*chokmah*' paints a living picture: *Within the fence of covenant, the open hand holds the flow of revelation and breath.* Wisdom, then, is not just thought; it is relationship. It is the divine mind opening its hand to those who will hold rest carefully. When Solomon asked for a listening heart, this is what heaven heard:

"Therefore give to Your servant an understanding heart to judge Your people,
that I may discern between good and evil.
For who is able to judge this great people of Yours?" 1 Kings 3:9

And God's answer was to pour the same '*chokmah*' that founded the earth into the heart of a man.

The Request for Wisdom

Gibeon shimmered in moonlight. The scent of sacrifice lingered in the air, cedar and smoke mingled with the faint sweetness of incense carried on the night wind. Thousands of burnt offerings crackled on the altar, their light flickering like a sea of stars fallen to earth. It was there that Solomon came, not to perform, but to perceive. He was not seeking formulas; he was seeking flow.

David had taught him that His Spirit is not earned but entered through rest. So, as the camp quieted and the priests withdrew, Solomon lay on his face before the altar, the dust cool beneath his hands, the fire warm on his skin. Between them, dust and flame, hovered the breath of God. That night, the dream came. But it was not just a dream. It was a visitation.

At Gibeon the LORD appeared to Solomon in a dream by night; and God said,
"Ask! What shall I give you?" 1 Kings 3:5

The question that shaped creation now fell again over the sleeping king. And in that timeless space, Solomon's heart answered what heaven had been waiting to hear since Eden:

"Give Your servant a 'lev shomea,' an understanding heart,
to discern between good and evil." 1 Kings 3:9

Not a grasping heart. Not a striving heart. A listening one that understands. The phrase *lev shomea* (לֵב שֹׁמֵעַ) is exquisite in Hebrew. '*Lev*' means heart; not emotion, but the seat of will, thought, and spirit. '*Shomea*' comes from '*shama*' and means to hear, to heed, to respond in alignment. Together, they mean a heart attuned to God's frequency.

A *lev shomea* is not wisdom possessed but wisdom received. It is the capacity to remain open to God without interference; a heart able to perceive divine movement before it becomes language. This kind of hearing is inward rather than intellectual, responsive rather than striving. Solomon was not asking for brilliance or strategy. He was asking for a heart that could stay attentive to God and carry what it received faithfully into the world.

Heaven's Answer

And God's response came like sunrise over water:

"Because you have asked this thing, and have not asked for long life or riches or the life of your enemies…behold, I have given you a wise and understanding heart (lev ḥakham ve-navon); so that there has not been anyone like you before you, nor shall any arise after you." 1 Kings 3:11–12

Solomon asked for a *lev shomea*. God answered by giving him the *chokmah* and *binah* that flow through a listening heart.

God did not hand Solomon wisdom as a possession. He formed within him the way wisdom moves. What Solomon received was not merely insight, but access; the ability to receive understanding from God and carry it faithfully into the world.

In Israel, the king was never meant to rule alone. He was a shepherd under the greater Shepherd, a visible expression of God's governance. Wisdom was not gathered from counsel chambers or strategy rooms; it descended from proximity. Judgment required intimacy. Leadership required nearness.

Solomon understood this instinctively. He was not asking how to govern well; he was asking how to remain close enough to hear. Israel's throne mirrored a higher throne, and ruling God's people required walking with God Himself. What he desired was not strategy, but attentiveness, a heart able to receive heaven's instruction and return with clarity for the people.

Step Inside: The Path Wisdom Travels

When Solomon confesses, *"I do not know how to go out or come in,"* he is not speaking about inexperience alone. In Hebrew, this phrase carries a deeper meaning: it describes the movement between realms; the ability to approach God for instruction and return carrying what has been received.

The language itself holds this movement.

The Hebrew letters that shape this phrase trace the inner journey Solomon longs to learn. *Tsade* represents the righteous one stepping beyond self, the posture of humility that initiates approach. *Aleph* is the breath of God that animates the ascent, the divine life that makes encounter possible. *Tav* marks completion, where intention becomes embodied action and what was received is carried back into the world.

Together, they describe a soul leaving the ordinary and entering divine encounter, and then returning changed.

Solomon was not merely asking how to govern well. He was asking how to remain close enough to hear. The king of Israel was meant to stand between realms: approaching God for instruction and returning with clarity for the people. Wisdom did not originate in the throne room; it descended there.

To go out was not departure from God, but movement toward Him. And to come in was not retreat but return, bringing what had been received back into human life intact.

Solomon understood that Israel's throne mirrored heaven's throne. Ruling God's people required walking with God Himself. He was not asking for strategy; he was asking for proximity. He was not just a king, but one called to move between heaven and earth.

This is the path wisdom travels.

Step Inside: The Cosmic Ladder of Wisdom

When Scripture says God gave Solomon wisdom *"greater than any man,"* the mystical reading hears something more than brilliance. It hears that Solomon was given access to the pathway wisdom travels; the movement of ascent and return, the divine circuit by which heaven's understanding enters the world.

Solomon's confession, *"I do not know how to go out or come in,"* becomes cosmic in scope. He is naming his awareness that leadership requires movement between realms. He knows wisdom does not originate in human reasoning. It must be received and then carried back intact.

This is the same ladder Jacob saw, stretched between heaven and earth. It is the same movement Moses lived as he entered the cloud and returned with instruction. Enoch walked it until the boundary between worlds dissolved. Isaiah stood within the heavenly court. Ezekiel was carried into the chariot realm. These were not metaphors. They were encounters that reshaped how these men spoke, led, and lived.

Solomon seeks this not for ecstasy, but for responsibility. He is asking for the inner capacity to ascend for counsel and descend with clarity for the people entrusted to him.

This is why the Temple mattered.

The house Solomon built was not merely sacred architecture; it was a physical echo of the ladder itself. A place where heaven and earth touched. A structure patterned after divine order so that wisdom could continually move between realms. For Solomon to build it, he had to understand not only the plans David handed him, but the pattern of heaven those plans reflected.

So, Solomon was not only a king. He was an architect of passage entrusted with guarding the way wisdom enters the world. To "*go out and come in*" was not a poetic phrase. It was the very calling his reign would embody.

Step Inside: Gibeon, The Threshold Between Tents

The place where Solomon prayed was *Gibeon* (גִּבְעוֹן), meaning hill, elevated place. It stood between Jerusalem (where the Ark rested in David's tent) and the old Tabernacle of Moses, which was still stationed there. This was not coincidence but divine choreography.

Gibeon was the in-between space of Israel's worship: where the memory of the wilderness met the promise of the kingdom, where sacrifice (Moses) and song (David) overlapped for one night. It was at that threshold that Solomon heard God speak. Wisdom always descends at the meeting of tents: the old fading, the new emerging.

In the geography of *Gibeon*, heaven declared a pattern: Before glory rests in a house, it first speaks in a tent. Before wisdom builds, it listens. Before creation forms, Spirit hovers. Solomon awoke with dawn breaking over the hills, the smoke rising from the altar like incense from a reborn Eden. He had asked for the heart of God and the heart of God had answered.

The Building of the House: Wisdom Made Visible

When Solomon woke, the dream still clung to him like dew. Its words pulsed behind every heartbeat: a listening heart. Now that inner hearing began to shape outer form. Months later, the mountain of Moriah was no longer bare. Stone upon stone, cedar upon cedar, the vision grew. It did not rise from ambition but from divine symphony; the same pulse that beat through Eden when God first spoke light into the dark.

The workers cut and carried in silence, for the Torah said:

> *"No hammer, no chisel, no iron tool was heard in the house*
> *while it was being built." 1 Kings 6:7*

Rest was literally built into its walls. Each material spoke its own language. The foundations of limestone held memory of the earth itself. Cedar beams from Lebanon brought the fragrance of the forest; echoes of the trees of life that once filled the garden. Every surface gleamed with gold, the color of dawn, the hue of revelation. Carved cherubim spread their wings above, not to bar the way as in Eden, but to invite God to dwell again among creation.

Solomon watched the craftsmen work as if they were guided by an unseen cadence. He recognized it: the same rhythm that had filled his dream, the same breath that moved through his father's harp. '*Chokmah*' was no longer an idea; it had become architecture. Wisdom had learned to take shape.

Step Inside: A Temple Built in Silence

The Temple rose without noise. No striking. No shaping. No correction sounds echoing through its courts. This was not because tools were unnecessary but because the shaping had already been done elsewhere.

Scripture tells us that every stone was quarried, cut, and prepared before it ever arrived at the site. What entered the Temple mount was not raw material but finished offering. Each stone arrived already knowing its place.

The house of God was assembled, not forged. This is wisdom's way of building. God does not form His dwelling through friction, pressure, or public display. He shapes in the hidden places such as quarries, wildernesses, wombs long before anything is set into position. By the time the stones reached Jerusalem, their becoming was complete. The work of noise had already yielded to the work of rest.

The Temple was raised in silence because silence is the sound of trust. No hammer was needed because nothing was being forced. No chisel was required because nothing was being corrected. No iron rang out because nothing was being resisted.

Iron in Scripture often signifies warfare, dominance, and human strength. But God's dwelling is not built through conquest or striving but through consecration and surrender.

This is why the Temple could only be assembled in peace.

David, a man of war, gathered the materials and Solomon, whose name carries *shalom*, was the one permitted to assemble it. The house of rest cannot be constructed with the instruments of battle. Even the sound of iron was excluded.

What rose instead was alignment so complete that assembly required no adjustment. Stone met stone. Space received presence. Wisdom rested. And the greatest mystery is this: God is still building this way.

He shapes His dwelling stones in quiet places. In seasons that feel unseen. In lives that feel delayed. And when the time comes to set them into place, there is no noise, only recognition.

The house rises because the stones are ready.

When the last beam was set, seven years had passed. Seven, the number of completion, and the Sabbath woven into time. Solomon looked at the finished house and saw the Sabbath made visible: walls that rested, spaces that breathed, gold that glowed without consuming.

Step Inside: The Temple as Creation Replayed

The Temple's pattern followed the structure of Genesis itself.

Creation Day	Temple Element	Revelation
Day 1: Light	Golden Lampstand	Divine illumination; wisdom's sight.
Day 2: Firmament	Veil dividing holy and most holy	Heaven and earth distinguished yet joined.
Day 3: Land and Fruit	Carved palms, lilies, pomegranates	Earth's fertility redeemed.
Day 4: Lights	Cherubim of gold	Celestial guardians, glory reflected.
Day 5: Living creatures	Priests moving within courts	Life serving the divine order.
Day 6: Man	The High Priest	Image of God standing before the God's presence.
Day 7: Rest	The Ark within the Holy of Holies	God dwelling with man.

Each chamber narrowed the worshipper's focus toward stillness: outer court (*earth*), inner court (*heavens*), holy of holies (*unseen*). At the center, silence became sanctuary. It was the same hush that followed "*Let there be light.*" The house itself was breathing and the breath of God enclosed in space and form.

The Moment of Filling

When the priests placed the Ark beneath the wings of the cherubim and withdrew, a cloud descended. Scripture says,

"And it came to pass, when the priests came out of the holy place,
that the cloud filled the house of the LORD,
so that the priests could not continue ministering because of the cloud;
for the glory of the LORD filled the house of the LORD." 1 Kings 8:10–11

The Hebrew word for filled, '*male*' (מָלֵא), is the same used in Genesis when the seas were filled with living creatures. Creation was happening again, not in wilderness, but in worship. The sound of shofars rolled across the city like thunder softened by joy. David's harp had become Solomon's house. The same Spirit that once hovered now rested.

'*Chokmah*' and '*menuchah*,' wisdom and rest, met and produced '*kavod*', a glory with the tangible weight of divine peace. Solomon lifted his hands and said:

"…The LORD said He would dwell in the dark cloud.
I have surely built You an exalted house, And a place for You to dwell in forever."
1 Kings 8:12–13

That phrase, "a settled place," '*mekon le'shivtekha olamim*,' is the echo of '*menuchah*,' the resting of God. The invisible Eden had finally found walls.

Wisdom's Rest

When the cloud filled the temple, time itself paused. What began in the garden's breath, the ark's ribs, and David's heart had come to completion. Rest had built a dwelling for glory; wisdom had given it form. But it was never about gold, cedar, or stone. It was about pattern; how heaven teaches earth to breathe again. Wisdom builds what love dreams. Rest fills what wisdom forms. That is the architecture that still creates worlds.

The Queen of Sheba: The Nations Come to Listen

Imagine heat shimmering over the dunes like molten glass. From the far south, beyond the Red Sea and the spice roads, a royal caravan was moving north; its camels were heavy with gold, myrrh, and the scent of frankincense. At its center rides a woman cloaked in linen the color of sunrise. Her eyes, dark and steady, hold the light of a mind that questioned everything and feared nothing.

She is the Queen of Sheba, sovereign of a kingdom that traded in the world's rarest perfumes and wisdom. And yet, rumor had reached her of another fragrance, the wisdom of a king whose words opened the air like dawn after long night.

> *"Blessed be the LORD your God, who delighted in you,*
> *setting you on the throne of Israel!*
> *Because the LORD has loved Israel forever,*
> *therefore He made you king, to do justice and righteousness."*
> *1 Kings 10:9*

But until that moment, she did not yet believe. So she came, as all true seekers come: to test the fragrance for herself.

The Journey of the Seeker

Before her confession, there was a summons. Scripture in 1 Kings 10:1 says, *"And the Queen of Sheba heard of the fame of Solomon concerning the name of the LORD."*

The Hebrew word for 'heard,' *'shama'* (שָׁמַע), is the same used for "hear, O Israel" in the *Shema* (Deuteronomy 6:4). It means more than sound entering the ear; it means listening with the intent to obey, or to align.

So, the Queen's journey begins not in curiosity but in response. She has heard the echo of Eden again. Wisdom, spoken through a king at rest, calls to the wisdom sleeping in her own spirit. And like the nations Isaiah foresaw, she rises and travels toward the mountain of understanding.

Step Inside: The Meaning of Sheba

The Hebrew word *Sheba* (שְׁבָא) is from the root *'sheva'* (שָׁבַע), meaning seven, oath, or fullness. It is the number of covenant and completion and the pulse of divine rest itself. To come from *Sheba*, then, is to come from the place of oath, from the idea of fullness searching for its source. So, prophetically, the Queen of Sheba represents the nations returning to covenant and the earth's scattered wisdom seeking reunion with heaven's rest. Her name, her kingdom, her journey are all a mirror of what happens when creation starts listening again.

The Exchange of Wisdom

When the Queen entered Jerusalem, the sound of her caravan mingled with temple music. The air smelled of myrrh, cassia, and the cedar of Lebanon. Solomon's court shimmered with light; every vessel reflected gold and water. But what stunned her most was not the splendor but the order. The Scripture says:

> *"When she saw the house that he had built, and the food on his table,*
> *the seating of his servants, the attendance of his ministers,*
> *their apparel, his cupbearers, and the ascent by which*
> *he went up to the house of the LORD,*
> *there was no more breath in her."*
> *1 Kings 10:4–5*

That phrase, "no more breath in her," in Hebrew reads *"v'lo hayah bah od ruach"* (וְלֹא־הָיָה בָּהּ עוֹד רוּחַ): literally, "her spirit left her." The same *'ruach'* (breath) is used in Genesis 2 when God breathed life into Adam. In Solomon's ordered peace, she encountered the same breath that first animated humanity. She was not impressed; she was undone. For what she witnessed was not architecture but a divine symphony; a kingdom where every servant moved like a note in a single song, every gesture, every cup, every ascent another syllable of praise. She realized then: *Wisdom is not the mastery of knowledge but the harmony of rest. It is when the seen and unseen worlds move together as one.*

The Overflow of Rest

The Queen came bearing gold and questions. She left bearing revelation.

> *"Then she said to the king: 'It was a true report which I heard*
> *in my own land about your words and your wisdom.*
> *However I did not believe the words until I came and saw with my own eyes;*
> *and indeed the half was not told me.*
> *Your wisdom and prosperity exceed the fame of which I heard."*
> *1 Kings 10:6–7*

This confession is the awakening of every soul that has encountered divine rest: I had heard but now I have seen. The same language Job would one day use when his own striving fell silent. The same language of worship when wisdom becomes encounter.

And what does she give in return? Gold: a purity refined. Spices: fragrance of devotion. Precious stones: clarity through pressure. It is creation offering back to its Source the beauty it received.

Step Inside: Prophetic Mirror

Her coming fulfills the pattern Isaiah later declared:

"Nations shall come to your light, and kings to the brightness of your rising."
Isaiah 60:3

Even Yeshua would later invoke her as the witness of wisdom received rightly:

"The Queen of the South will rise up at the judgment with this generation and condemn it, for she came from the ends of the earth to hear the wisdom of Solomon; and behold, something greater than Solomon is here." Matthew 12:42

In other words, she becomes a prophecy of the Bride: the global heart that rises and comes when Wisdom calls. What began in a desert caravan ends in worship. The nations that once wandered after Babel's confusion are now reuniting under one sound: the sound of rest ruling again.

The Magnetic Power of Stillness

Solomon never sought to advertise his wisdom. He did not send word to kingdoms or parade power. Wisdom at rest draws without striving; it attracts by resonance. Creation recognizes the voice that first called it into being. The Queen's visit shows us this divine paradox: when the human heart becomes still enough, nations begin to move. When rest reigns, wisdom travels farther than any chariot. That is why the ark rested before it radiated. That is why Eden breathed before it blossomed. And that is why the world came to Jerusalem: to hear once more the language of peace.

The Song of Songs: Wisdom Transformed into Love

The palace was silent again. Years had passed since the Queen of Sheba's visit. The builders were gone, the gold polished, the sacrifices rhythmic as breath. Solomon walked through the colonnades of cedar that smelled of forests long vanished. He had built the greatest dwelling the world had ever seen. But something in him began to ache, a quiet longing not for walls, but for wonder. For the first time, he understood what wisdom had been trying to teach him all along: the goal of knowledge is intimacy.

From Wisdom to Union

Solomon had spent a lifetime immersed in the understanding of *chokmah* with the patterns of creation, and the structure of peace bubbling within his being. But now *chokmah* itself began whispering a deeper secret: *You can build the house of rest, but you cannot hold the heart of it unless you love.*

So, he took up his pen again. But this time, his words did not calculate or advise. They sang. Out of the stillness rose a new kind of revelation: the wisdom that moves as affection, is the mind of God spoken through the heart.

He called it שִׁיר הַשִּׁירִים (*Shir HaShirim*): the Song of Songs. It is not merely a song about love; it is love itself finding language.

> *"Let Him kiss me with the kisses of His mouth,*
> *for Your loves are better than wine." Song 1:2*

In Hebrew, the word translated "loves" here is *dodim* (דֹּדִים). It does not speak of love as a concept or a virtue, but of beloved closeness, love known through presence. *Dodim* is the language of mutual delight, of affection that moves toward union simply because nearness itself is life. It is not love proven by effort or endurance, but love revealed through shared space, shared breath, shared attention.

This is why the Song begins here. Wisdom does not open with instruction but with desire. Before covenant is named, before devotion is tested, love is experienced as invitation. What Solomon once studied from the outside now draws him inward. Wisdom becomes relational. Understanding gives way to encounter. The Song opens not with explanation, but with closeness.

Step Inside: The Hebrew Mystery of Love

Solomon's love language mirrors Eden's original breath. Every phrase in The Song of Songs reverses the fracture of Genesis 3. Where Eve once hid, the Bride now cries, *"Draw me after You, let us run."* Where Adam once blamed, the Bridegroom now calls, *"Behold, you are altogether beautiful; there is no flaw in you."* Each verse unravels the old shame and rewrites it with communion. The beloved garden returns:

> *"Awake, O north wind; and come, O south!*
> *Blow upon my garden, that its spices may flow out." Song 4:16*

The Hebrew word for 'garden' is '*gan*,' the same word used in Genesis 2. This is not coincidence. The garden of Eden has become the garden of hearts. The Spirit now blows not over waters, but over the soul; it has become a reawakening rest.

The Bride and the Blueprint

If David was the heart that longed for God, and Solomon was the mind that understood Him, then the Song of Songs is the breath that unites both. It is where wisdom takes on the tone of worship and rest becomes relationship.

Here, Solomon becomes both teacher and lover, both king and bridegroom. And in his voice, we begin to hear another echo: one far beyond him:

"I am my beloved's (dodi), and my beloved is mine." Song 6:3

The Hebrew root *'dod'* (דוד) is the same way in which David's name is formed. The circle closes. What began as David's heart of love now finds its completion in Solomon's wisdom of intimacy. The Beloved (David) and the Lover (Solomon) are two halves of the same revelation: *God's desire to dwell in union with His creation.*

The Tree and the Flame

There is a moment near the end of the Song when the Bride declares,

"Many waters cannot quench love, nor can the floods drown it." Song 8:7

The Hebrew phrase *'mayim rabbim lo yuchlu lechabot et-ha'ahavah'* is a direct reversal of the flood narrative. Where once waters covered the earth in judgment, now waters cannot extinguish love. The ark of rest has become the heart of the Bride. Covenant no longer floats above the waters, it burns within them.

And then comes the verse that seals it all:

"Its flames are flames of fire, A most vehement flame." Song 8:6

The Hebrew words *'shalhevethyah,'* "the flame of Yah," appear nowhere else in Scripture. It is the only place where the name *Yah* (יה) is joined directly to love. This is Eden's final secret: *God Himself is the fire that rests without consuming.* The same flame Moses saw in the bush, the same glory that filled Solomon's temple, now burns between two hearts that move as one.

Love as the Final Wisdom

When Solomon sang the Song of Songs, he was not writing poetry. He was completing the pattern wisdom shaped in Eden, where *chokmah* reaches its fulfillment not in instruction, but in *dodim*, the shared life between beloved and beloved.

Wisdom orders creation; love sustains it. Wisdom builds the house; love fills it. Wisdom speaks, and love listens. Together they form the unbroken pattern of rest.

And so the last word of Solomon's wisdom is not command, but communion. The greatest mind in history ends not with a lecture, but with a love song. Because in the end, the wisdom of rest becomes the worship of union.

The Turning Point: When Wisdom Forgets Rest

There came a time when the songs grew quieter. The same palace that once glowed with God's presence now shimmered with distraction. The courts that had echoed with praise began to murmur with politics, treaties, and alliances. Solomon, who had once asked for a listening heart, began to listen elsewhere. Scripture names the moment with quiet sobriety:

"For it was so, when Solomon was old, that his wives turned his heart after other gods; and his heart was not loyal to the LORD his God, as was the heart of his father David." 1 Kings 11:4

The text does not say his mind failed. It says his *lev*, the center of trust, devotion, and rest, became divided. Influence entered where attentiveness had thinned. And when rest fractures, wisdom no longer governs.

Solomon multiplied horses from Egypt, gold from Ophir, and wives from foreign lands. Each abundance whispered the same subtle lie: *you must now sustain what you have built.* But the temple had never been upheld by Solomon's strength. It was sustained by the Spirit that once filled him.

Here the equilibrium broke. Striving began to maintain what only rest could hold. Solomon had built a house for the Lord but forgot that he himself was meant to be one. And when inner stillness gives way to management, outer splendor becomes noise. The kingdom of peace trembled beneath the weight of its own beauty.

Step Inside: The Cost of Divided Rest

In Hebrew, the word for turned away is '*natah*' (נָטָה) and also means to stretch, to bend, or to incline. It is the same root used when describing the heavens being stretched out at creation. The same motion that once created space for light now creates space for shadow. Even in falling, the pattern of creation continues: God allows the bending so that His mercy can straighten.

Every covenant must pass through its test: *Will wisdom remember the womb of rest? Or will it try to rule without relationship?* Solomon's decline was not punishment but revelation. It showed the world what happens when structure outpaces surrender, when the mind outruns the heart.

The Hidden Hope: Wisdom's Seed Still Lives

Yet even here, grace hums beneath the failure. God had promised David that his seed would never be cut off. That seed is the Hebrew word '*zera*' (זֶרַע) and means not only offspring, but also potential, beginning, and germination.

While the kingdom divided, wisdom's seed remained buried, waiting to sprout again. The prophets would later carry that seed in their mouths, and from the stump of Jesse a new shoot would rise; a Branch who would embody the wisdom and rest both David and Solomon foreshadowed.

> *"And the Spirit of the LORD shall rest upon Him,*
> *the Spirit of wisdom and understanding,*
> *the Spirit of counsel and might,*
> *the Spirit of knowledge and the fear of the LORD."*
> Isaiah 11:2

Wisdom had not perished; it was merely pregnant again. Rest was not lost; it was gestating in silence.

Selah Meditation: The Quiet Room

Find a place where you can sit without being needed for a few moments. It does not have to be beautiful. It does not have to be sacred. Let the door close physically or inwardly. Notice how much sound you have been carrying. The low hum of expectations. The static of unfinished thoughts. The pressure to respond to the lists. You do not need to push any of it away. Instead let it lose its urgency. This is not a place for insight. This is not a place for prayers. This is a place for you to simply be present.

Breathe slowly. Then again. Feel how quiet does not arrive all at once. It gathers around you. In this stillness, you are not alone. You never were. God does not need volume to be near. He does not compete with noise. He waits for space.

Let yourself be here without shaping the moment. Without searching for the sensation of His presence. Without asking for meaning. Just remain.

If a thought passes through, let it go by without following it. If nothing happens, let that be enough.

This room, this pause, this simple act of staying is already your meeting place and your garden. You do not have to feel Him to be with

Him. You only have to stay.

Rest here for a few breaths longer than feels necessary. When you rise, do not take anything with you. Let the quiet remain where it belongs, within you.

Notes:

_____

_____

_____

_____

_____

_____

_____

_____

_____

_____

_____

_____

_____

_____

_____

_____

_____

_____

12

ISAIAH

The Root and The Rest

**"And in that day there shall be a Root of Jesse,
Who shall stand as a banner to the people;
For the Gentiles shall seek Him,
And His resting place shall be glorious."
Isaiah 11:10**

Vision and Ruin: The Temple Falls Silent

The year King Uzziah died, the air in Jerusalem was heavy, not just with grief, but with disillusionment. For fifty-two years, Uzziah had ruled. He was brilliant, visionary, and blessed with strength. He built towers, dug wells, trained armies, and fortified cities. Israel prospered beneath his hand until his heart lifted above the Giver of his strength.

Second Chronicles 26 tells the story. When Uzziah entered the temple of the Lord with a censer in his hand, he crossed the one boundary that even kings were never meant to cross. Eighty priests followed him in, a number not of coincidence, but of covenant. Eighty: ten times eight, order multiplied by new beginning.

They were the living guardians of divine pattern, the priesthood standing as the final gate between presumption and God's holy presence.

151

"Uzziah, it is not for you," they pleaded. *"It is for the sons of Aaron to burn incense to the LORD. Get out of the sanctuary, for you have trespassed."* But Uzziah would not turn.

He had known victory in every battle, and his heart told him that proximity could be claimed by strength. He wanted to draw near to God but on his own terms. He wanted intimacy without surrender, authority without obedience.

The censer in his hand glowed with coals; his forehead burned with pride. And there, beside the golden altar, leprosy broke out upon his skin. It began on the forehead; the very place the high priest once bore the inscription "HOLY TO THE LORD." Where the sign of consecration should have shone, corruption appeared instead. The body revealed what the heart had already done.

In that moment, the temple itself became a mirror of Eden. Pride had reached for what only love could give, and again humanity found itself shut out from God. Uzziah fled, covering his face, and from that day lived in isolation. He died a leper, remembered as both builder and breaker of the covenant order.

The Temple's Silence

And now, in the year that Uzziah died, the temple stood quiet again. The altar of incense was cold; its fragrance had long since faded. The priests moved softly, their robes brushing the stone like whispers. The same holy place that once trembled with pride now echoed with vacancy.

It was into that silence Isaiah came. He was not a priest, not a ruler, he was a listener. He entered not to offer incense, but to breathe again the air where heaven once walked with earth. Every breath in that space carried memory and the smoke of presumption, the ache of absence.

But heaven had not left. The Spirit never abandons the places man profanes; it simply waits for humility to open the door again.

"In the year King Uzziah died, I saw the Lord sitting upon a throne, high and lifted up, and the train of His robe filled the temple." Isaiah 6:1

The same temple that had been defiled by ambition now burned with uncreated light. Above the throne hovered seraphim, burning ones, whose song restored what pride had silenced.

"Holy, holy, holy is the LORD of hosts; the whole earth is full of His glory."
Isaiah 6:3

The incense that once rose from man's defiance arose from heaven's own fire. God's presence had returned, not to demand, but to dwell. Where Uzziah's striving reached for the altar and was struck, Isaiah's surrender received from the altar and was sent.

A divine reversal and the story of pride turned to purity, and leprosy turned to lips touched with flame.

Why Uzziah Stormed the Temple

Uzziah's fall was not merely the result of arrogance; it was the confusion of calling. He was a king, anointed to govern and guard the people, but he reached for the incense of the priesthood.

In that moment, he blurred the boundary God had drawn between rule and worship. Both were sacred offices, meant to move in harmony like the right and left hands of creation. The king represented God's authority on earth; the priest represented earth's adoration before God. When those two harmonize, heaven and earth touch. When they compete, pride is born.

Uzziah wanted to merge the two by strength rather than submission and to hold proximity without purity. His hand grasped what could only ever be received. In doing so, he distorted his identity and the order of worship that protected intimacy itself.

This is not ancient history; it is the same fracture that divides hearts now. Whenever we attempt to take spiritual authority without surrender, or lead without listening, we repeat Uzziah's act. And, as then, something in our sight begins to dim.

The Line He Crossed

In the Torah, only the sons of Aaron were permitted to offer incense (Exodus 30:7–8; Numbers. 16–18). Uzziah ignored that pattern. He tried to stand between God and man on his own merit, to mediate instead of yield. The altar he approached symbolized communion; by storming it, he fractured it.

His forehead, the seat of perception, bore the mark of that fracture. The skin manifested what the spirit had done: separation. The golden plate on the high priest's turban read "Holy to the LORD." That inscription once sanctified Israel's approach. Now leprosy occupied that space, a living sign that holiness cannot be claimed; it must be carried through obedience.

The Eighty Priests: Guardians of Covenant Order

The eighty priests who confronted him were more than men; they were the embodied boundary of covenant faithfulness. Their number eighty (שְׁמוֹנִים / *'shmonim'*) in Hebrew speaks of new beginnings (8) multiplied by completion (10). Eighty is the perfection of renewal. When they stood between Uzziah and the altar, covenant itself stood guard.

"They withstood King Uzziah." 2 Chronicles 26:18

The Hebrew word *'amad'* (עָמַד) means to stand, or to take one's appointed place. It is the same verb used for angels standing before God. These priests were, in effect, cherubim at the temple's threshold, defenders of divine order. Their courage preserved the pattern through which intimacy could one day be restored. If they had yielded, Israel might have lost the distinction between calling and ambition altogether.

Why Incense?

Incense is the fragrance of nearness. Throughout Scripture incense symbolizes prayer, relationship rising, unseen yet real. Uzziah's desire to offer it reveals the ache for intimacy that still lived in him; but intimacy without surrender becomes idolatry. He sought the nearness of God's presence through performance rather than trust. The censer he held became the mirror of his own striving and smoke without spirit.

Reflection: Sight Restored

Uzziah's forehead was touched with leprosy; Isaiah's lips will soon be touched with fire. One was silenced in exile; the other will speak for nations. One reached upward by strength; the other will bow in awe. This is the divine reversal of pride to purity, of blindness to vision.

Whenever the Church loses sight of her identity, whenever she confuses position with God's glory, the same mercy that marked Uzziah's forehead still calls her back, not to shame, but to surrender.

Isaiah: The Man Before the Vision

Isaiah does not burst onto the scene as a nobody. He was born into Jerusalem's upper class and possibly even of royal descent.

Jewish tradition (*Talmud and early rabbinic commentaries*) identifies his father, *Amoz* (אָמוֹץ), as the brother of King Amaziah, which would make Isaiah a cousin to King Uzziah.

Isaiah was not just some onlooker; he was inside the royal house. He had watched, perhaps from childhood, how power distorts faith and how kings rise in glory and fall through pride.

So, when the text says, *"In the year King Uzziah died, I saw the Lord,"* it is not just a chronological note, it's personal. He had seen Uzziah's leprosy up close. He had felt the tremor of that scandal through the palace walls.

And now, in the wake of that fall, the call comes to him. Isaiah's story begins where human kingship ends. It is as if God waits until the throne of man is empty to reveal the throne of heaven.

Step Inside: The Meaning of Isaiah's Name

The Hebrew name 'Isaiah' (יְשַׁעְיָהוּ / *Yeshayahu*) means "God is salvation."

- *Yesha* (יֶשַׁע) = salvation, deliverance, rescue.
- *Yahu* (יָהוּ) = a contracted form of the divine name, God.

So, every time someone spoke his name, they were declaring the message he would live to proclaim: "The LORD saves."

In a time when kings like Uzziah and later Ahaz trusted in alliances, armies, and idols, Isaiah's very name became confrontation and comfort in one breath. It was a message sealed into the man, written into his identity. Even the structure of Isaiah's book mirrors his name:

- The first 39 chapters echo judgment (the revelation of our need for salvation).
- The final 27 ring with redemption (the revelation of God as salvation).

The embodiment of Isaiah's name.

Step Inside: Moriah, The Place of Seeing

The temple stood on Mount Moriah, a name that carries the meaning to see, to be shown, or to be provided for by sight. The Hebrew root רָאָה (*ra'ah*) means to see, but not merely with the eyes. It speaks of perception, of something being revealed because one has arrived willing to look.

Moriah is first named in the story of Abraham and Isaac:

"Go to the land of Moriah… and offer him there."

It is the place where Abraham lifted his eyes and saw that provision was already waiting. The ram did not appear because Abraham understood everything; it appeared because he was willing to trust without seeing first. On Moriah, faith does not begin with clarity. Clarity follows surrender.

That meaning never left the mountain.

David later ascended this same height carrying repentance, and the plague stopped, not because judgment was argued away, but because mercy was seen. Solomon built the temple here, shaping a house around the truth that God allows Himself to be encountered where reverence replaces control. And here when Isaiah entered the temple, he stood on ground that had learned how to reveal God only to those emptied enough to perceive Him.

Moriah is not a place of explanation. It is a place of unveiling.

This is why Isaiah does not reason his way into vision. He does not analyze, strive, or ascend by effort. He simply sees. *"I saw the Lord,"* he says. The seeing itself is the gift. On Moriah, revelation does not come through grasping but through yielded attention.

The mountain teaches the same lesson across generations:

God is not hidden because He is distant.

He is hidden because He is holy and holiness requires sight shaped by humility.

To step onto Moriah is to stand where God has always been willing to show Himself, but only to those ready to let their striving fall silent long enough to see.

Why Isaiah Entered: The Inner Prompting

Isaiah does not say why he entered the temple that day and that's part of the mystery. But we can read the silence as the language of grief. The nation was in mourning for King Uzziah. Perhaps there was a memorial service. Perhaps Isaiah went to pray for the nation, or to seek direction. What we know is that his entrance was not planned for vision, it was born of longing. Something in him needed to see more than politics, more than failure, more than the hollow rituals that had replaced God's presence.

He came to listen. And in his posture of listening was what opened the veil.

Every divine encounter begins with a question that does not have words. Isaiah's question was not *"What should I do?"* but *"Where are You?"* And God answered not with instruction, but with Himself.

Sometimes the greatest visions come not in pursuit of calling, but in the ache for communion. Isaiah did not step into the temple to find a mission. He stepped into the silence to find God.

The Coal and the Call: Purified for Presence

The temple trembled. Smoke filled the air, thick and fragrant, not from man's incense but from heaven's own altar. The sound of the seraphim's cry rolled like thunder through Isaiah's bones. Their song was not for performance but purification.

Every "holy" struck his heart like a blade of light, cutting through the shadows that pride had left behind.

> *"Woe is me! For I am undone; because I am a man of unclean lips,*
> *and I dwell among a people of unclean lips;*
> *for my eyes have seen the King, the LORD of hosts." Isaiah 6:5*

This is where the contrast with Uzziah becomes perfect and painful. The king had stormed the temple to offer incense; Isaiah confesses that even his words are impure. Uzziah lifted his hand in presumption; Isaiah covers his mouth in repentance.

And yet this is what opens the door. When Isaiah surrenders to his own smallness, grace rushes toward him.

The Touch of Fire

Then one of the seraphim flew to him, holding a live coal taken with tongs from the altar. That altar, the same place where Uzziah reached and was struck, now becomes the place of Isaiah's healing.

> *"And he touched my mouth with it, and said: 'Behold, this has touched your lips;*
> *your iniquity is taken away, and your sin purged.'" Isaiah 6:7*

The coal is no mere ember. In Hebrew, the word is *'rîtzpâh'* (רִצְפָּה) and it shares a root with *'ratzon,'* meaning divine favor, and delight. This is not the fire of destruction but of desire; the fire that restores communion, not consumes it. Where Uzziah's forehead burned with judgment, Isaiah's lips now burn with grace.

One tried to create his own offering; the other becomes one. Isaiah's mouth, the instrument of prophecy, is baptized in the fire of God's presence, so that what comes forth carries the fragrance of heaven itself.

Step Inside: The Altar as Heart

In Hebrew imagination, the altar is always a mirror of the heart. It is the inner place where offering and God's presence meet. Uzziah's leprosy began at the "forehead," the seat of perception. Isaiah's cleansing begins at the "lips" which is the gateway of expression. Perception and proclamation, sight and sound, both are restored through fire.

The coal does not cleanse for perfection's sake; it consecrates for purpose. Isaiah is not purified so he can be pure; he is purified so he can speak.

The Voice That Calls

The fire settles. Smoke still lingers in the upper reaches of the room, thinning slowly as it rises. The air carries warmth, weight, and a quiet that feels alert rather than empty. Isaiah remains where he is, aware that something has shifted not only around him, but within him.

The coal has touched his mouth. Whatever once stood between him and speech has loosened. Breath moves freely again. The silence that follows is not awkward or strained; it feels expectant, as though the space itself is listening.

Then the Voice speaks.

It does not shake the thresholds this time. It moves through the stillness with ease, as though the room has already been prepared to receive it.

"Whom shall I send, and who will go for Us?" Isaiah 6:8

The question rests gently in the air, an invitation waiting to be received. It opens space. Isaiah finds that the place within him that has been listening all along has reached its moment.

The words rise from there.

"Hineni."

Here I am.

They come because he is already present. The yes has been forming in him for years; shaped by nearness, softened by reverence, and strengthened by waiting. This is not obligation finding its voice. It is the call meeting a heart that has been quietly cultivated for it.

Nothing else needs to be said. The exchange completes itself, not because the path ahead is clear, but because the relationship is. Heaven has spoken, and a human heart has answered freely, without force, without haste.

The room holds that agreement.

Step Inside: Hineni, Presence That Answers

The word Isaiah speaks, *hineni* (הִנֵּנִי), is often translated, "Here am I." But in Hebrew, it carries far more weight than location or availability.

Hineni comes from the Hebrew root *hen* (הֵן), meaning "behold," joined with the first-person suffix *-ni* ("me"). It is not a statement of readiness so much as a presentation of the self. It means, *"Behold me. I am fully here."*

This word appears at moments of deep relational encounter throughout Scripture. Abraham speaks it when God calls his name. Moses speaks it before the burning bush. Samuel speaks it in the night. In every case, *hineni* is spoken before instruction is given, before outcomes are known, before consequences are named.

It is not a response to assignment. It is a response to recognition.

When Isaiah says *hineni*, he is not volunteering for a task but offering himself. The word describes a posture of openness and attentiveness, uncovered and unguarded, spoken by someone who has already been listening.

In Hebrew thought, hearing precedes speaking. One does not say *hineni* unless the inner ear has already been tuned. That is why this word cannot be forced. It does not rise from pressure or fear. It emerges from a heart that has been shaped over time by nearness.

Hineni does not mean, "I am capable or willing."

It means, "I am here in truth."

This is why God's call is framed as a question rather than a command. The call waits for consent. Heaven does not compel response; it brings invitation. And *hineni* is the sound of that alignment becoming audible.

Isaiah's life did not change in the moment he spoke the word. What changed was that his inward posture became visible. The listening he had practiced in hiddenness now had a voice.

In this way, *hineni* is not the beginning of Isaiah's calling but the unveiling of one already formed.

Reflection: The Call That Waits in Every Heart

The call of God does not arrive as a demand but as a place of encounter or meeting. It rises where surrender has already been practiced in quiet ways; where attention has learned how to stay, and where rest has softened the need to control outcomes. When a heart has been formed through intimate union, its response is not forced or hurried. It simply becomes naturally open and available. This is the posture that rest creates: openness and trust. A listening heart does not reach for purpose but recognizes the shift of seasons. And when the moment comes, the yes feels less like a decision and more like agreement with something that has been true and cultivated for a long time.

The Message and the Mystery: Hearing but Not Perceiving

The moment Isaiah says, *"Here am I, send me,"* he expects perhaps clarity, joy, revival. Instead, the Voice that thunders with holiness speaks words that ache with paradox:

> *"Go, and tell this people: 'Keep on hearing, but do not understand;*
> *Keep on seeing, but do not perceive.' Make the heart of this people dull,*
> *Their ears heavy, And their eyes blind;*

Lest they see with their eyes and hear with their ears,
And understand with their heart, And return and be healed." Isaiah 6:9-10

The first task of the purified prophet is to speak into deafness. It is not judgment alone but mercy in disguise. Heaven does not harden to punish; it veils so that humanity can learn desire again. The same fire that cleansed Isaiah's lips now becomes the light that blinds those who will not yet love.

The Prophetic Paradox

The Hebrew phrase "make the heart dull" (שָׁמֵן / *shamen*) literally means to make fat, or to thicken. It is not cruelty but the divine principle that hearts must sometimes be numbed before they can be renewed. Like calloused hands that first lose feeling, only to one day be made tender again.

Isaiah's mission, then, is not to produce results but to preserve revelation so that the word can faithfully be carried until a generation arises with ears to hear.

He is sowing seeds that will sprout in centuries, his prophecies echoing down to John the Baptist, and to Yeshua Himself, who will later quote this very passage when the crowds see miracles and miss Messiah.

"Therefore I speak to them in parables, because seeing they do not see,
and hearing they do not hear, nor do they understand."
Matthew 13:13

Isaiah's voice becomes the bridge between the old blindness and the new sight. In the face of such an impossible call, Isaiah whispers the question of every weary heart:

"Then I said, 'Lord, how long?'" Isaiah 6:11

And God answers not with a calendar but with a picture: *until the cities are emptied, until the land lies desolate, until only a stump remains.* But then, like a seed buried beneath winter, He adds:

"…The holy seed shall be its stump." Isaiah 6:13

The vision that began with death ends with promise. The tree cut down will grow again. Life will come from what looks lost. Isaiah's entire ministry will unfold from this mystery: *the seed of holiness is hidden inside judgment, and the promise of rest will be concealed inside ruin.*

Step Inside: The Stump and the Seed

In Hebrew, the word for "stump" here is *'matzevet,'* a term that also means pillar, memorial, or something firmly set. So even in the image of devastation, there is structure, remembrance, and permanence. And the "holy seed" (*zera qodesh*), the same phrase used of Messiah's line, is God's assurance that His covenant structure cannot be broken.

Out of the ground of surrender, from the root of ruin, a new Eden will begin to rise.

It is the same promise that will later bloom as Isaiah 11:1: *"A shoot shall come forth from the stump of Jesse, and a Branch shall grow out of his roots."*

The prophet who saw glory in the temple will now see it reborn in a child.

Reflection: The Rest Between the Roots

Isaiah did not leave the temple with answers neatly arranged. What he carried was a vision that would take generations to unfold. He saw that what had burned in the sanctuary would one day bloom far beyond it. The wilderness itself would begin to flower, light would rise where despair had settled, and glory would no longer be confined to a single room or mountain.

Again and again, his words return to the same promise: desolation is not the final state. Dry ground can sing. Ruins can shine. What appears dormant is often only waiting for the right season to awaken. Even the command to *"arise"* is not a call to strain, but to stand into a light that has already arrived.

Isaiah understood something profound; that God was not seeking larger structures or louder offerings, but a dwelling shaped by humility and listening. Heaven may be His throne and earth His footstool, yet His attention rests where hearts remain tender, where reverence has not hardened into control.

The vision stretches beyond Isaiah's lifetime, beyond Israel's borders, beyond the temple itself. What began as a garden, and later rested between cherubim, moves steadily outward until creation itself becomes the dwelling place. The story does not end with glory returning to humanity but with glory filling the earth.

And all of it begins the same way it always has with rest making room for life to rise again.

The Song of the Vineyard: Rest Forgotten

"Let me sing for my Beloved my love song concerning His vineyard:

My Beloved had a vineyard on a very fertile hill..." Isaiah 5:1

Long before the Branch appears, Isaiah shares a song: an echo of rest forgotten. It begins not as a decree but as a love ballad: *"My Beloved had a vineyard."* The vineyard is not abstract. It is a kingdom carefully raised. A reign patiently established. A king strengthened by provision that did not originate in himself.

God chose a fertile hill; ground already positioned for success. He cleared away obstacles, removed resistance, and secured the borders. He built a watchtower, not to control from afar, but to remain near. And then He hewed a winepress before fruit ever appeared, preparing in advance for abundance. Nothing was lacking or withheld. Every condition for flourishing was given freely.

This is what Scripture records of Uzziah's reign: he was marvelously helped until he became strong. His fame spread. His defenses increased and fields prospered. His army grew. The vineyard thrived.

God expected fruit that matched the care: justice shaped by humility, strength held in dependence, authority exercised in reverence. But when the harvest came, it told a different story.

The grapes were bitter.

Isaiah calls them *be'ushim*; not merely wild, but sour and corrupt. Fruit grown from strength that forgot its Source. Prosperity that turned inward. Success severed from surrender. What had been given as stewardship was seized as possession.

The vineyard had produced but not what love had prepared it for.

The Soil of the Heart

In Isaiah 5:3–4, God speaks not as a distant judge, but as one who has invested Himself fully:

"What more could have been done for My vineyard that I have not done for it?"

This is not rhetorical flourish but the voice of covenant grief. God recounts a history of provision: strength given, protection supplied, opportunity multiplied, and then asks where the fracture occurred.

The soil had been prepared. The conditions were right. The kingdom had flourished. Yet something within the heart of the vineyard turned inward. Strength began to stand on itself. What had once depended on God's nearness now relied on its own momentum.

This is the moment 2 Chronicles 26:16 names plainly: *"When he was strong, his heart was lifted up, to his destruction..."* The issue was never the strength. It was the direction of the heart that carried it.

Isaiah's song exposes the quiet danger of blessing received without continued surrender. The vineyard did not fail because it lacked care, but because its center of trust shifted. Authority detached from reverence and union. Fruit appeared without the reflection of the Gardener's nature.

God had hoped for *mishpat*: a justice shaped by His ways. Instead, He witnessed *mispach*: bloodshed born of misuse. He looked for *tsedaqah*: righteousness rooted in relationship. But instead came *tse'aqah*: the cry of those crushed beneath power no longer restrained by humility.

The lament is not over loss of productivity, but loss of correspondence.

The Vineyard as Eden Remembered

Isaiah chooses Eden's language to interpret what has just happened in history. Eden enters the story quietly, not as nostalgia, but as pattern.

The failure is not agricultural but relational. This is the fracture Eden introduced, and Israel's kings repeated: structure without surrender, authority without abiding, blessing that no longer listens. The vineyard does not collapse because God withheld care, but because strength turned inward. Rest was forgotten and nearness was assumed. The heart lifted itself.

Isaiah's revelation cuts beneath behavior and exposes orientation. Eden cannot be restored by provision alone. Correction does not heal separation, and law cannot produce intimacy. Even when everything is done rightly for a people, something must still remain rightly ordered within them.

What is missing is not effort, but *union*: a life shared from the inside out.

God waits for a people who can receive rest not as entitlement, but as indwelling, for fruit that grows because the vine and the Gardener finally share the same life.

The Wine of Toil and the Wine of Trust

Scripture knows a wine pressed by striving and a wine poured from rest. One ferments beneath anxiety and control, is sharp on the tongue, and becomes numbing rather than nourishing. It is the taste of self-will working the soil without intimacy.

The other flows from abiding. It ripens slowly, drawn up from shared life rather than forced effort. Yeshua shares of this kind of fruit when He says,

"I am the vine, you are the branches. He who abides in Me, and I in him, bears much fruit; for without Me you can do nothing." John 15:5

Isaiah's song of the vineyard stands as the quiet threshold to that promise. It reveals the sorrow of producing without nearness, of growth pursued apart from love. The fruit God seeks cannot be manufactured. It emerges only where union has taken root.

When Rest Is Refused

Across generations, the pattern unfolds quietly. God plants a place meant for communion, and over time it becomes a field managed by effort as rest is slowly reorganized again into labor. What is given by His Spirit is converted into systematic structures. Altars meant for the meeting of the heart turn into self-sustaining structures to appease the masses.

In Isaiah's song, the shift is almost imperceptible at first. The melody does not break, but bends. Love gives way to grief. The vineyard opens into wilderness. The hedge is lifted, not in anger, but in sorrow. What is released is not punishment, but control.

A vineyard cannot be forced to love its Gardener and fruit cannot be demanded into being. So, the ground is allowed to rest, to lie open, to feel what absence teaches. The hope of longing returns where striving once ruled.

It is only in this place of softened soil that the Branch spoken of in Isaiah 11 will take root. Life must grow from shared union and breath as rest waits patiently for a heart ready to receive it.

Whispers of the Coming Vine

Even within the sorrow, something quieter remains. The song does not end in silence; it thins into promise. The Beloved who tended the vineyard does not abandon it. He waits.

Isaiah's lament carries a future within it. One day, the Gardener will speak again, not through song but through presence:

"I Am the true vine, and My Father is the vinedresser."

The image that once held grief will open into communion. What could not grow through striving will flourish through union and fruit will emerge.

Revelation: The Heart's Soil

Isaiah's song of the vineyard reveals something tender about God's way with humanity. Love does not advance by command. It waits. It invites. It grows only where the heart is willing to receive it.

Fruit cannot form in hardened ground. So, God does not force the vineyard to yield. He tends it, sings over it, and allows seasons where nothing seems to grow, trusting that beneath the surface, something is still alive.

Even when the song turns heavy with grief, mercy does not withdraw. It keeps working quietly, pressing seeds into the dark places of the heart, waiting for softness to return. The garden is never forgotten. It is simply being prepared for fruit that can only grow through love and rest.

When the Voice Grows Gentle

"Behold My Servant, whom I uphold; My chosen one, in whom My soul delights.
I have put My Spirit upon Him; He will bring forth justice to the nations.
He will not cry out or lift up His voice, nor make it heard in the street."
Isaiah 42:1–2

After the thunder of judgment and the ache of the vineyard, Isaiah hears a new sound not in fire or storm, but stillness. The Holy One who once shook thresholds now whispers, *"Behold My Servant."*

The Hebrew word for servant, *'eved* (עֶבֶד), means both servant and worshiper. It is not a term of subjugation but a description of devotion. This Servant does not serve from duty, but delight and a life so surrendered that obedience itself becomes adoration.

"A bruised reed He will not break, And smoking flax He will not quench;
He will bring forth justice for truth." Isaiah 42:3

This is the tone of divine rest returned to flesh and strength expressed through gentleness, authority through humility, rule through relationship.

When Isaiah says, *"I have put My Spirit upon Him,"* he implies more than empowerment; the verb carries the sense of settling where the Spirit finds its resting place.

In creation, *Ruach* hovered. In Noah, it drifted. In Solomon's temple, it filled the house. But here, in the Servant, *Ruach* abides. This is the convergence of breath and stillness, movement and dwelling and the pattern of Eden incarnate.

The Wisdom of Stillness

The world expects deliverance by domination. But Isaiah's Servant redeems by restraint. He brings justice not through conquest but through constancy: a quiet fidelity that refuses to crush weakness. In Hebrew, '*mishpat*' (justice) means "restored order." So, when the Servant "brings forth justice," He is not enforcing law but re-establishing harmony and returning creation to its original tempo.

This is the wisdom of rest: *the capacity to hold power without hurry, to heal without demand, to let love accomplish what effort never could.*

The Servant's Song

Isaiah's earlier song of the vineyard ends in wilderness; this song begins in wilderness reborn. The same voice that once lamented, *"My beloved had a vineyard,"* now sings, *"Behold, I will do a new thing, Now it shall spring forth; Shall you not know it? I will even make a road in the wilderness And rivers in the desert." Isaiah 43:19* The Servant is that "new thing" yielding restoration and the Branch bearing fruit where the vineyard failed.

Later, in Isaiah 53, the Servant will *"open not His mouth."* His silence will not be weakness, but wisdom. It is the stillness of one who knows the outcome. The lamb does not argue with the shearer; the Redeemer does not justify Himself before the unjust. In that silence lies the power to absorb chaos without echoing it. This is the essence of divine rest.

Every wound becomes womb; every stripe becomes seed; every death becomes doorway.

"But He was wounded for our transgressions, He was bruised for our iniquities; The chastisement for our peace was upon Him, And by His stripes we are healed." Isaiah 53:5

Revelation: The Rest That Walks

Isaiah sees the pattern clearly now: The Servant is not only the messenger of rest; He is rest embodied. The '*nuach*' of creation, the '*kaphar*' of atonement, and the '*chokmah*' of wisdom all converge in a single heartbeat.

Where Uzziah reached for glory and was struck with leprosy, this Servant lowers Himself and becomes glory itself. Where kings built houses for God, this Servant becomes God's dwelling. The vineyard that once withered now finds its Vinedresser.

Isaiah's vision has moved from fire to fruit, from judgment to joy, from noise to stillness. He is glimpsing the face of the One who will one day say,

"Come to Me, all you who labor and are heavy laden, and I will give you rest." Matthew 11:28

The Glory to Come: Eden Prophesied Again

"The wilderness and the wasteland shall be glad for them,
And the desert shall rejoice and blossom as the rose;" Isaiah 35:1

Isaiah's voice, once trembling with lament, now rises like a hymn. He sees the impossible miracle: the wilderness singing. The prophet who saw nations crumble now beholds creation healing. Sand turns to soil, dryness to delight. It is Eden regrown from the dust. What was once *"Ichabod,"* the glory departed, becomes *'kabod shuv,'* the glory returned. The curse was never meant to be reversed by human effort. It was always meant to be redeemed, once and for all, by the Servant God would send.

Even the parched ground remembers how to bloom when God draws near. The imagery is so lavish it nearly bursts the page: waters breaking out in the wilderness, streams in the desert, the burning sand becoming a pool. It is Genesis sung backward as chaos is reordered into communion.

Step Inside: The Word "Blossom"

In Hebrew, the verb used for *"blossom"* in Isaiah 35:1 is *'parach'* (פָּרַח). And means to bud, to burst forth, or to sprout suddenly. It is the same root used for Aaron's rod that blossomed inside the tabernacle. That connection is no accident.

Aaron's rod bloomed as a sign of divine election: life from death, and choice from decay. Now Isaiah sees that miracle multiplied across creation. The wilderness becomes a global sanctuary, every thorned branch now bearing fruit again.

Arise, Shine: The Light of Rest Returns

Isaiah's vision does not end with nature; it widens to nations.

"Arise, shine; For your light has come!
And the glory of the LORD is risen upon you." Isaiah 60:1

The same verb *'qum'* (קוּם), "arise," returns. It is the echo of God's first command to light itself. It is the same word He spoke to Joshua after Moses died, the same energy that raised David from obscurity, the same resurrection breath that will one day lift the Son of Man from the grave. This is not the light of domination; it is the light of dwelling.

Isaiah 60 pictures the nations walking by radiance, not out of fear but out of recognition. They are drawn, not driven. Rest has become gravitational. Gold and frankincense appear again: the language of kings and worship. Even creation joins the procession: flocks, ships, forests, all converging toward the place where His presence rests.

Heaven's Home on Earth
Then God asks a question that unravels the last thread of religion:

"Thus says the LORD:
"Heaven is My throne, And earth is My footstool.
Where is the house that you will build Me?
And where is the place of My rest?
For all those things My hand has made,
And all those things exist," Says the LORD.
"But on this one will I look: On him who is poor and of a contrite spirit,
And who trembles at My word."
Isaiah 66:1–2

The Father is not seeking another temple; He is seeking hearts that have become resting places.

It is the final reversal of Uzziah's sin, no longer storming the sanctuary, but becoming one. The cosmos itself becomes a tabernacle of peace. The Holy of Holies is no longer confined behind curtains of gold; it is within hearts of flesh. Eden has expanded. God's presence that once dwelt between cherubim now fills the whole earth with glory.

"They shall not hurt nor destroy in all My holy mountain,
For the earth shall be full of the knowledge of the LORD
As the waters cover the sea." Isaiah 11:9

That is not the end but the beginning again.

Revelation: The Full Circle of Rest
In the end, Isaiah sees not destruction, but renewal. The coal that once burned his lips now glows in every redeemed life. The vineyard that withered now overflows with wine. The branch that sprouted becomes a forest of righteousness. And the prophesy of the Servant's silence becomes a symphony of nations.

This is Eden, not remembered, but realized. Not a return to the past, but the unveiling of the purpose that was hidden in every seed, every exile, every waiting heart. When Isaiah cried, *"How long, O Lord?"* this was the answer. Until the wilderness sings again. Until every root remembers its Maker. Until the whole earth hums with Sabbath breath.

Selah Meditation: A Place to Rest

Pause here. Let the movement of the chapter settle. You do not need to revisit the images or hold the meaning together. Simply notice the quiet that remains after revelation has passed. He is here sitting with you.

There may be places in you that feel overworked, overgrown, or dry. Do not rush to figure out how to change them. Rest begins when you stop managing what needs to heal.

Sit with who is present. Yeshua. See Him and just let the ground of your heart soften without effort. Breathe in the fragrance of His presence and let stillness do the hidden work you cannot.

Nothing is being asked of you in this moment and no fruit or response is expected. Know that He sees you and loves you deeply.

Remain here for a few breaths longer than feels necessary. His rest is present. His wilderness within you blossoms.

Notes:

_____

_____

_____

_____

_____

_____

_____

_____

_____

_____

_____

_____

_____

_____

_____

_____

_____

_____

_____

13

THE BRIDE

The Rest of Love

**"Let Him kiss me with the kisses of His mouth,
for Your loves are better than wine."**
Song of Songs 1:2

The Wilderness Before the Kiss

The desert wind carried no song. For years, her life had been labor;
tending other vineyards, watching over fruit that was not her own.

The sun had darkened her skin; her hands had forgotten softness.

She had walked in the heat of others' harvests until her heart felt as
brittle as the branches she pruned. And yet, hidden beneath the weight
of those days, something unseen had been growing; roots reaching down
through dry ground, a secret garden taking shape in the soil of surrender.
She did not know it, but every act of service, every silent "yes," had been
making room for something holy. In the wilderness, love had been
waiting.

Then came the scent. It was not dust or sweat this time, but oil.
Fragrance moved through the air before any voice spoke, the sign that

the King had drawn near. Her breath caught. The desert around her seemed to hush, as if listening. And from the stillness, she felt Him, not a stranger, but the One her soul somehow remembered.

The ache of exile met His nearness. She bowed low, the heat of the earth under her palms, and whispered the only prayer her heart could form:

> *"Let Him kiss me with the kisses of His mouth,*
> *for Your loves are better than wine."*
> Song of Songs 1:2

It was not a plea, but surrender. The phrase *"let Him"* was her yielding, her final release of control. She bent, not in shame, but in adoration. In that posture, Eden reopened. The kiss she spoke of was not passion; it was breath. The nearness that revives what has gone dry. Love Himself had come to awaken what wilderness could not kill.

And so begins the Song.

It is not merely Solomon's melody; it is the echo of God's first love call; the same sound that once walked in the cool of the garden, now returning to find the heart that has learned to be still.

His Loves Are Better Than *Yayin* (Wine)

When the Shulamite whispers, *"Your loves are better than wine,"* she uses the Hebrew word יין (*yayin*), a word that flows like what it names: a picture of two Hebrew letter *yods* (י י) cupping the Hebrew letter *nun* (נ).

In Paleo Hebrew the *'yod'* is the arm or hand, and the letter *'nun'* is the seed of life, continuation, or offspring. Together, *'yayin'* paints the image of two hands cradling life: a drink poured from intimacy, not indulgence.

Wine, in Israel, was not a symbol of excess; it was the essence of joy born from process. Grapes had to be crushed. Sweetness came through surrender. Fermentation required time hidden in darkness. The ancients understood this rhythm: transformation happens in waiting.

So, when she says, *"Your loves are better than wine,"* she is confessing something deeper:

> *Your love has done what even the finest process of earth cannot; it has pressed my*
> *pain into joy, my delay into sweetness, and my surrender into song.*

In their culture, wine also sealed covenant. At weddings, it was the cup of union; the same image Yeshua would later raise and say, *"This is My blood of the new covenant."*

So, her declaration is not poetic flattery; it is covenantal awakening.

She has tasted earthly covenant and found it lacking. Now, in the presence of the Bridegroom, she drinks from His cup of rest: love fermented in eternity and poured fresh into her wilderness-weary heart.

The world drinks to forget. The Bride drinks to remember; to return to Eden's joy, where presence itself was the only intoxication. Her thirst is finally met by His embrace. This is the wine that restores sight, that steadies the soul, that teaches wisdom through sweetness. This is '*Yayin*': joy cradled between two hands, the very hands that formed her from dust, and now lifts the cup to her lips.

Step Inside: The Kiss (נָשַׁק, *Nāshaq*)

The first word spoken from her lips is "*Let Him kiss me.*" In Hebrew, kiss is נָשַׁק (*nāshaq*), and it carries a weight that the English language cannot hold. It means not only to kiss but also to join, to equip, to fasten together. It is used elsewhere for the touch of weapons being readied for battle, or for lips meeting in covenant greeting.

At its root in Hebrew, '*nāshaq*' describes the moment of connection when two become one in purpose. In the Song, the word moves from battlefield to bridal chamber. The touch once used for war becomes the touch of union. This is how heaven redefines power: intimacy replaces striving, communion conquers conflict.

But '*nāshaq*' also hints at breath. In the ancient Near Eastern world, a kiss was an exchange of breath: the giving and receiving of life. So, when the Bride says, "*Let Him kiss me,*" she is yielding to that same breath that once moved over the waters in Genesis 1. She is asking, not for passion, but for something greater: for His Spirit and breath to fill her again.

To be kissed by God is to be reanimated by love. It is the restoration of the divine exhale that formed Adam. It is Eden revisited through affection. And notice her phrasing:

"*Let Him...*"

She does not demand; she yields. The verb is passive, a prayer of surrender. She has reached the end of striving; she bends in trust. Love is no longer something to chase; it is something to receive. This is the first true rest: the rest of being breathed upon.

In rabbinic thought, '*nāshaq*' also shares a linguistic echo with '*nesheq*': armory, weapons, tools of readiness. Even this is a secret of wisdom: the one who has received the kiss of God is fully equipped.

Affection becomes armor. Union becomes authority. The breath that revives her is the same that empowers her.

The Shulamite's surrender is remembrance. She is rediscovering what

Adam lost, the nearness of divine breath. Her heart becomes the new garden where God walks again.

Your Name Is Flowing Oil (שֶׁמֶן נִשְׁפַּךְ שְׁמֶךָ)

After the kiss, the first thing she perceives is fragrance:

"Because of the fragrance of Your good ointments, Your name is oil poured out…"
Song of Songs 1:3

The Hebrew language paints a vivid picture.

- שֶׁמֶן (*shemen*) is oil, anointing, and richness.
- נִשְׁפַּךְ (*nishpakh*) means to pour forth, to spill over, to flow without restraint.
- שֵׁם (*shem*) means name, reputation, essence, identity, and renown.

Put together, her cry becomes: *"Your very identity flows like anointing oil."*

In Hebrew thought, '*shem*' is not a label but the manifestation of essence. To know someone's name is to perceive their nature. So, the Bride is not saying His name smells nice; she is confessing that His being saturates everything. His presence cannot stay contained; it moves, it perfumes, it consecrates.

Oil in the ancient world was the mark of chosenness. Kings, priests, and prophets were anointed and set apart by its fragrance. Every anointing released an aroma that clung to skin and garment, announcing identity long before the crown or robe was seen. The oil of anointing said: *this one carries presence.*

So, when she says, *"Your name is oil poured out,"* she is proclaiming that He is the Anointed One before any title was spoken. His nature is self-giving, and He pours Himself out. He does not hoard holiness; He spills it into the air so that all who breathe may live.

In that single sentence, the Shulamite recognizes what generations of seekers have missed: *rest is the fragrance of yielded identity.* When the Beloved breathes upon her, His essence mingles with hers until she begins to smell like Him. The oil that once marked kings and prophets now marks the Bride.

Step Inside: *Shemen* and *Shem*

The Hebrew words, '*shemen*' (oil) and '*shem*' (name) share the same root sounds and the sages noticed this: שׁ-מ.

"Wherever the Name dwells, oil flows."

Oil symbolizes the Spirit, the outpoured presence of God; the Name is the revelation of His nature. Together, they tell one story: *the Spirit flows wherever identity is revealed.*

In the garden of her soul, the Bride is discovering who He is and in doing so, she begins to remember who she is. His name is not a word to repeat but a fragrance to inhabit. She breathes it in until it becomes her atmosphere.

Every exhale carries a trace of Him. This is why the virgins love Him. This is why hearts run after Him. Because where His Name is known, His presence rests.

Draw Me Away: The Invitation of Rest (מָשְׁכֵנִי, *Moshkeni*)

"Draw me after You; let us run. The King has brought me into His chambers."
Song of Songs 1:4

After breath (*the kiss*) and oil (*the fragrance*), comes movement. The first stirrings of rest always pull the soul closer. In Hebrew the word for "*draw me*" is מָשְׁכֵנִי (*moshkeni*), from the root מָשַׁךְ (*mashakh*), meaning to draw, pull, stretch toward, or anoint.

It is the same root used for drawing oil over a king's head to anoint him. So, her cry is not desperate; it is prophetic. She is asking, *"Anoint me with Your nearness and pull me into who You are."*

This word '*mashakh*' also carries a physical tension: to stretch. To be drawn is to be expanded, and to leave what was known. The Shulamite's prayer is the prayer of every soul called from striving into surrender, *"Stretch me into union; pull me out of the narrowness of self."*

Then she says, *"Let us run."* Notice the shift: from me to us. The kiss of rest has joined her to the Bridegroom so deeply that her language changes. Love dissolves separation. This is no longer a solo pilgrimage: it has become a shared movement. Her run is not toward, but with. And where does He lead her?

"The King has brought me into His chambers." Song of Songs 1:4

The Hebrew word חֲדָרָיו (*chadarav*) means the innermost rooms, the secret place, and the heart within the house. This is the first temple imagery of the Song. Just as David longed to *"dwell in the house of the LORD,"* and Solomon built chambers for the Ark of Rest, the King here brings the Bride into His inner sanctuary.

What Eden lost, intimacy restores. She has been called back into the holy of holies of love. But note she does not walk in; she is brought. *He carries her* into this place. Rest is always received. Love's gates are never forced open. Love cannot be attained by effort or claimed by will. It is love's gravity, not effort's reward.

Breath awakens awareness. Fragrance releases remembrance. Drawing invites surrender. Dwelling fulfills rest. Her *"draw me"* is the echo of God's own invitation:

> *"I drew them with gentle cords, With bands of love,*
> *And I was to them as those who take the yoke from their neck.*
> *I stooped and fed them." Hosea 11:4*

Love does not force; it pulls gently until desire becomes motion. The Shulamite is learning that rest moves not lazily, but lightly and carried by affection, not ambition. She is being drawn back into Eden's rhythm: the sound of footsteps in the cool of the day, the running that feels like flying, the heart unafraid of closeness.

The Shulamite: The Mirror of the Beloved

After the pull of *"Draw me"* comes the moment of recognition.

> *"I am dark, but lovely, O daughters of Jerusalem,*
> *like the tents of Kedar, like the curtains of Solomon." Song of Songs 1:5*

For the first time she speaks of herself, and she speaks in paradox. *"Dark, yet lovely."* In Hebrew: שְׁחוֹרָה אֲנִי וְנָאוָה (*shechorah ani v'naavah*), *shechorah* means blackened, weathered by sun, and shaped by labor. *Naavah* comes from the Hebrew root *na'ah*: to be beautiful, fitting, and dwelling-worthy. She names both her weariness and her worth in the same breath. The *"tents of Kedar"* were woven of black goat hair; they speak of exposure, impermanence. The *"curtains of Solomon"* were linen veils of the Temple: pure and luminous.

Between them lies her truth: *she is the meeting place of dust and glory, earth and sanctuary. She has carried the wilderness in her skin and yet contains her Lover's presence in her heart.*

Then comes the hidden key of her name: Shulamite (שׁוּלַמִּית *Shulammît*) is the feminine form of Solomon (שְׁלֹמֹה *Shlomo*), whose name arises from *shalom*: peace, wholeness, and rest. The Shulamite is Solomon's reflection.

The Song is not two voices in tension; it is one wholeness speaking to itself: masculine and feminine, giver and receiver, spirit and soul.

Where he is *Shlomo*, the embodiment of peace, she is *Shulammît*, peace restored. He is rest extended; she is rest received. Together they complete the circle of *shalom*: creation reunited with Creator.

In rabbinic midrash the sages wrote that the Shulamite represents Israel, and Solomon the Divine Lover. But in the light of the full story, she is the Bride of humanity: the echo of Eve, the heart of the Church, the soul that remembers Eden.

Her confession, *"I am dark but lovely,"* is the gospel in miniature: scarred by toil yet chosen by tenderness. Each verse here answers the ache of generations: Adam hid; the Shulamite stands unveiled. She names her shadows but refuses shame. Love has taught her that exposure is not exile; it is invitation.

"Do not gaze at me because I am dark, because the sun has looked upon me. My mother's sons were angry with me; they made me keeper of the vineyards, but my own vineyard I have not kept." Song of Songs 1:6

She tells her story, the weight of duty, and the neglect of her inner life. She has labored under others' expectations, lost her own garden in the process. But even here, wisdom is working beneath the surface. The neglected vineyard has become the soil of authenticity. Her exhaustion is the doorway through which true rest will call her home.

She is the Shulamite: the soul in restoration, the Bride awakening, the mirror in which the Beloved sees His own reflection. Her darkness does not disqualify her; it becomes the canvas for glory.

The Shepherd's Invitation: Following the Tracks of Rest

"Tell me, O You whom my soul loves, where You feed Your flock, where You make it rest at noon; for why should I be as one who veils herself beside the flocks of Your companions?"

"If you do not know, O fairest among women, follow in the footsteps of the flock, and feed your little goats beside the shepherds' tents." Song of Songs 1:7-8

The dialogue shifts: she who was silent now speaks freely. The Shulamite has been kissed, perfumed, drawn, and seen; now she asks. This is not distance; it is desire seeking direction. She has glimpsed love but longs to abide in it. Her question carries the ache of every awakened soul:

"Where do You feed? Where does Your flock rest?" Song of Songs 1:7

The Hebrew word for feed is רָעָה (*ra'ah*) and means to shepherd, to nourish, and to pasture. And the Hebrew word for rest here is רָבַץ (*rābats*) and means to lie down, or to settle. Together, they form the ancient rhythm of care and calm: nourishment leading to stillness, and fullness producing rest. She is not asking about location, but lifestyle: *"Where do You dwell in peace, so that I may live in that same rhythm?"* She adds, *"Why should I be like one who veils herself?"*

In her culture, a veiled woman among the flocks could imply shame or distance: one hiding identity, or a harlot seeking attention. But the Shulamite does not want the counterfeit of intimacy; she wants the real nearness. She has left pretense behind in the vineyards of her brothers. The Bridegroom's response is tender and practical:

"If you do not know, O fairest among women, follow in the footsteps of the flock, and feed your goats beside the shepherds' tents." Song of Songs 1:8

His answer is not abstract mysticism; it is embodied wisdom. He tells her three things; the same pattern that sustains all who walk with Him:

First, follow the tracks of the flock and do not wander alone. Rest grows in community. The Hebrew word for footsteps is עָקְבוֹת (*'iqvot*) and means heel prints. It is the same Hebrew root as 'Jacob' (*Ya'aqov*) who is the one who followed in faith until rest became reality. So, the Bridegroom is saying: *Follow the path of faithfulness. Walk where love has already left tracks in the dust.*

Next, feed your little goats: care for what is entrusted to you. Do not despise small stewardship; tend your daily field. Goats were the humble companions of the shepherd's life and a picture of everyday ministry. The Bride learns that rest is not withdrawal from responsibility; it is finding presence in it.

Lastly, stay near the tents of the shepherds; remain in fellowship, in guidance, and in worship. The tents are where communion happens and the temporary sanctuaries of those who live led by God's presence. The Beloved is saying: Stay near My shepherds, where My voice still speaks through song, story, and shared flame.

The King's answer is a shepherd's wisdom: *Rest is not found in isolation, but in orientation. Follow. Feed. Stay near. The path of peace is traced by love's footprints.*

In Hebrew, the word 'imagination,' (*noon*), the time she mentions, represents the zenith of light, and the place where shadows vanish. So, when she asks where He makes His flock rest at noon, she is longing for life without shadow but unbroken communion.

And His answer is a map to that reality: rest in light by walking with those who walk in light. The Shulamite begins to learn that divine intimacy is not escape from the ordinary; it is the sanctification of the ordinary by His presence. The same fields that once burned her skin will soon bloom under her care.

Hebrew Connection: רָעָה, *Ra'ah* and רָאָה, *Ra'ah*

In Hebrew, the two verbs רָעָה (*ra'ah*) and רָאָה (*ra'ah*) are nearly identical in sound and form.

They differ only by a subtle shift in the middle letter:

- Ra'ah (*feed*) has the Hebrew letter *ayin* (ע): the letter pictographically meaning eye, or to perceive insightfully.
- Ra'ah (*see*) has the Hebrew letter *aleph* (א): the silent letter symbolizing oneness, divinity, breath, source.

Even visually, the two words mirror one another and is not a coincidence but revelation. In Hebrew thought, to shepherd well is to see rightly, and to see truly is to nourish life. Feeding and perceiving are two sides of the same act of care. The good shepherd provides because he perceives what is needed. Vision births provision.

Now listen again to the Shulamite's question:

"Tell me, O You whom my soul loves, where You feed (רָעָה ra'ah) Your flock..."
Song of Songs 1:7

What she is really asking is, *"Where do You see Your flock? Where do You behold them with care?"* She is not just longing for food but for the gaze of love. Her heart remembers Eden, where to be "seen" by God was sustenance itself. Before there was toil, there was sight; before there was bread, there was breath.

In this hidden pun, the Spirit reveals the economy of rest: *We are fed where we are seen. We are nourished by the gaze that knows us.*

It is the same truth Yeshua later unveils when He calls Himself *"the Good Shepherd"* (ὁ ποιμὴν ὁ καλός). He is the One who both sees and feeds, who knows His sheep by name and gives them pasture (John 10). The Hebrew mind would have heard that echo immediately. Every act of divine feeding is also divine seeing.

When God provided manna in the wilderness, He was saying, *"I see you."* When the Beloved feeds His flock at noon, His gaze becomes the bread. So the Shulamite's question, *"Where do You feed?"* is also asking, *"Where may I be seen again?"*

And the Bridegroom's answer to the Shulamite, *"Follow the footsteps of the flock,"* is His way of saying: *Walk in the light of My seeing; feed others as you have been fed; let My gaze become yours.*

The King's Affirmation: You Are My Dove

"I have compared you, my love, to a mare among Pharaoh's chariots.
Your cheeks are lovely with ornaments, your neck with chains of gold."

"Behold, you are fair, my love; behold, you are fair! You have dove's eyes."
Song of Songs 1:9,10, 15

The first sound she hears from the King is not command but delight. He calls her *"My love"* and in Hebrew, רַעְיָתִי (*ra'yati*) is a term drawn from *ra'ah*, the very same root we just explored meaning to feed, or to shepherd. So even in His address, there is nourishment hidden inside His affection.

His response could be rendered: *My nourished one. My companion in pasture. My beloved who rests where I feed.*

He compares her to a mare among Pharaoh's chariots. This is an image that to modern ears may sound strange, but in Hebrew idiom it is rich with layered symbolism. Pharaoh's horses were renowned for their strength, beauty, and disciplined unity. The image evokes not wildness, but grace harnessed by love.

The Bridegroom sees in her not chaos, but capacity for communion. Her cheeks and neck are symbols of expression and surrender and are adorned with ornaments and chains of gold. Gold, in Hebrew thought, represents divinity refined by fire. It is not decoration but sanctification.

He is saying, *you have let Me refine you, and now My light rests on your countenance.*

Then He looks deeper.

You have dove's eyes.

In Hebrew, 'dove' is יוֹנָה (*yonah*) which is the same word used for the dove that Noah sent out from the ark. The dove always seeks rest. So, when the King says, *"You have dove's eyes,"* he is saying: *Your gaze has learned to look for peace, not for performance. You know how to find rest.*

The eye of the dove sees in simplicity and is focused, single, and unfractured. It cannot look in two directions at once. Yeshua makes a similar reference later when He says, *"If your eye is single, your whole body will be full of light."* (Matthew 6:22) This is the same vision of rest. The Bride's eyes mirror His own. Her seeing has become one with His seeing.

Step Inside: The Dove and the Ark

The dove first appeared in Scripture over the waters of judgment. Noah released it from the *tevah*, the ark, and it returned carrying an olive leaf: a sign that rest had been restored. Here, in the Song, the dove has found its resting place again, not on an ark of wood but within the gaze of love.

The Hebrew name '*yonah*' (dove) shares a root with '*yayin*' (wine) and '*yom*' (day) which are images of joy, light, and renewal.

So, the Beloved's words carry a triple blessing:

"Your eyes carry the dawn. Your gaze carries joy. You have become the place where My peace lands."

In the presence of that voice, her shame begins to melt. The very parts she once hid with darkened skin, labor-worn neck, and cheeks weathered by sun; He names as beautiful.

He speaks to her soul until her self-perception aligns with His affection. The Bridegroom does not teach her rest; He gazes her into rest. His love restores what striving had taken. This is always how transformation begins: by allowing ourselves to be seen through the eyes of the Beloved.

The Language of Surrender: Cheeks and Neck

When the Beloved describes her cheeks and neck, He is not fixated on outward beauty but pointing to where yielding has taken root.

In Hebrew imagery, the 'neck' (צַוָּאר, *tsavvar*) is the hinge between head and body and the meeting point between will and obedience. It is the place that either stiffens in pride or bends in humility.

To be "stiff-necked" in Scripture meant to resist God's leading (Exodus 32:9). To bow the neck was to surrender to divine will. So, when He adorns her neck with chains of gold, He is crowning her surrender. Gold represents what has passed through fire without losing purity: the refinement of trust.

Where she once carried burdens, she now carries beauty. The yoke of striving has become the necklace of communion. And her cheeks, the Hebrew word for '*lehi*,' is related to the root for jaw or mouth and speaks of expression, speech, and communion.

They are where breath becomes sound: the place of words, prayer, and response. In the wilderness of self-effort, her mouth once carried complaint, but in the nearness of His gaze, her language changes. Her cheeks, once burned by the sun, now bear the glow of encounter. Her words become worship. The ornaments He mentions are not trinkets but testimony. Every syllable of love adorning her is proof of where she has been refined. So, when He says,

"Your cheeks are lovely with ornaments, your neck with chains of gold…"
Song of Songs 1:10

He is saying: *"I see your surrender and the beauty of the burdens you have released, the music in the mouth that once murmured. What you gave Me in humility, I have turned to radiance."*

This is the anatomy of rest: the stiff neck softened, and the weary mouth re-tuned. Even the body of the Bride echoes in delight: where you yield, you shine.

The Garden Awakened: The Bed Is Green

Something shifts in her. The shame that once whispered *"I am dark"* is gone. Now she sees what He sees. Her eyes are open, and she begins to perceive creation again.

"Our bed is green..." Song of Songs 1:16

The Hebrew word for bed here is מִטָּה (*mittah*), which can also mean resting place, couch, or marriage chamber. It is not just furniture but fellowship. This is the first time since Eden that the word "resting place" and "green" share a sentence.

The Hebrew word green רַעֲנָן (*ra'anan*) means fresh, flourishing, alive with sap. It is the same word used in the Psalms to describe a tree planted by rivers of water (Psalms 52:8; 92:14).

She is standing again where life flows freely, where love and rest grow from the same root. In the wilderness, everything was toil. Now, in His nearness, even the ground breathes again. The "bed" is not about passivity but the communion of stillness, the mutual resting place where Creator and creation sing again in unison. Then she notices the structure around them:

"The beams of our house are cedar, and our rafters are fir." Song of Songs 1:17

These are not random details. Both cedar and fir were the very woods used to build Solomon's Temple. In Hebrew, '*erez*' (cedar) symbolizes incorruptibility and resists decay. '*Berosh*' (fir) speaks of strength and fragrance. Together they represent durability and delight: a house whose architecture mirrors both Eden and the Temple.

It is as if the Shulamite, still reeling from grace, suddenly remembers creation's blueprint. She is seeing with the same sight Adam once had: to look upon the world and say, *"It is good."*

Her rest has become a portal back into wisdom's rhythm: the garden and the temple overlapping once more. She is realizing that union is not only spiritual but environmental. When love is rightly ordered, even the rafters sing.

This is the full circle of Genesis 2: *"Then the LORD God planted a garden..."* Now the Bride's heart has become that garden: green again, fragrant again, and filled with song. Creation is answering her restoration. The curse is reversing through her worship.

Even the trees remember Eden, and in their grain and scent they join her in praise.

The King's Table and the Banner of Love

"I am the rose of Sharon, and the lily of the valleys.
Like a lily among thorns, so is My love among the daughters.
Like an apple tree among the trees of the forest, so is my Beloved among the sons.
In His shade I sat down with great delight, and His fruit was sweet to my taste.
He brought me to the banqueting house, and His banner over me was love."
Song of Songs 2:1–4

The Shulamite begins this scene by naming herself: something she could not do before. No longer does she define herself by the sun's burn or her brothers' anger; now she identifies with creation's beauty: a rose of Sharon, a lily of the valleys. Both flowers grow untended. They bloom without cultivation, and without striving in rested growth. In Hebrew, *'ḥăḇaṣṣeleṯ'* (חֲבַצֶּלֶת), translated "rose," means meadow-flower or crocus; a bloom that appears in springtime after winter's dormancy. It is the language of renewal, of life returning through stillness. Then the Bridegroom responds, *"Like a lily among thorns, so is My love among the daughters."*

It is His way of saying: Your purity is enduring. The lily survives surrounded by harshness. It thrives where others pierce. This is the mystery of holiness: beauty preserved in adversity. And then the Shulamite answers again, her gaze fully awakened:

"Like an apple tree among the trees of the forest,
so is my Beloved among the sons..."
Song of Songs 2:3

She has found shade. The Hebrew word *'tzel'* (צֵל), means shadow, protection, covering. The same word appears in Psalm 91:1, *"He who dwells in the secret place... shall abide under the shadow (tzel) of the Almighty."* To sit in His shade is to dwell in His covenant. Notice the posture: *"I sat down with great delight."*

In Hebrew, the phrase can also mean I sat and rested with joy. This is *'nuach'* in motion: the rest of intimacy. No fear, no striving, just joy under

His covering. Then comes the fruit, *"His fruit was sweet to my taste."* This is the fulfillment of Eden's reversal.

The first woman took and ate in disobedience; the restored Bride receives and eats in communion. Wisdom's fruit, once stolen, is now shared. Love redeems what rebellion lost. He brings her to His table, the house of wine (בֵּית הַיַּיִן, *beit ha-yayin*).

Wine in Hebrew symbolism always represents joy, covenant, and the inflowing of Spirit. The same wine she mentioned in chapter one, the wine of His loves, now becomes her shared feast.

Above the table flutters His banner, דֶּגֶל (*degel*), meaning standard, ensign, or flag carried by a tribe to mark identity and belonging. He declares over her not a doctrine, not a duty, but a name: אַהֲבָה (*ahavah*): love. She no longer strives to earn it; she sits beneath it. Rest has turned into rejoicing. Her identity is sealed beneath the canopy of affection.

When she sits beneath the apple tree, she is not simply resting in shade; she is returning to the rhythm of the first garden. In Eden, Adam and Eve ate from the trees without sweat or striving. Their sustenance came from communion, not labor. The fall broke that rhythm causing rest to turn into toil, and breath into effort.

Now the Shulamite is re-learning what was forgotten. The "house of wine" is the garden reopened. The fruit she eats is not forbidden but freely given. She eats from Him, not apart from Him. This is the restoration of wisdom's order: union before action, rest before fruit.

Even her breath changes. The Hebrew play between '*tappuach*' (apple tree) and '*naphach*' (to breathe) reminds us that what she inhales is the same breath that made humanity alive. But now it is mingled breath: His life moving through hers. The Song of Songs becomes the sound of Eden breathing again through the human heart. There is no strife here. No serpent. Only the quiet intelligence of wisdom at work beneath everything and turning former toil into hidden flourishing. What grows now grows by grace.

Step Inside: The Apple Tree in Hebrew Thought

The Hebrew word for apple tree is '*tappuach*' (תַּפּוּחַ), not merely the fruit we know today, but a symbol for fragrance, breath, and awakening. Its root, '*naphach*,' means "to breathe, to blow." It echoes Genesis 2:7, *"God breathed into Adam the breath of life."* So, when she says, *"I sat in His shade and His fruit was sweet,"* she is breathing again receiving the same *Ruach* (Spirit) that animated humanity in the beginning. This is not just divine romance; it is re-creation.

At the King's table, all striving ends. Love becomes both her covering and her nourishment. The feast is not food but fellowship. She has finally found what Eden lost: the unbroken communion between Creator and creation, between rest and delight.

The Voice of My Beloved: The Season of Singing

"The voice of my Beloved! Behold, He comes leaping upon the mountains, skipping upon the hills. My Beloved is like a gazelle or a young stag. Behold, He stands behind our wall; He is looking through the windows, gazing through the lattice.

My Beloved spoke and said to me: 'Rise up, My love, My fair one, and come away. For lo, the winter is past, the rain is over and gone. The flowers appear on the earth; the time of singing has come, and the voice of the turtledove is heard in our land.'"
Song of Songs 2:8–12

The moment opens with sound, *"The voice of my Beloved!"* The Hebrew word for voice is *'qol'* (קוֹל); it is the same word used in Genesis 3:8 for the *"sound of God walking in the garden in the cool of the day."* The echo is deliberate. Eden is being replayed, redeemed, restored. The Bride hears again the same footsteps that Adam once heard walking among the trees. What was terror to the fallen heart is now tenderness to the awakened one. He comes leaping upon the mountains; it is the imagery of joyful urgency.

The mountains in Hebrew thought are barriers, boundaries, and also meeting places. His love overcomes them all; nothing obstructs His approach. Then she sees Him behind the lattice. The word *'harakkim'* implies a woven screen: a boundary of intimacy, not separation. He looks through it; He is near yet giving her space to respond.

This is how divine romance always works: He approaches, but He never forces. Love waits for love's answer. And then the voice comes; the same word we have met before: *"Rise up (qum), My love, My fair one, and come away."*

This *qum* is the rhythm of resurrection. It is the same call that sounded to Joshua after Moses, the same command to the prophets when they were called to speak, and the same word Yeshua used when He said to the sleeping girl, *"Talitha koum."* Here it is no less miraculous. He is calling the Bride to rise out of dormancy: from remembrance into participation, from contemplation into communion.

Winter had its purpose: the hidden work of wisdom beneath the frost. But now the rains are over, and the season of song begins. The Hebrew meaning for singing here can also mean pruning. Even joy has its

185

discipline; even blossoming has its refinement. But this pruning is gentle, it is the loving hand that shapes beauty, not pain that punishes.

The Hebrew word for turtledove is *'tor'* (תּוֹר) and is the bird of fidelity; it mates for life and migrates by seasons. Its voice announces spring. It is as though creation itself joins the Bridegroom's call, affirming: *"Rest has returned. The garden is alive again."* This is the call every soul eventually hears: *"Arise, My love, and come away."* Not to escape but to emerge. It is the invitation to live from the inside out, to let the song of love become the sound that governs every step.

Step Inside: *Qol* (קוֹל), The Voice That Walks

In Hebrew, *'qol'* means "voice," but it also means sound, vibration, resonance, thunder, or breath in motion. It is not merely speech but His sound moving through air. The first time *'qol'* appears is in Genesis 3:8, *"And they heard the 'qol' of God Elohim walking in the garden in the cool of the day."*

This is the same moment humanity first hid. The sound that was meant to bring joy became something they feared. Now, in Song of Songs 2:8, that same word returns *"The 'qol' of my Beloved!"* The voice that once revealed distance now restores intimacy. The sound that once exposed sin now awakens love. The echo of Eden is redeemed; the garden no longer trembles but sings.

In Hebrew thought, *'qol'* also carries the idea of vibration that brings forth. It is the creative frequency of God's word: *"By the word (qol) of the LORD were the heavens made."* (Psalms 33:6) Every time His voice sounds, something is born.

So, when the Shulamite hears the qol of her Beloved, the sound reaches deeper than her ears. Something within her stirs and answers. Breath recognizes breath. Her body, her longing, her will begin to move together again. She is not being persuaded or informed. She is being reawakened and drawn back into harmony with the One whose voice shaped her from the beginning.

The Harmony of the *Qol* and *Qum*

'Qol' is the sound that calls, the divine vibration that stirs what is hidden. *'Qum'* is the answering movement, the human spirit rising in response to the call. Renewal is born in this meeting. The voice sounds, and something that was sleeping stands.

Every new creation begins this way. In Genesis, God speaks and light rises. In the Song, Love speaks and the Bride rises. In the Gospels,

Yeshua breathes and life awakens.

The Bride of the Song is learning what resurrection feels like. It does not arrive with thunder or upheaval, but with the quiet certainty of being called by name. Wisdom restores rest by speaking until what sleeps within us remembers how to rise.

The Secret in the Cleft of the Rock

"O my dove, in the clefts of the rock, in the secret place of the steep pathway,
let me see your face, let me hear your voice;
for your voice is sweet, and your face is lovely."
Song of Songs 2:14

The tone softens here. After the wild joy of mountains and springtime, the Beloved lowers His voice. It is no longer the shout of "Arise" but the whisper of "Come closer." He calls her "My dove." It is the same word, *'yonah,'* that He used before: the bird of rest, of peace, of homecoming. But now, the dove is in the rock. Something has changed.

The cleft of the rock is the place of safety and revelation. The Hebrew phrase literally means "the split or hollowed places." These spaces are carved by pressure, time, and hidden waters. They are not built but formed. This is where love hides us when the noise of the world is too loud. In Exodus 33:22, Moses stands in that very place when God says, *"I will put you in the cleft of the rock and cover you with My hand while My glory passes by."*

Now the same language returns, not for a prophet, but for a bride. The intimacy once reserved for one man becomes the inheritance of every heart. Here the Shulamite enters the revelation that Moses glimpsed, glory revealed through gentleness. He says, *"Let me see your face, let me hear your voice."*

This is one of the most profound truths in the Song: *God longs to be loved back. The Creator who spoke galaxies into being now waits for the sound of her voice.* The Hebrew word for see is *'ra'ah'* is the same word that also means to shepherd and to feed. The word for voice is *'qol,'* the same one that walked in Eden.

Even here, the language folds in on itself: to be seen is to be nourished, to speak is to echo creation. The Lover wants her face: the place of expression, honesty, and encounter. He wants her voice, the sound of her being awake. He says her voice is sweet, literally "melodious," and her face lovely, "beautiful in form."

When the Bride speaks, the world hears what Eden sounded like. Her voice is the instrument through which Wisdom's rest becomes audible again.

Step Inside: The Rock of Revelation

In Hebrew, the word for rock is *'tsur'* (צוּר) and means not just a stone, but a stronghold, a foundation, the unshakable one. It is the same word used for God Himself: *"He is the Rock; His work is perfect." (Deuteronomy 32:4)*

When the Bride hides in the rock, she is hiding in Him. The cleft is not separation; it is union. It is the space love makes for safety and refuge. The same imagery unfolds again when Yeshua's side is pierced, and a cleft opens in the true Rock.

From it flows water and blood as the new rivers of Eden pour out from His heart. That cleft becomes the everlasting hiding place for His beloved. Every time the Bride withdraws into stillness, she is stepping into that same opening, where love both shelters and reveals.

The Little Foxes: Guardians of the Vineyard

Immediately after the call into intimacy, the Beloved warns her:

"Catch for us the foxes, the little foxes that spoil the vineyards, for our vineyards are in bloom." Song of Songs 2:15

The timing is precise. The vineyard is blooming, and the heart is fruitful again. This is when the foxes also begin to appear. In Hebrew, *'shualim'* (foxes) come from a root meaning to burrow or hollow out. They represent subtle compromises, distractions, small fractures that hollow intimacy from within.

Love's greatest threats rarely roar; they nibble. They are not always sins; sometimes they are simply substitutes for presence. He says, *"Catch them for us."* Notice the pronoun: *us.* Intimacy's work is always shared. The Bridegroom is not demanding she fix herself; He is inviting her to guard the garden with Him. It is the restoration of Eden's commission: tend and keep it together.

Bether: The Mountains of Covenant Pieces

The chapter closes with her whisper:

"Until the day breaks and the shadows flee away, turn, my Beloved, and be like a gazelle or a young stag upon the mountains of Bether."
Song of Songs 2:17

'*Bether*' means separation, division, covenant pieces. It is the landscape of longing between promise and fulfillment. The Bride asks Him to move over these mountains and to keep leaping, to keep bridging the distance until morning comes and union is complete. Even in her longing, she is resting. She no longer runs in fear; she watches in faith. Her love has learned to wait, and her waiting has become worship.

The word בֶּתֶר (*bether*) comes from the Hebrew root '*batar,*' meaning "*to cut, to divide, to make a covenant by sacrifice.*" It is the same verb used in Genesis 15, when God cut covenant with Abram:

> "*He took for Him all these and divided (batar) them in the midst…*
> *and behold, a smoking furnace and a burning torch passed between those pieces.*"
> *Genesis 15:10–17*

That night, a deep sleep fell on Abram; the same sleep (*tardemah*) that fell on Adam before God formed Eve. Both are covenantal sleeps. Both are moments when God does the work of union while man rests. So, when the Bride in Song of Songs 2:17 says, "*Turn, my Beloved, and be like a gazelle or a young stag upon the mountains of Bether,*" she is invoking that same ancient imagery. The "*mountains of Bether*" are not random hills; they are the high places of divided sacrifice, the landscape of covenant. She is saying, in essence:

> "*Move, my Beloved, across the very covenant that binds us.*
> *Leap across what divides us. Let Your promise bridge the separation between us.*"

Just as the smoking firepot and flaming torch, symbols of God's presence, passed between the halves of the covenant pieces, so the gazelle and the stag (images of swift, living fire) move upon the mountains of *Bether*.

It is the same scene, but now in the language of love. God once walked between covenant pieces to unite Himself with Abraham's seed; now the Bridegroom leaps across covenant divides to unite Himself with His beloved Bride.

The Word "Turn": Love's Circle of Revelation

The Hebrew verb for "turn," '*sur*' (סוּר), can mean to depart, but it also means to turn aside, to approach from another angle, to appear again. It is the same word Moses used before the burning bush:

> "*I will now turn (sur) aside and see this great sight.*" *Exodus 3:3*

The Shulamite's plea is not rejection but reverence. She is saying,

*"Keep circling me with Your presence. Show me another facet of Your glory.
Teach my heart to bear the weight of Your nearness."*

Love moves in spirals, not straight lines. Every "turn" is another revolution of revelation. He turns toward her, and in that turning she learns another aspect of beholding. Even her restraint is worship. She is still becoming; her heart is tender, her form unfinished. So, she invites Him to turn rather than to stay, not because she doubts His love, but because she honors its holiness.

The rhythm of approach and retreat keeps longing alive until dawn. And when the light finally breaks, it fulfills what the prophets once saw from afar:

*"Arise, shine, for your light has come,
and the glory of the LORD has risen upon you." Isaiah 60:1*

The Covenant Pattern of Union

From the beginning, union has always been born the same way; through rest, not reach.

In Eden, Adam falls into deep sleep, and from his resting side, life is formed. Union begins not with pursuit, but with surrender. Later, Abraham is drawn into that same stillness as a deep sleep settles over him. While he rests, God alone moves between the sacrificed pieces, binding promise without demand. Covenant is carried by God while man is held.

Now, in the Song of the Bride, the pattern appears again. The Bride remains at rest while the Beloved moves toward her, crossing distance with delight; union unfolds not through pursuit, but through being drawn into love.

And finally, the pattern reaches its fullness as Yeshua offers His body freely. Sleep gives way to death, and from His opened side, covenant is completed once and for all. What began in Eden's rest is fulfilled in redemption's gift and union is forever secured.

Every covenant sings the same song.

The mountains of *Bether* become the landscape of that song. They hold Eden's memory, Abraham's promise, and Yeshua's sacrifice together in one terrain of love. Distance is never the point but the canvas upon which reunion is revealed.

Unveiling the Rhythm of Turning and Departure

In Song of Songs 2:17, the Bride says: *"Turn, my Beloved, and be like a gazelle or a young stag upon the mountains of Bether."*

The Hebrew word *'sur'* meaning "turn" or "turn aside," invites Him to circle around, to appear from another angle. But in doing so, the Beloved actually withdraws into mystery. His "turning aside" is not rejection but the divine rhythm of intimacy that teaches the heart to love by faith, not by feeling. Immediately afterward, in Song of Songs 3:1, the scene shifts as the Bride shares,

"By night on my bed I sought the one I love; I sought him, but I did not find him."

She now experiences what mystics call *the night of love* as she experiences the first taste of absence after overwhelming nearness.

Love matures through hiddenness. In chapter 2, the Bride is intoxicated by new affection with the joy of being seen, called beautiful, and awakened. But at this stage, her love depends on His nearness. She has not yet learned to trust His silence and arise. So, when He "turns," what is interpreted as departure is actually invitation. He withdraws so she will rise from the bed of comfort and seek Him.

"I will rise now and go about the city." Song of Songs 3:2

The same Hebrew verb appears here again, *'qum'* ("arise"). Do you see the pattern? Every apparent distance from God becomes the next arising of the soul. The Lover's "turn" is the Beloved's training. He hides only long enough for her hunger to awaken. She learns that His presence she felt beside her bed is now calling her to walk through the streets, through the night, and through searching. The intimacy of rest becomes the intimacy of pursuit.

The Divine Dance of Love

This rhythm of revelation, concealment, revelation again is the dance of divine love seen throughout Scripture:

- Eden: God walks with Adam, then withdraws; the cry of longing begins.
- Abraham: God speaks promise, and then is silent for years, until faith matures.
- Israel: God fills the Temple, then departs, to awaken repentance.
- The Gospels: Yeshua says, *"It is good for you that I go away,"* because His departure opens the way for indwelling union.

This same pattern unfolds in the Bride's story as He turns not to abandon her but to make her move. It is in the seeking that she discovers

His presence not as an external visitor, but as the pulse within her own heart.

Mystical Insight: The Bed and the Streets

The "bed" symbolizes comfort, passivity, spiritual infancy. It is where she once rested in His gifts rather than in His being. When He turns aside, she realizes that rest without pursuit becomes stagnation. The "streets and broad places" symbolize life itself; the world where love must now be lived, not merely felt. Her search in the night is the training ground of mature rest: *Rest that walks.*

In this way, what seemed like absence was actually the next stage of Eden's restoration; learning to walk again with the Beloved, not just recline beside Him.

The Night of Turning: When Love Teaches the Soul to Arise

"By night on my bed I sought the one I love; I sought him, but I did not find him."
Song of Songs 3:1

The Beloved's final leap across the mountains of *Bether* leaves the garden trembling with silence. The Shulamite feels the air shift as His nearness folds inward like twilight. She called for Him to turn, and He did. In the Hebrew of her song, she calls Him *'tzevi'* (gazelle) and *'ayyal'* (stag).

Both names carry the sense of radiant beauty and swift motion. The Hebrew root of *'tzevi'* (gazelle) is related to *'tzvi,'* and means "glory" or "splendor." This is the same word later used in Isaiah for *"the glory of Lebanon."* And the Hebrew word *'ayyal,'* (stag) is from the Hebrew root meaning *"to ascend or bound upward,"* which evokes the image of life rising with effortless grace.

This same root also forms *'ayil,* the "ram" provided for Abraham on Moriah, strength offered in surrender, life rising from the place of sacrifice. In this way, ayyal carries both the power of ascent and the memory of substitution, motion born from yielding.

Together they describe the quick, living movement of God Himself, the way His presence appears and vanishes like light across water, never heavy, always alive. So when she says, *"Turn, my Beloved, and be like a gazelle or a young stag,"* she is not asking for escape but for swiftness: *"If You must veil Yourself, let it be quick as light, so I may yet glimpse Your glory in motion."*

The same image appears again in the song of the prophets: *"He makes my feet like the deer's; He causes me to walk on my high places." (Habakkuk 3:19)*

What once described divine movement now becomes the shaping of the human soul, strength taught to move lightly in trust.

She knows deep within that the next revelation always comes disguised as absence. Her plea is not resistance to His turning; it is yearning for grace in the hiddenness. Even His retreat is beautiful when seen through love. The Hebrew word '*sur*,' to turn aside, holds both motion and mystery.

The bed that once held rest now holds longing. Her hands grope for the One whose fragrance still clings to her hair, and the empty space where His voice had been becomes the birthplace of pursuit. The "bed" is infancy; rest that still depends on sight. The "streets" are maturity; rest that moves through trust.

When she rises from the bed to walk into the city, she is learning that the garden was never lost; it simply moved inside her. The same voice that once called to Adam in the cool of the day now whispers within her own heartbeat.

The turning was never absence. It was the circle of love completing its revolution. He turns that she might rise; she rises that He might return. And thus the night of love becomes the dance of union.

The Breath Between the Lines

The Song does not end. It simply softens, the way evening softens into stillness. The Shulamite's last words linger like the scent of myrrh: a world once divided now bound together by love's gaze. Nothing more must be explained. Wisdom has spoken through the quiet of surrender. Rest answers her with breath. Together they move in rhythm as two currents meeting, and two voices echoing the same name. The ancient psalm sings what the garden now knows:

"Mercy and truth have met together; righteousness and peace have kissed."
Psalm 85:10

This is that kiss. In Hebrew,

- *chesed* (mercy, covenant love)
- *emet* (truth, faithfulness)
- *tzedek* (righteousness, alignment)
- *shalom* (peace, wholeness, rest)

It is the Psalmist's own picture of Eden restored and the attributes of heaven reuniting upon the earth. That verse is, in essence, the Song of Songs in miniature: heaven's affection and earth's faithfulness embracing again. It is also the very breath of exhale; the moment where rest (shalom)

193

and wisdom (truth) finally meet and kiss.

The meeting place of Eden restored with love and order, fire and stillness, and the wisdom that builds with the rest that dwells. The air feels holy again, as though creation itself remembers how to breathe. You are no longer a listener at the edge of the garden.

You are inside it and are the living echo of His voice in the cool of the day.

Selah Meditation: The Rest of Love

Pause here.

Let the noise thin, the way mist lifts from the ground at morning. Nothing needs to stop all at once. Just enough space for breath to widen. Feel the hush of His breath near, the quiet that has always been holding you.

Breathe slowly. Between one heartbeat and the next, there is space; an opening you do not have to search for. Remain there.

Imagine the leaves stirring above you, soft and unhurried. Cedar and fir carry their scent on warm air. The ground beneath you is steady, ancient, and alive. It does not rush you.

Now let your awareness rest on the One who is already here. His nearness carries no weight and makes no demand. His breath moves in rhythm with yours as time settles and love remains. Stay in this place. Let longing soften into belonging. You are seen. You are held.

This place does not close when you leave the page. He waits for you in the quiet moments of your day; in the pause before words, in the stillness that follows surrender. When the world presses in, return here.

His garden does not fade. The rest of His love remains within you.

Notes:

14
YESHUA
Rest Made Flesh

**"In the beginning was the Word,
and the Word was with God, and the Word was God...
In Him was life, and that life was the light of men."
John 1:1–4**

The Dawn of Return: The Gardener of Eden

It was still dark when she came. The stars had not yet faded; the earth still held its breath between night and day. Mary Magdalene walked to the tomb, the jar of spices in her hands, her heart heavy and aching with love's memory. The Sabbath was over, but silence still wrapped the garden.

"Now on the first day of the week, while it was still dark, Mary Magdalene came to the tomb and saw that the stone had been taken away." John 20:1

She ran to tell Peter and John, and they came racing through the gray dawn. They saw the grave clothes folded, the head covering rolled apart, and then they left, their minds torn between fear and wonder.

But Mary stayed.

The others had looked and gone. She lingered. The garden held its breath with her. And that lingering, her refusal to leave love's last trace, opened a door between worlds.

"But Mary stood weeping outside the tomb,
and as she wept she stooped to look into the tomb." John 20:11

The moment she bent down, heaven bent with her. Two angels sat where His body had been, one at the head and one at the feet, as though guarding the mercy seat of a new covenant. They asked, *"Woman, why are you weeping?"*

But before she could answer fully, she turned and saw someone standing there.

"When she had said this, she turned around and saw Jesus standing there,
but she did not know that it was Jesus." John 20:14

Her eyes were veiled by grief, but the veil itself was thin. She stood in the narrow space between shadow and sunrise; the same thin place where Eden once breathed with God's voice in the cool of the day.

The Gardener was near.

"Jesus said to her, 'Woman, why are you weeping? Whom are you seeking?'
She, supposing Him to be the gardener, said to Him,
'Sir, if You have carried Him away, tell me where You have laid Him,
and I will take Him away.'" John 20:15

Her words were mistaken, yet prophetic.

Her eyes saw a Gardener because that is who He truly is: the Keeper of soil and soul, and the Restorer of what was planted and lost. Yet, He is the One who walks again in the garden, tending the first sprouts of resurrection. Then He said her name:

"Mary."

The garden seemed to still around her as if creation leaned close.

"She turned and said to Him, 'Rabboni!' Teacher." John 20:16

She turned once in confusion; she turned again in revelation. That second turning was *teshuvah*, the kind of return that realigns the heart. It was not motion but awakening, the inward turning of humanity back toward its Source. Where Adam turned away and hid, Mary turns to behold. The garden that once heard footsteps of searching now hears the sound of recognition.

Eden's exile ends with a name spoken in love.

"Do not cling to Me," He said, "but go to My brothers and say to them, 'I am ascending to My Father and your Father, and to My God and your God.'"
John 20:17

No thunder, no spectacle; only breath meeting breath in the morning wind. It was the cool of the day again, the hour when labor yields to stillness, when the Spirit walks among trees and hearts. The same *Ruach* that once moved through Eden's twilight now moves through resurrection's dawn. Creation exhaled, and heaven inhaled.

The Gardener had returned to His Garden. Every root beneath her feet seemed to stir, as if the soil itself had heard resurrection.

Step Inside: The Cool of the Day (לְרוּחַ הַיּוֹם)

Genesis 3:8 says,

"They heard the sound of the LORD God walking in the garden in the cool of the day."

In Hebrew, this phrase is '*l'ruach ha-yom*' and means "in the breath or wind of the day."

- *Ruach* (רוּחַ) is breath, wind, Spirit; the same word used when the Spirit hovered over the waters (Genesis 1:2).
- *Ha-yom* (הַיּוֹם) is "the day," especially the soft light when heat surrenders to rest.

Together they describe the transition hour when creation exhales; when light softens, sound stills, and His presence becomes near. It is the Sabbath within the day; the time appointed for communion. God walked then because it was the hour when everything rested. At dawn, the mirror hour, He walks again: night giving way to day, and death giving way to life. The *Ruach* that once searched for Adam now calls Mary by name.

Twilight sealed the first garden; sunrise opened the second. And into that light He spoke her name. Mary. Before restoring the world, He restored the one before Him. Her name was the doorway.

Step Inside: The Meaning of Mary's Name

Miryam (מִרְיָם) is a name layered with memory. Its roots carry both ache and anticipation, holding together the long arc from loss to restoration.

One strand comes from *marar* (מרר), "bitterness." Scripture remembers bitter waters made sweet at Marah (Exodus 15:23), a place where sorrow met divine transformation. Mary's tears outside the tomb carry that same tension. What looks like grief is already becoming the moisture from which resurrection joy will rise.

Another echo rests in *mar* (מר), a drop or the sea itself. In Hebrew imagination, the sea is both depth and reflection, the surface that first catches light. Mary becomes the first mirror of resurrection, the one in whom the risen Son is reflected back into the world.

Later linguistic echoes soften the name further, carrying tones of beloved or wished-for. This, too, is fitting. She is the first to behold the Beloved alive again, the first heart steady enough to remain near when others have withdrawn.

So when Yeshua speaks her name, *"Mary,"* He is not only calling her attention. He is restoring her identity. Bitterness gives way to recognition. Grief yields to belonging. As He said, *"He calls His own sheep by name"* (John 10:3).

In that moment, resurrection is mutual. He rises from the grave, and she rises from the weight of the fall. A name spoken becomes a doorway, and Eden opens again through recognition.

Step Inside: The Garden Tomb

John alone highlights the garden (John 19:41) and calls it a *gan* (גן), an enclosed, cultivated sanctuary, derived from *ganan*, and means to protect or surround. In the Song of Songs, the Bride is called a *gan na'ul*, a locked garden. John's detail is not incidental. It is architectural.

The garden of beginnings has opened again.

Tradition whispers that Adam's skull lay beneath this hill of the Skull. If so, the Second Adam now rests where the first one fell; His blood seeping into the dust from which humanity was first shaped, breathing life back into the ground that once received a curse.

Eden is not merely remembered here. It is replanted.

And already waiting within the story is Joseph of Arimathea, not as an interruption, but as a keeper of the threshold.

Joseph, a Sanhedrin member, wealthy, hidden, and watching offers his own newly carved and unused tomb to Yeshua. As the first Joseph prepared a place of preservation when famine loomed, this Joseph prepares a resting place when death itself is about to be undone. Both appear at the hinge of history. Both hold space while God reshapes the future.

Joseph's garden-tomb becomes the cradle of new creation; the womb where the Second Adam sleeps before rising.

It is not a burial place; it is a seedbed. The garden holds Him the way soil holds a seed; only long enough for life to break open the ground. For if the first garden received a sentence spoken over dust, this garden receives mercy poured into it with blood.

The garden is no longer locked. What was once guarded by cherubim is now opened by love. The stone rolled, the gate stands open, and Eden is no longer be a place humanity is sent away from, but life humanity is invited into.

The Gardener has returned and this time, the garden cannot close again.

Reflection: The Remembering

Mary did not remain in the garden; she ran as He commanded. But as she ran, the garden remained in her. The earth still held His warmth where He had stood, and the echo of her name trembled inside her like a bell still ringing. She felt the moment replay within her: the turning, the Voice, the unveiling that opened her deeper than tears could reach.

And beneath that wonder, another memory rose like a buried ember catching wind. Not a memory of death, but of a table. It came to her gently; the scent of oil and roasted lamb, the glow of lamps flickering against the walls, the hush that fell whenever He lifted His eyes.

She had not slept much that night. None of them had. The weight in the room was too holy for rest, too tender for speech. And Mary... Mary had watched Him more closely than the lamps watched their flames. She remembered the way His hands moved; slow, deliberate, as though each gesture held a universe inside it. Hands that washed feet with the humility of a servant and carried authority that made angels tremble. Hands that reached for the bread. The memory came to her like a whisper against her ribs, as if her own heart were telling the story back to her.

He lifted the loaf as though it were a child. Not with force. With devotion. As if He were holding the breath of creation itself. And when He tore it, Mary felt the tear inside her chest now, as she ran from the garden, the same way she had felt it then. She did not know why the breaking hurt her; only that something ancient and sacred had been opened that night, something she still could not name.

It was not hunger that made her remember, nor sorrow, but longing. Longing for the moment when love had leaned close enough to place eternity between His fingers. Longing for whatever it was in His eyes when He looked at the bread and then at them as though He were inviting them into the deepest secret of His heart.

Mary pressed a hand over her own chest, as if to steady something rising inside her…she was remembering.

The Bread of Life: The Meal That Remembers Eden

Evening settled around the disciples like a cloak as they gathered in an upper room lit by trembling lamp flames. It was Passover before Yeshua was arrested.

The scent of roasted lamb lingered, mingling with the warmth of bodies pressed close; all of them sensing, though none could name it, that something ancient was about to be fulfilled.

Yeshua's eyes were quiet, but not the kind of quiet born of sorrow; the quiet of someone carrying a secret so old it predates the stars. He took the loaf in His hands.

Simple. Ordinary. Drawn from the same earth Adam once touched. The room hushed. It was the kind of silence that feels like waiting. He looked at them the way the Gardener looked at Adam when He showed him the fruit of every tree except one. Then He did something no prophet had ever done, something no priest ever dared:

> *"And He took bread, gave thanks and broke it, and gave it to them, saying,*
> *"This is My body which is given for you; do this in remembrance of Me."*
> *Luke 22:19*

The loaf cracked beneath His fingers. The sound was soft as a sigh, but heaven heard it like the breaking of a yoke that had burdened humanity since Eden's turning.

Hunger's First Echo

Adam once reached for food without trust, grasping instead of receiving, and taking instead of communing. Bread became toil. Hunger became fear. But tonight, the curse began to unravel by touch. Yeshua held the bread not as a demand, but as a gift, as if to say: *"What you once fought to earn, you now receive from My hands. What sweat once bought, love now provides."*

No sweat of the brow. No thorns in the soil. No separation between hunger and fulfillment. The One who once shaped Adam from dust now offered Himself as the meal that would restore him.

The Bridal Cup: Covenant of the Bridegroom

As Yeshua lifted the cup, the room held its breath for a moment. The wine inside caught the lamplight; dark, deep, shimmering like the heart of a pomegranate and every disciple felt something ancient stir. In

Galilee, everyone knew what it meant when a man offered a cup like this. It was the moment of proposal. Not with flowers or poetry, but with wine. A Galilean bridegroom would pour a cup and hold it out to the woman he loved.

The cup spoke for him: *"This is My covenant with you. I offer you My life. Do you receive Me?"*

And the woman, the bride, at that moment had a choice. She could lift the cup to her lips and say yes with her whole being. Or she could push it back, shaking her head, and walk away. Everything rested on the cup. Yeshua knew this. The disciples knew this. The room knew this. So, when He lifted the cup that night, He was not closing a Passover meal or instituting a sacrament, He was speaking the language of lovers, the language of covenant and choosing. He lifted the cup the way a Galilean bridegroom would, and the words He spoke were the vows of Eden restored:

"This cup is the new covenant in My blood."

Not a covenant. The covenant. Not written on stone, written in veins. Not enforced by fear but sealed by union. Then He did what no bridegroom had ever done: He offered the covenant before paying the bride price.

In Galilee, the groom paid the price first with silver or gold given to her family. But Yeshua offered the cup and then said quietly with His eyes: *"I am the price."* And the disciples, young men, still trembling between faith and confusion held the cup knowing what it meant: To drink was to say yes to being His. To drink was to receive His life as their life, His destiny as their destiny, His path as their path. To drink was to become the Bride.

One by one, they lifted the cup with hands that did not yet know what they were agreeing to. Wine touched lips, sweet, warm, alive, and slipped into them like a vow. Heaven leaned close. The angels, who once guarded a flaming gate in Eden, watched the gate open inside eleven trembling men. The wine was no longer just wine. It was a doorway. A covenant. A marriage begun.

And Yeshua watched them drink with the tenderness of the Bridegroom who had waited since the beginning for His Bride to say yes. He would finish this covenant alone within hours; crushed like these grapes, pressed until blood and water flowed, breathing out His life so they could breathe it in. But for now, in this dim, intimate upper room, He offered them the cup of Eden restored, the cup of love stronger than death, the cup that turned wandering disciples into covenant partners of the Messiah.

And the room, for one sacred moment, became a wedding. Not the wedding of Cana, and not the final marriage supper of the Lamb, but the quiet middle place, where covenant is spoken in bread and wine. It is here that the meaning of the meal must unfold. Because what He placed in their hands that night was not a ritual but the reversal of Eden's ache. To understand the weight of His offering, we must return to the very first word ever spoken over bread.

Step Inside: *Lehem*, The Ancient Mystery of Bread

Bread is one of the oldest words in Scripture, yet it carries a mystery most have never seen. *Lehem* (bread), comes from the root *lacham* (to fight, to struggle, to wage war). The very word for bread carries the echo of battle. This is astonishing, because Eden knew no battle. No striving. No resistance between soil and seed.

Before the fall, Adam received food as gift, not grind. Work was delight, not sweat. The earth cooperated with his touch like a friend responding to a friend. But when union fractured, when wisdom was traded for self-definition, the relationship between humanity and the ground changed. God told him:

"By the sweat of your face you shall eat bread (lehem)." Genesis 3:19

He did not say, *"You will sweat because you are cursed."* He said: *"The ground will resist your rest."*

Bread, once the symbol of communion, became the symbol of struggle. Every generation of Israel tasted this memory. Every loaf carried the ache of exile. Bread whispered with each bite: You are no longer in Eden. You must fight for what was once freely given.

But the story of bread goes deeper still.

Lehem and Adam: The Word That Remembers the Dust

The name Adam in Hebrew is אָדָם (Adam) and is from the Hebrew root *adamah* and means אֲדָמָה (ground).

Bread rises from the very soil Adam was formed from, and the soil he now must battle to survive. Hebrew imagination makes the pattern unmistakable:

Word	Meaning	Connection
Adam	humanity	formed from the ground

Adamah	the ground	the place of origin
Lehem	bread	what rises from the ground
Lacham	battle	what humanity now must do to obtain bread

Bread becomes humanity's struggle with its own origin; Adam reaching into the dust that birthed him and finding resistance instead of rest. But hidden inside the same word is a prophecy: the fight would not last forever.

The Hidden Echo Inside the Word Lehem

Ancient Hebrew was not heard only with the mind but felt with the body. When Israel spoke the word לֶחֶם (*lehem*), they did not hear "bread" alone. They felt the weight of survival and the warmth of provision carried in its sound.

The Hebrew letters themselves that make up with word *lehem* tell the story. *Lamed* lifts hunger toward learning and dependence. *Chet* encloses life in warmth: the hearth, the home, the inner place where strength is restored. *Mem* carries the memory of hidden waters and slow formation, the long patience required before nourishment can appear.

It is no accident that the same root that forms *lehem* also forms *milhamah* which is the Hebrew word for "struggle." Bread remembers the fight to live, even as it promises rest from that fight.

This is why the Bread of the Presence mattered. It was bread that no longer struggled. It rested before God's face, warm, whole, and complete. It was a table set in advance for the day when divine life would sit and eat with humanity again.

Bread was never only food. It was memory. And it was prophecy.

Yeshua and the Reversal of *Lehem*

When Yeshua lifted the bread at Passover, He was not redefining it. He was fulfilling everything it had ever ached for. He took the bread of struggle into His hands and spoke the words that ended the fight forever:
"This is My Body."

And in that moment, He was saying: *"The battle ends in Me. The ground ceases its resistance in Me. Adam's exile ends in My flesh."*

He becomes the *lehem panim*, the Bread of the Presence, God's face made edible, communion made flesh, and Eden restored in a loaf. When the disciples eat, they are not observing a ritual. They are eating the return of rest.

"Do This in Remembrance of Me": Remembering Eden

In Hebrew, *zakar* means "remember" but not in the way of thinking back. Instead, it means to draw what was into what is ... to pull the past into the present moment. So, when He says, *"Do this in remembrance of Me,"* He is not asking them to memorialize a supper. He is asking them to re-enter a Garden.

Everything Adam forgot of relationship, rest, and union is restored in the breaking of bread. The table becomes the doorway back to Eden. The bread becomes the body of rest. The wine becomes the drink of wisdom.

And Mary, standing in the resurrection garden, feels this remembering rise in her, not as recollection, but as recognition. Her heart knows the Gardener long before her eyes do.

The Rest of Wisdom

When Yeshua said, *"Take... eat,"* He was answering the first taking in Eden. Adam reached for the fruit in self-will, grasping life apart from God. At the table, Yeshua offers Himself and says, *"Take."* Not to seize, but to receive freely. The disciples eat in surrender what Adam took in fear. One taking fractured wisdom; the other restores it from within.

When Yeshua lifted the cup, He lifted the world back into communion. The bread restores rest. The wine restores union. Together they reopen the inner garden.

Mary's remembering was not nostalgia but revelation. Wisdom had walked with them. Rest had reclined beside them. And now Wisdom and Rest stood resurrected in the Garden.

And what Mary met in the garden, the disciples were about to meet in a locked room. Wisdom does not stay in one place: she moves until every heart is awakened.

The Breath Restored: The Ruach of New Creation

When evening fell on that same resurrection day, the disciples gathered behind locked doors. Fear held their chests tight, their hearts beating like animals trapped in the thicket of uncertainty. The room was heavy, not just with grief, but with the suffocating ache of absence. And then, without a footstep or a shadow, the Gardener entered the room.

"Peace be with you." John 20:19

The word did not just cross the air. It unwound the room. Peace. Shalom, the word that means wholeness, nothing missing, nothing broken. It was the sound Eden once knew before shame learned to speak. Only then did they see Him. And Yeshua, with hands still bearing the memory of nails, drew close enough that they could feel His nearness. He did not raise His voice, nor spread His arms like a king issuing proclamation. He simply breathed.

> *"And when He had said this, He breathed on them and said, 'Receive the Holy Spirit.'" John 20:22*

The moment He exhaled, the air in the room thickened with eternity. It was Genesis all over again; dust receiving breath, humanity animated by the Spirit moving through a human chest. This was the cool of the day restored, the breath of God walking again among hearts instead of trees.

To understand what filled that room, we must listen to the Hebrew language itself; the language that first described the breath that made humanity alive.

Step Inside: *Ruach* and *Neshama*, The Twofold Breath

In Hebrew thought, breath is never merely air. It is the carrier of life, awareness, and divine nearness. Scripture speaks of breath in two distinct but intertwined ways: *ruach* and *neshama*.

Ruach (רוּחַ) is wind, spirit, movement and the animating force of God that stirs creation. It is the breath that hovered over the waters in the beginning (Genesis 1:2), the wind that parts seas, the Spirit that empowers prophets and kings. *Ruach* is God's life in motion.

But *neshama* (נְשָׁמָה) goes even deeper.

Genesis tells us that when God formed the human from dust, *"He breathed into his nostrils the breath of life, and the man became a living being" (Genesis 2:7)*. The word used there is *neshamat chayyim*, the breath of lives. This is not mere animation. This is the breath that awakens consciousness, the inner knowing that allows humanity to recognize God, respond to Him, and walk with Him.

Scripture consistently links *neshama* to awareness and communion:

> *"The neshama (breath) of the Almighty gives understanding." Job 32:8*

> *"The neshama (breath) of man is the lamp of the LORD, searching all the inner chambers." Proverbs 20:27*

> *"Thus says God the LORD... who gives neshama (breath) to the people on the earth, and ruach to those who walk on it." Isaiah 42:5*

Scripture reveals a pattern:

Ruach gives life its movement. *Neshama* gives life its inward light.

Ruach empowers. *Neshama* awakens.

Ruach animates the body. *Neshama* opens the soul to God.

Now return to the locked room where the disciples are.

When Yeshua stands among the disciples and breathes on them, John is not describing symbolism; he is recording a deliberate act of new creation. The same verb used in the Greek (*emphysaō*, "to breathe into") is used in the Septuagint of Genesis 2:7. John is pointing backward on purpose.

The Second Adam breathes again.

But this time, the breath does not enter dust. It enters hearts already shaped by grief, fear, and love. The breath that once awakened Adam's awareness now reawakens communion. This is not Pentecost power yet. This is Eden restored within.

Ruach is given when Yeshua breathes on them and says, "*Receive the Holy Spirit.*" *Neshama* is rekindled as their inner lamp is lit again. The disciples do not run. They do not speak. They simply receive.

The breath does what words cannot: *it reopens Eden's garden within.* Not outside them, but within them. The cool of the day returns, not among trees, but among trembling hearts. Humanity is no longer animated merely to live but awakened again to abide.

Creation begins again, not with command, but with breath. Not with distance, but with nearness. Not with dust and ground, but with surrendered lungs. And the room that once held fear becomes a sanctuary as *Ruach* awakens lives and *neshama* awakens intimacy.

The Heart Becomes the Garden

As that breath moved through them, something ancient quietly unlatched inside. Fear fell away like leaves in wind. Shame loosened its grip. The door Adam once closed in Eden, the one he tried to hide behind with leaves and excuses, opened softly inside each disciple.

The garden was no longer outside them; it was unfolding within them.

The first temple was being rebuilt inside ribs. The veil within them had torn from top to bottom; not with force, but with His breath.

And the Creator that once walked among trees was now walking within them.

Before they could speak, He spoke, and the first word of the new creation rose in the room like dawn breaking over water.

The First Word of the New Creation: Peace

"Peace be with you."

Not comfort. Completion. *Shalom* is the world mended. *Shalem* is the heart made whole.

When Yeshua spoke *shalom*, He was not soothing fear, but reversing the fracture of Eden. Where the first man hid from God's breath, the disciples now inhaled it. The room itself became Eden, a sanctuary where the Gardener walked again in the cool of restored communion.

But the peace He spoke had a history because that breath had once been given away. And now, it was being given back.

The Breath Given Back

On the cross, Scripture says He *"gave up His spirit." "Father, into Your hands I commit My spirit." And having said this, He breathed His last. Luke 23:46*

The Greek is *paredōken* to *pneuma*. He handed over the breath. The breath He surrendered to the Father was now the breath He returned to humanity. Seed returned as harvest. Surrender returned as communion. The breath that left His body at death returned multiplied in resurrection.

Every inhale since that moment carries that rhythm: from the Son to the Father, from the Father through the Son, from the Son into the Bride.

Breath becoming union. Union becoming life. Life becoming rest.

The Door Within: The Inward Eden Reopened

When He breathed on them, the real resurrection happened inside the disciples. Not in the tomb. Not even in the room. But in their hearts.

The locked door within each one, the one guarded by fear, swung wide open. His Spirit moved in without resistance. Every disciple became a small Eden, a secret garden restored, a sanctuary filled with wind and flame.

This was always His desire: not a tabernacle of wood, but a temple of ribcage and breath. *"Within you"* was not metaphor, but a blueprint. The Gardener had returned to plant rest inside His beloved. The breath restored their hearts; the blood had already restored the earth beneath them.

For resurrection does not renew only the human heart; it renews creation itself. The disciples inhaled the new world, but the soil had felt it first.

The Ground Redeemed

This is the place where the curse breaks, where the story turns. Mary did not know it, but as she stood in the garden that morning, she was standing on ground that had already begun to heal. Before she recognized His voice, before she saw His face, the earth beneath her feet had already responded to the One who made it. Creation had been the first to feel Him rise. For when His blood touched the soil, the story shifted. The fracture that began in Eden met its restoration in a single downward drop. The ground had been waiting longer than any living heart.

And then came the moment everything changed.

The Moment Everything Changed: Blood Meets Soil

John 19:34 says simply: *"And immediately blood and water came out."*

But heaven felt the weight of those words in full. Blood did not fall into the air, it fell into earth. Geographically. Physically. Intentionally. The Second Adam's blood touched the very element from which the first Adam had been formed. And the moment it did, creation recognized its Maker. The soil that had groaned under the curse felt Life reenter its depths.

This is why Matthew 27:51 says: *"The earth quaked..."*

The ground was not trembling in fear. It was responding in recognition. For the first time since Eden, the curse was breaking.

Step Inside: When the Earth Itself Shakes

Matthew writes, *"And behold, the earth quaked, and the rocks were split..."*

He chooses the word *seismós*, a word reserved for moments when foundations do not merely tremble but give way. This is the same word he uses for the storm that threatened to swallow the disciples at sea, and again for the moment the stone is rolled away at the resurrection. In Matthew's telling, the earth shakes only when something irreversible is taking place.

Scripture has always known this kind of movement. Hebrew carries two verbs for it. *Ra'ash* (רָעַשׁ) speaks of quaking, trembling, a deep vibration that unsettles what once felt stable. *Ga'ash* (גָּעַשׁ) goes further, describing a surging roar, a storm-like upheaval that rises from within. These are not descriptions of weather, but of creation reacting to nearness.

"The earth quaked and the heavens poured rain at the presence of God," the psalmist sings. *"The mountains quaked at the presence of the LORD,"* Deborah remembers. When God draws near, the land does not remain neutral. It responds.

So when Yeshua breathes His last and the ground convulses beneath the cross, Matthew is not recording an atmospheric detail. He is announcing that something has shifted at the deepest level of reality. The old order has been breached. What once held has given way.

This is not creation overreacting.

It is creation recognizing its Maker.

What Is the Earth Responding To?

Not pain. Not violence. Fulfillment.

The earth quakes when His blood touches the soil. It quakes when the veil is torn. It quakes again when the stone is rolled away (Matthew 28:2). Boundaries are being redrawn. Heaven and earth are being rewoven.

This is not the first time the ground has reacted to human blood. Scripture remembers the moment clearly:

"The voice of your brother's blood cries to Me from the ground." Genesis 4:10

Abel's blood cried out for justice. Yeshua's blood speaks a different word,

"the blood that speaks better things than that of Abel." Hebrews 12:24

The ground hears that better word.

The quake is its answer.

The Ground as the First Intercessor

Abel's blood caused the ground to accuse. Yeshua's blood causes the ground to intercede. The *seismós* at the cross is creation's "Amen" to the end of the curse, as if the earth itself were saying:

"This is the One we have been waiting for.
This is the blood that heals what was broken in us too."

So, when the stones split and the graves open, it is not chaos; it is the ground doing what humans often struggle to do: respond rightly to the presence of God.

The quake is not threat; it is release. The soil is letting go of what it was never meant to hold. Redemption has reached all the way into the foundations.

Mary in the Garden: Standing on Redeemed Soil

When Mary mistook Yeshua for the gardener, she was more right than she knew. She was standing in the first garden of the new creation; the first soil of the renewed world, the first place where the curse had already begun to reverse.

Her feet pressed into the proof: Rest had returned to the earth. Wisdom had returned to the dust. Eden had begun to breathe again.

This is why He speaks her name in a garden. Not beside a temple. Not on a throne. Not in a synagogue. In the soil. The same ground where the story began. The same ground where the story fractured. The same ground where the story turns.

The ground felt resurrection before human eyes did. Something within the tomb had risen, had stood up. Creation answered with movement of its own.

Step Inside: *Qum* (קוּם), When Rest Stands Up

Before anyone saw Him, before a voice cried out, before Mary whispered His name, there was an earthquake. Not violence. Recognition.

Matthew records it simply:

> *"And behold, there was a great earthquake, for an angel of the Lord descended from heaven and rolled back the stone." (Matthew 28:2)*

The earth moved first. The same soil that once opened to receive Abel's blood. The same ground that held Adam's tears and bore the weight of exile. Now it trembles in relief, because something inside the tomb has shifted. Something has stood.

The Hebrew word for "stand" is *qum* (קוּם). It is the word spoken over Joshua, "Arise." The word Isaiah speaks over Zion, "Arise, shine." The word the Bridegroom whispers to the Bride. *Qum* is not effort but alignment, a rising into what was always intended, an awakening that comes from rest rather than strain.

On resurrection morning, no human ear heard it, but creation did. The stone moved because the earth responded to the One who had risen. The Greek word *egēgertai* carries the same meaning: He has been raised, awakened, stood upright. Not resuscitated. Not revived. Set back into right order.

Mary does not witness the moment itself; she sees its aftermath. The trembling ground. The displaced stone. The garden breathing differently. His rising is not spectacle but restoration.

The ground that once absorbed the curse now feels a weight lift from it as the Second Adam stands upon its surface, not in conquest but in rightness. This is *qum*. The world returning to its posture.

When Mary finally sees Him standing there, not in the tomb but in the garden, she sees what resurrection looks like when it touches soil. A Man upright. A ground awakened. A story restored.

The Eyes Restored

The ground grew still beneath Mary's feet as His breath faded into morning light. Her heart was awake; the garden inside her had opened. But Yeshua did not remain with her long. Love never stays only where it is recognized; it goes where sight is dim, where hearts burn but cannot yet name the flame.

Even as Mary turned to run and tell the others, He was already on another road walking beside two disciples who could not see Him, their eyes open in grief but closed in revelation. They did not know it, but their blindness had been anticipated years earlier in a small village called *Bethsaida*, where Yeshua first taught the world that sight comes in stages. And now, on the road to *Emmaus*, He would finish what He began.

Seeing as Eden Once Saw

The road stretched quiet beneath the fading afternoon, dust rising under weary sandals, hearts bowed beneath disappointment. Two disciples walked with heads lowered, their steps heavy with dreams undone. They spoke of death, of hopes dashed, of a kingdom that had slipped through their fingers like sand.

And then a Stranger drew near. No announcement. No radiance. Just a presence keeping pace with their sorrow. Luke writes: *"Their eyes were restrained." (Luke 24:16)* Not blinded. Not punished. Held. As though heaven itself waited for the moment when revelation would not crush them but heal them.

He asked what they were discussing. They poured out their grief. He listened, not as one uninformed, but as One gathering up every broken syllable and turning it into the tinder of awakening.

"One of them, named Cleopas, answered Him…" Luke 24:18

Cleopas: The Name That Interprets the Moment

Cleopas's very name becomes a doorway into the story. In Greek, it comes from *Kleopatros*, from *kleos* (glory) and *pater* (father): *"the glory of the Father."*

On the Emmaus road, that meaning quietly takes on flesh. The radiance of the Father's glory (Hebrews 1:3) walks beside a man whose name carries that same weight. He listens to his questions. He matches his pace. And as they walk, He opens the Scriptures that reveal the Messiah.

Glory beside glory. The image of God returning to those who could not yet see it. Eden's likeness being restored, step by step, breath by breath.

A Second Layer: The Semitic Echo

Some trace the name *Cleopas* to roots connected with the Hebrew words *heleq* (portion, inheritance) and *halaph* (to change, pass over, exchange). If so, his name holds an additional meaning: *"the one whose portion is changed," "the one who receives exchange," "the one who passes over into inheritance."* This is precisely what happens on the *Emmaus* road.

The whole journey is a Passover of revelation: from blindness to sight, from sorrow to burning, from confusion to communion. Another tradition goes deeper still: many believe *Cleopas* is the same as *Clopas* in John 19:25 who is the husband of one of the Marys standing at the cross.

If that is true, the disciple on the Emmaus road is likely Yeshua's own uncle by marriage. This means resurrection begins not with strangers, but with family. Tenderness before triumph. Kinship before clarity. Cleopas becomes a living prophecy: *The glory of the Father walks beside the blind until sight returns.*

The Unveiling on the Road

Then Yeshua began to speak. As He opened the Scriptures, their hearts began to burn; not with fear, not with shame, but with a warmth older than Sinai, older than Abraham, older than Eden's first sunrise. Still, their eyes remained closed. Some revelations must ignite the heart before they can illumine the eyes. Sight ripens slowly under the heat of His voice.

As they neared the village, they begged Him to stay. He agreed, entering their home the same way He had entered the world: quietly, humbly, carrying eternity inside His humanity. At a simple wooden table, He took bread not as a guest, but as the Host of Creation.

He blessed it. He broke it. He gave it.

The same motion He had given them the night before His death. And in the breaking the veil inside them tore.

"Then their eyes were opened, and they recognized Him." Luke 24:31

Eyes that once opened in shame now open in recognition. This was Eden in reverse: wisdom restored, union restored, rest restored. They did not see Him in thunder. They saw Him in communion. In the bread.

Because sight returns not through force, but through fellowship. Because Wisdom reveals herself in the ordinary places where rest becomes real. And then He vanished. Not as absence. As fulfillment. Recognition had done its work. The second touch had come.

The veil had lifted. They saw. And in seeing, they rested.

Step Inside: Emmaus, The Geography of Revelation

Most readers imagine Emmaus as a village on a map. But Scripture rarely gives distance without intention.

Luke tells us,

> *"Emmaus was about sixty stadia from Jerusalem."*
> *Luke 24:13*

Sixty stadia. About seven miles.

Seven.

The distance itself begins to speak. This is Sabbath ground. A measured walk between fracture and wholeness. The road to Emmaus is not a commute; it is a passage where despair loosens with each step and grief slowly releases its hold.

What began beneath the weight of crucifixion opens, mile by mile, toward communion. Sight does not return all at once. It awakens as the body keeps moving.

Revelation does not arrive suddenly here. It walks. It listens. It keeps pace with wounded hearts until rest has room to breathe again.

And even this is only the surface.

The Name: Emmaus, "Warm Spring / Hot Waters"

Emmaus comes from the Hebrew/Aramaic root *ḥammath* (חַמַּת), meaning warm spring, healing waters, hot fountain.

This is astonishing. The first place the resurrected Yeshua chooses for a long revelation is not a throne room, a synagogue, or the Temple. It is a place named for healing waters, a town whose very name means: *"Where the waters rise warm."* The outer landscape mirrors the inner landscape. What is happening around their feet is happening within their chests: hearts once cold are warming, eyes once dim are clearing, and souls once numb are beginning to burn.

> *"Did not our hearts burn within us...?" Luke 24:32*

Emmaus is not merely a geographic destination. It is the map of resurrection moving through the human heart.

Emmaus Was a Place of Past Defeat

In Jewish memory, Emmaus carried the stain of loss. During the Maccabean revolt in 165 BC, Israel suffered a crushing defeat near this very place. Emmaus became synonymous with national humiliation, the ground where hope collapsed.

Yeshua chooses that road for the first long conversation of the new creation.

He walks resurrection into land marked by failure so that history itself becomes healed ground. His presence reframes the landscape. Where Israel once lost hope, Hope Himself walks again. Where the people were scattered, the Word gathers. And where the past recorded sorrow, wisdom begins to write joy.

He could have appeared anywhere. He chose Emmaus.

Because resurrection often begins where humanity is least expecting God to walk.

Emmaus Was Outside the Main Roads

Emmaus was not a major city. It was not a trade route or a place of influence. It was a side road, quiet and easily overlooked.

Resurrection rarely begins in crowded sanctuaries or public platforms. It begins where hearts are breaking. *The Rest of Wisdom* does not announce itself over nations. It walks beside unnoticed travelers on obscure paths.

Emmaus is the geography of hidden encounter.

The revelation of Yeshua's identity does not occur in the Temple. It unfolds in a humble house, at a modest table, with ordinary bread. Wisdom has always chosen the small door.

"Sixty Stadia": The Measure of Transition

Sixty stadia. About seven miles.

Luke does not give this distance casually. In Hebrew symbolism, sixty corresponds to the letter *samekh* (ס), a form that signifies enclosure, support, and the unseen work of protection. *Samekh* is the circle that holds life while it matures. It is the support that surrounds without drawing attention to itself.

The disciples walk sixty stadia as the old world closes and the new one begins to form.

Emmaus becomes a place of gestation. Awakening does not arrive suddenly here. It ripens. Faith matures into sight along the way. This road becomes the corridor of becoming, where revelation grows quietly before it is recognized.

Emmaus Happens Away from Jerusalem

Jerusalem was thick with pressure. Religious expectation, political tension, fear, disappointment, and unfulfilled hope crowded its streets.

Emmaus stood far enough away for the noise to thin.

Sometimes God reveals Himself only after we step out of the environment that taught us how not to see. Emmaus becomes the place of exhale after trauma. The disciples leave the pressure and discover His presence. They leave the crowd and find communion. They leave the city and encounter the Gardener.

Revelation meets them not where they were supposed to stay, but where they finally slowed enough to walk.

The First Touch: Bethsaida, Sight in Outline

What unfolded in Emmaus had a shadow years before. In *Bethsaida*, a blind man was brought to Yeshua. But instead of healing him there, Yeshua took him out of the village, out of noise, out of familiarity, out of distraction, because some healings require solitude.

There, outside the crowded square, He touched the man's eyes.

"Do you see anything?"

The man blinked into the light.

"I see men... as trees... walking."

Not wrong. Not right. In-between.

A glimpse of Eden's memory, where humanity once stood like living trees rooted in God's breath. Then came the second touch. Vision sharpened. Shapes became faces. Blurry life became beloved life. *Bethsaida* was the first dawn of restored sight. *Emmaus* was the sunrise.

The first touch opened his eyes to the world around him. The second opened the world within him. The first restored the organ of sight. The second restored the capacity to behold.

Step Inside: "Eyes Opened," from *Ómma* to *Diēnoichthēsan*

In Bethsaida, Mark tells us that Yeshua heals a blind man in stages. The first touch brings partial sight. The second brings clarity. Mark uses the word ómma, the physical eye, the organ of perception. Sight returns, but it arrives gradually, as though the world must be learned again.

On the road to Emmaus, Luke chooses a different word entirely.

After the bread is broken, Luke writes, *"Then their eyes were opened."* *(Luke 24:31)*

The word he uses is *diēnoichthēsan*. It does not describe eyesight. It describes unveiling. To open fully. Thoroughly. All the way through. Not a flicker of recognition, but the removal of what was closing them.

Luke uses this word carefully. Throughout Scripture, *diēnoichthēsan* appears only in moments where God Himself removes a barrier that human effort cannot. It is used when heaven opens, when Scripture opens, when wombs open, and when understanding awakens. In every case, the action belongs to God. These openings are not forced. They are granted.

So when Luke says the disciples' eyes were *diēnoichthēsan*, he is telling us something precise. This was not improved perception. It was revelation.

Bethsaida shows us healing that restores sight. Emmaus shows us resurrection that restores recognition. In Bethsaida, they see again. In Emmaus, they know.

The same Yeshua walked beside them before the bread was broken. The same voice explained the Scriptures. But only in the breaking did the veil fall away.

This is how wisdom moves. Light comes first. Seeing follows. And sometimes the eyes must wait for the heart to open.

Revelation: The Eyes of Eden

In Hebrew, the words for seeing and feeding are intertwined. The Hebrew word *ra'ah* means to see, to perceive, to behold. From the same sound comes the word for pasturing, for nourishing, for being fed.

The sages said that we feed from what we see.

In Eden, humanity saw God and lived. After the fall, humanity learned to look at fear and fed on it instead. But in the garden of resurrection, sight is restored. The disciples see the Gardener and are nourished by His presence. Recognition becomes sustenance.

This is Eden's gaze returned. To behold Love without fear. To recognize Wisdom not through control or certainty, but in the breaking of bread and the quiet companionship of a Stranger on the road.

Step Inside: Bethsaida, The Geography of Half-Sight

Bethsaida in Hebrew is *Beit-Tsayda* and means House of the Hunt. House of the Chase. House of Striving for Provision. Bethsaida is the antithesis of Eden; a place where provision is earned, not received; and where sight is labored for, never resting into clarity. No wonder Yeshua said: *"Woe to you, Bethsaida..."* *(Matthew 11:21)* Bethsaida witnessed miracles, but never learned rest.

A Threshold Place

Set on the northern rim of the Galilee, Bethsaida sits on a liminal frontier between Jewish and Gentile lands, between solid ground and deep water, and between familiar villages and ungoverned wilderness.

Thresholds are thin places. Places where revelation is close, but clarity feels far. Bethsaida is the geography of almost seeing. Perfect soil for a half-healing.

A Village of Beginnings and Resistances

Bethsaida was a place of beginnings, but also of resistance.

Peter, Andrew, and Philip came from its shoreline streets; apostles destined for nations were raised in its sand. Yet the same soil that birthed world-changers resisted the revelation they would one day carry. It was the paradox of a village caught between awakening and apathy.

Bethsaida is paradox with miracle soil that refuses to awaken, calling soil that refuses to respond, and seeing soil that refuses to behold.

It is the perfect symbol of the human heart before the second touch.

Why Yeshua Led the Blind Man Out

Mark tells us plainly: *"He took the blind man by the hand and led him out of the village."* *(Mark 8:23)* Yeshua healed multitudes in the open, but not here. Because the soil resisted sight.

The air in Bethsaida carried a certain weight: too familiar, too noisy, too restless. It was a village shaped by pursuit more than presence, a *"House of the Hunt"* where hearts learned striving instead of stillness.

This was the perfect geography for a half-healing. A place where sight could begin but not yet bloom.

You cannot restore sight inside the atmosphere that blinded it. So, Yeshua leads the man out: out of striving, out of noise, into stillness, into quiet, into Eden-space.

Only there does the first touch come.

Why He Saw "Men as Trees Walking"

In threshold places, vision blurs. But it blurs into memory. The man sees humans as walking trees, not mistake, but revelation. A flash of Eden's way of seeing humans like trees, rooted in divine breath, branches lifted to the Light, and living conduits of glory.

It is true vision, but not yet whole. Bethsaida sight. First-touch sight. Outline without essence. Awakening without revelation. He sees rightly…just not fully.

From Bethsaida to Emmaus: The Two-Touch Gospel

Bethsaida shows us what sight looks like when it first awakens: shapes coming into view, truth outlined but not yet embraced. Emmaus shows us what sight becomes when love finishes its work: recognition, communion, the heart remembering what the eyes forgot.

Bethsaida is the first touch: a world perceived in outline, a glimpse of Eden's memory and "men as trees, walking."

Emmaus is the second touch: the veil dropping, the Stranger revealed as the Lord and known in the breaking of the bread.

Bethsaida draws us out of the familiar, the noisy, the striving. Emmaus draws us into the table, where bread becomes revelation. Two places. Two touches. One Gardener.

Healing our vision from the outside in…then from the inside out.

Leading humanity from blur to belonging, from pursuit to presence, from the House of the Hunt into the cool-of-the-day rest we were made for.

Presence Walking in Flesh

The disciples in the Upper Room were still trembling from fear, from hope, and from the quaking of the earth itself. Mary had seen Him in the garden. Cleopas had walked with Him on the Emmaus road. And earlier, long before the resurrection dawned, the blind man of Bethsaida had already shown the world what resurrection sight would one day look like: vision returning in stages, outlines first, then clarity.

Now, all these threads converged. Every whispered report carried the same breathless confession: He is not gone. He is moving. He is breathing. He is with us.

God's presence they once knew behind a veil, hidden within acacia and gold, guarded by wings and shadow was now walking through walls of fear as easily as He once walked among the fig trees of Eden.

And suddenly, He stood among them. Not with thunder. Not with blazing fire. But simply there, the way His presence once pooled in the Holy of Holies, heavy and quiet and unmistakably near.

"Peace be with you," He said.

The same word spoken over the formless deep. The same breath that cooled Eden's morning. The same syllable that had quieted storms and stilled frantic hearts. They stared: some with wonder, some with disbelief, all of them hushed.

Then He lifted His hands; hands that once shaped dust, steadied fishermen, fed wanderers, and wrote mercy in the sand. Now they bore the marks of the Tree that held Him. But these were not signs of death; they were the memory of every tree that had carried God's presence since Genesis. His wounds were not an end; they were a doorway. They invited the disciples into a story older than the flood, older than Sinai, older than exile. A story written from a Tree and fulfilled in His flesh. For the Cross was not merely timber; it was the final place where the Tree that once guarded Eden opened the way back into union.

Step Inside: The Wood, Two Arks Fulfilled in One Tree

Scripture holds the story the way an ancient tree holds its rings: quiet, layered, remembering. Lean in closely. In Yeshua's body, Eden's ancient path converges.

Scripture never tells us what kind of wood held the body of the Messiah, perhaps because the point was never the species, but the story. And if you lean close to that story, close enough for breath to warm the grain, you begin to hear the whisper inside it: the Cross was not a random beam.

It was a return. It was a remembering. It was the place where every tree in Scripture bent toward the same center, like branches reaching for their root. Let us look gently. Let us listen deeply.

The wood will tell the truth.

The Ark of the Covenant, the vessel of glory, the resting place of the *Shekinah* was crafted from acacia wood (*shittim*, שִׁטִּים):

"Make an ark of acacia wood..." Exodus 25:10

Why acacia? Because acacia is incorruptible. It does not rot. It resists decay. It survives desert heat and wilderness storms. It is the wood that cannot be destroyed.

Early believers recognized the resonance immediately: If the Ark that carried God's presence was made of incorruptible wood, how much more the Cross that carried His presence-in-flesh?

Some ancient communities even believed the crossbeam itself was acacia; the same wood that once bore God's glory now bearing God in human form. Not provable. But profoundly fitting.

Gopher: The Wood That Saved the World

Long before Moses shaped acacia, Noah shaped something older.

"Make for yourself an ark of gopher wood..." Genesis 6:14

We do not know the species. But we know this: God chose it to carry creation through judgment into a world reborn in rest. The Ark was not merely a boat. It was a womb: a *tevah*, a vessel of breath, a container of beginnings.

Early Jewish Christians began to see the pattern:

- Noah's ark carried creation through water.
- The Ark of the Covenant carried God's presence through wilderness.
- The Cross carried the world through death into resurrection.

Three arks. One story. Three woods. One pattern. Three vessels. One Gardener. Some traditions even whisper that the vertical beam of the Cross was gopher wood, the wood of deliverance. Not archaeology. But an ancient echo.

The Tree That Healed the Waters: The Wood of Marah

In the wilderness, Israel came to *Marah*. Its waters were bitter, undrinkable, and poisoned by curse.

"The LORD showed him a tree..." Exodus 15:25

Moses cast the wood into the water, and bitterness became sweetness. Jewish tradition teaches this was acacia. If so, the pattern becomes breathtaking: The same wood that healed the waters of *Marah* now heals the waters of humanity at the Cross. The world's bitterness touches the tree, and sweetness returns. The curse meets the wood, and Eden's flavor rises again.

The Cross as the Tree of Life Itself

The early fathers of the Church were bold enough to say aloud what Scripture had whispered all along: *"The Cross is the Tree of Life."*

Not symbolically. Ontologically. The Tree humanity lost in Genesis is the Tree humanity finds at Golgotha. Yeshua does not merely hang upon the Tree of Life, He is the Tree of Life rooted in the soil of a cursed world, bearing fruit for the healing of the nations.

So, when the thief breathes, *"Remember me..."* he is reaching for fruit again. And the Gardener does not refuse him. All creation strains toward this moment: the moment when Wisdom hangs on the Tree, when Rest pours its final breath into Adam's soil, when the curse trembles beneath the weight of mercy.

The Mystery

We do not know the name of the wood because the Cross is the meeting place of every tree in Scripture and the fulfillment of all of them. It is the place where the story bends toward its center and where Eden's memory touches humanity's future. And the moment His blood touched that wood, the curse on every tree, every vine, every seed, every field, every generation... unraveled.

The ground is redeemed. The tree is redeemed. The story is redeemed. The Gardener has returned to His Garden. His Presence no longer behind curtains. The Ark no longer in a temple.

And in that moment, the wood held the Son, cradled the story of creation, anchored every covenant ever spoken, shouldered the deliverance of the world, and lifted the very presence of God before human eyes.

The Ark was standing before them alive.

What had always appeared as separate stories, arks and altars, wood and vessels, shelters and sacrifices now revealed themselves as a single pattern. With the mystery unveiled, history itself could be reread. What once looked like preparation was fulfillment waiting for its moment. What once seemed symbolic now stood embodied. The veil had not only been torn in the temple; it had been lifted from the story itself.

The Living Ark: The Body That Carried the World

When Yeshua vanished from the table in Emmaus, He did not slip into absence but into the ancient pattern. Into the story older than rain, older than angels, older than Eden's first dawn. The disciples saw only an empty chair. Heaven saw an Ark standing at the center of creation.

For the first time in history, God's presence was not resting on an object but breathing, laughing, walking, alive. The Living Ark had taken form.

The First Whisper of the Ark

Long before His hands broke bread, those same hands shaped gopher wood into refuge.

"Make for yourself an ark (tevah) of gopher wood..." Genesis 6:14

Tevah means ark, but it also means word, the vessel that holds life, the Word that holds worlds. Noah did not simply build a boat. He built a prophecy. Plank by plank, he formed the silhouette of the One who would one day hold all creation within His own ribs. When the rain began and the deep burst open, Noah entered the *tevah* and God Himself shut the door (Genesis 7:16). Inside, creation slept. Outside, the waters cleansed. And when the ark came to rest, Scripture uses the word *nuach*. Rest.

Echo of Eden. Echo of Yeshua. The first ark was a womb, cradling the seeds of a new world.

The Second Whisper: The Ark of the Covenant

Centuries later, another ark appeared, this time shaped from acacia wood, the incorruptible tree of the desert.

"They shall make an ark of acacia wood…" (Exodus 25:10)

Acacia refuses decay. It endures wilderness heat and barren soil. Its heartwood is guarded by thorns. It mirrors the sinless flesh the Messiah would one day wear. This ark was overlaid with gold, divinity embracing humanity, and crowned with the *kapporet*, the mercy seat, where two cherubim overshadowed atonement.

Within it rested manna, the bread from heaven; Aaron's rod, the branch that budded with life; and the tablets, the word written in stone. God's presence dwelled there, within a wooden vessel clothed in glory, waiting for fulfillment.

Two Arks, One Echo: The Body That Would Come

Noah's ark carried creation through death. The covenant ark carried God's presence through wilderness. Yeshua carries both.

He is the refuge. He is the throne. He is the manna. He is the resurrection branch. He is Wisdom in flesh.

Every story that ever saved the world was leaning toward Him. When He said, *"One greater than the temple is here,"* He was revealing that every sacred shadow was tracing His outline.

His Ribs: The Timber of the Final Ark

Just as Noah shaped gopher wood, the Father shaped the humanity of His Son, incorruptible as acacia and yielding under divine will. Every rib in His side was a curved beam of mercy, forming the shelter of the world.

When the soldier pierced Him, it was not merely a wound. The Ark was opened.

"Immediately blood and water came out." John 19:34

Blood for atonement, the mercy seat in motion. Water for cleansing, the flood that makes all things new. Where Noah's ark released a dove in search of rest, the Living Ark released the Spirit to fill the earth with rest. Where the high priest sprinkled blood once each year, the Great High Priest offered His own body once for all time.

The mercy seat was no longer a place.

It had become a Person.

And once mercy took on flesh, only one unveiling remained: the opening of His side.

Step Inside: The *Kapporet* and the Pierced Side

The *kapporet*, the mercy seat, was the place where heaven and earth met through blood. The rabbis called it the throne of rest and the place where heaven bends low.

When Yeshua's side was pierced, that blood fell onto the earth, the first mercy seat of creation. The soil that once drank Adam's curse now received Adam's redemption. His body became the meeting place between God and humanity. Just as the high priest passed behind the veil, the soldier's spear passed into the living temple and the veil inside His flesh tore open.

The mercy seat became human. God's presence found a body.

The War that Ended in His Side

The hill where Yeshua hung had grown strangely quiet. The kind of stillness that comes after shouting has spent itself and no one knows what to say next. The sky hung low and dull, as if even the light had grown cautious. The air tasted of iron and dust and sweat.

The three crosses loomed above the crowd, dark shapes against the sky. Bodies sag. Wood groans. Women are weeping and wailing. Somewhere else, laughter breaks out, sharp and brittle, and then stops just as suddenly.

A soldier steps forward.

There is nothing dramatic about him. No anger. No hatred. Just routine. That was how the days end and bodies are checked. The soldiers hand grips the spear the way it always has. He does not look at the man's face. He looks at the ribs.

The spear rises.

The crowd leans without realizing it. The point enters flesh.

There is a sound, not loud, not violent, but unmistakable. A yielding. A release. And then something no one expects.

Water pours out.

Not a trickle. Not a stain. But a flow.

Blood follows it, darker, heavier, soaking into the soil at the base of the cross. The dust drinks it in. The ground that once resisted now opens easily, as if it has been waiting.

The crowd gasps, feeling it before understanding it. A shudder passes through the people, not fear, not revulsion, but astonishment. This is not how death behaves. Bodies do not do this. Corpses do not give.

Someone whispers. Someone else falls silent mid-breath.

The soldier steps back, startled now, his routine broken. He stares at the spear as if it has betrayed him. The centurion's face tightens. The mocking has stopped.

No one speaks. The ground is quiet.

For the first time since Eden, blood touches the soil and the soil does not cry out.

It receives.

Something in the air loosens, like a clenched fist opening slowly. The war embedded in bread, in sweat, in survival, in every meal wrested from reluctant ground releases an ancient exhale. Water has touched the soil first, not as flood or judgment, but as life returned.

The Bread has been pierced. And the struggle ends here.

Bread no longer means struggle. Bread now means rest.

Before any human understood what had happened, the ground already knew.

Three Days: The Womb of the New World

Three days followed. Not decay, but gestation.

The Seed lay within the earth, hidden from sight, while Wisdom worked in silence. Nothing appeared to change. No movement announced itself. Yet beneath the surface, life was being arranged where no eye could see, held in the dark like breath waiting for its moment.

Scripture had already named this rhythm:

> *"On the third day He will raise us up."* Hosea 6:2

When the Living Ark stepped from the tomb, creation inhaled as one. The ground that had received blood and water now felt life rise through it. Rest returned to the earth. Wisdom stood again with wounded hands. And Yeshua began walking, no longer behind veils or within sanctuaries of stone, but within human hearts, carrying the new world with Him.

Within Us

The Ark walks with us: breath in our breath, rest in our bones, wisdom in our dust. The Living Ark has found His home. The breath of the risen One still lingered in the morning air, light as dawn, steady as promise.

Mary carried it as she ran. The disciples carried it as they trembled. The earth carried it as it waited. Nothing in creation was untouched.

And then, the moment the ages leaned toward, the moment the garden held its breath for, began to unfurl. Resurrection does not bloom in a vacuum. It blossoms from a story planted long before dawn ever touched the garden soil.

A sign had already been given: quiet, bridal, and veiled in joy.

Not thunder.

Wine.

And the one who recognized it was a woman.

The Woman at the First Sign: Cana's Whisper

Before the garden of resurrection, before Mary Magdalene mistook Him for the Gardener, there was another Mary standing in another threshold.

A wedding. Cana. A feast for joy now trembling with lack. Mary saw the truth before anyone else. Not empty jars. Not anxious hosts.

She saw Him.

"They have no wine."
"Woman, what is this to Me? My hour has not yet come." John 2:3-4

Not distance, but revelation. He calls her "Woman" because He is speaking to her as Eve restored.

She turns and says, "Whatever He says to you, do it." John 2:5

This is not obedience. It is consent. The first "yes" of the restored Bride. Water becomes wine. Joy returns. The future tastes its own beginning. The first sign belongs to her. The last sign belongs to another Mary.

Two women. Two gardens. Two revelations. One Bridegroom. Cana opens the story. The Garden completes it.

Mary Magdalene ran from the garden, her heart burning, her footsteps echoing the Song she did not yet know she was fulfilling.

"On my bed I sought Him whom my soul loves…" But now the search was over. With every stride, the Song of Songs rose inside her: *"Arise, my love… come away."* And the garden answered: The Bride is awakening. And as she ran, the moment replayed inside her: the turning, the name, the breath that awakened her world.

What awakened in Mary's heart is the same place Yeshua named as the fountain of living water; the inward chamber where desire becomes river.

Step Inside: The Belly, Where Desire Becomes River

In Hebrew imagination, the belly is never merely anatomy. It is the seat of longing. The inner chamber of desire. The hidden place where hunger becomes direction. Scripture uses three intertwined words:

בֶּטֶן *beten*: the belly, the womb, the place of formation.

מֵעֶה *me'eh*: the inner chambers, the guts, the place where emotions churn and intuition speaks.

קֶרֶב *qerev*: the innermost center, the place where God meets the soul.

This is why Yeshua chose the belly, not the mind, not the mouth, not the heart, when He declared:

"He who believes in Me, out of his belly will flow rivers of living water." John 7:38

The belly is where desire lives and desire are where worship begins. Not the worship sung from lips, but the worship that vibrates through bone and breath as a frequency of union. But there is another story hidden beneath this one.

The Serpent and the Belly

In Eden, the serpent is cursed:

"On your belly you shall go…" Genesis 3:14

The place of the serpent's humiliation becomes, in Yeshua, the place of the Bride's restoration. The very realm where deception once whispered becomes the chamber where the Spirit now flows. The curse falls downward. The river rises upward.

What once crawled, now becomes the place where heaven wells within. This is why Yeshua points to the belly: He is reclaiming the seat of desire. He is purifying the chamber where longing lives. He is turning the womb of appetite into the fountain of communion.

Desire, once twisted by fear, becomes aligned with Eden again. The Bride does not awaken in her mind; she awakens in her desire when the river begins to move.

Eden in the Inward Parts

When Mary heard her name, her desire turned. Her innermost place, *beten, me'eh, qerev* opened like a spring struck by the staff of God. Desire became river. Longing became recognition. The waters moved where the serpent once coiled. This is the Bride awakening: Not with a song from the mouth, but with a frequency rising from within, a resonance of the river that once flowed through Eden now flowing through her body.

And one day, when the Bride rises fully into this river, John hears the sound again:

"The voice of many waters...the sound of a great multitude." Revelation 14:2; 19:6

The sound is not a choir. It is a people. One body. A Bride whose innermost chambers flow with the same river that flows from the Lamb. David felt it. The prophets foresaw it. Mary tasted it. The Bride will embody it. The serpent was lowered. The Bride is raised. And desire becomes the dwelling place of God.

What rises in the Bride began with one woman's encounter.

The Bride Awakens: The Moment the World Remembered

The garden held its breath as Mary drew near. Morning gathered softly over the dew, and the air trembled as if creation remembered the sound of His voice. Her steps barely stirred the softened earth. Her heart beat with a rhythm she did not yet understand, the rhythm of a world beginning again. She had come looking for the dead. She was about to meet the Living.

The Turning That Unmade the Fall

She leaned toward the tomb, blinded by grief, vision blurred by tears. Her whole world was the hollow place where His body had lain. But heaven was not looking at the tomb. Heaven was looking at her.

"Woman, why are you weeping?" the angels asked (John 20:13).

Not out of curiosity, but because sorrow is the doorway to revelation. Then she turned.

That turning was the hinge of creation. The same Hebrew movement in *shuv*: to turn, to return, to come home. In Eden, the first woman turned away from the Voice. Here, the second woman turned toward it. And she saw Him yet did not see Him. She thought He was the gardener (John 20:15). And she was not wrong.

He was the Gardener of all gardens, standing in the soil He had just redeemed.

He Spoke Her Name and Eden Exhaled

Then came the moment the world had been waiting for since Genesis: *"Mary." (John 20:16)*

Not thunder. Not command. Not prophecy. A name.

The same Voice that once said, *"Where are you?"* now whispered, *"I know where you are... come out of hiding."*

Her whole being turned again, this time not toward a stranger, but toward her Beloved. Her eyes opened, and the deep place of desire within her awakened, the same place Yeshua promised rivers would flow, now filling suddenly with His living waters.

The Bride stood up inside her.

"Rabboni!"

Not a title. A recognition. The first healed word spoken by redeemed humanity.

The sound of a soul restored to its Source.

Eden breathed again.

Step Inside: The Name that Rebuilds the Heart

In Hebrew, a name is never a label. *Shem* is essence, breath, and inner nature voiced aloud. A true name is revelation, not designation. When Yeshua speaks Mary's name, He returns her to herself. He restores what sorrow tried to steal. He calls forth the garden within her and awakens the Bride.

This is why in Song of Songs 1:3 it says: *"Your name is flowing oil..."*

His voice pours identity into her. She is not clinging to memory. She is stepping into origin.

The Healing of the Edenic Identity

With one word, the risen Yeshua heals Eden's wound. He restores the first gift ever lost: identity as communion, identity as belonging, identity rooted in Love. Her name becomes the doorway back into union. This is why she awakens. This is why the Bride rises. Mary is the first witness of resurrection because Eve was the first witness of the fall.

Where the story fractured in a garden, it is healed in a garden. Where a woman once listened to a lie, a woman now listens to Love. Where sorrow first entered the world, joy first returns. Mary becomes the threshold between Genesis and Revelation, prophecy fulfilled in flesh and tears.

Step Inside: "Do Not Cling to Me" (John 20:17)

These words have puzzled many. But in Hebrew thought, to cling (*taphas*) can mean: to seize, to grasp, to hold in fear of losing. Yeshua is not rebuking affection. He is reorienting love:

"Do not cling to what I was. Receive who I have become."

He is no longer the Rabbi outside her. He is now the Life within her. This is the moment faith shifts from dependence to union.

The Bride awakens.

The First Commission of the New Creation

"Go to My brothers…" John 20:17

The first evangelist of resurrection is not Peter, not John, not a priest or prophet, but Mary, the one who mistook Him for a gardener. Because she was not mistaken. She was prophetic.

She saw Him as He is, the Tree of Life, the One who walks again in the cool of the day, the Restorer of Eden's song.

Eve and Mary: The Seed That Brings the Story Full Circle

Long before Mary walked into the dawn of the new creation, another woman stood in another garden, hearing a sentence fall not upon her but upon the serpent and upon the ground beneath her feet.

"I will put enmity between you and the woman, and between your seed and her Seed; He shall crush your head…" Genesis 3:15

Eve was not cursed; she walked out into a world where the ground itself had fallen, and her body, still blessed and chosen, would experience sorrow within that fractured soil. But her womb remained the vessel of promise, the chamber through which the Seed would come.

Only the serpent was condemned. Only the soil was burdened with sorrow. And the Seed, the promised One, was foretold. From that moment on, every daughter of Eve carried two things inside her: the ache of exile and the whisper of a promise.

Eve's tears were never the end of the story. They were the womb of it. And so, when Mary stands in the resurrection garden, she is not simply a grieving disciple, she is the one chosen to receive the fulfillment of the very promise spoken in Eden's first dawn.

Eve heard a prophecy about a Seed who would crush the serpent. Mary hears the Voice of that Seed speaking her name.

Eve watched the ground fall under sorrow. Mary stands on soil already healed by the blood of the Second Adam.

Eve felt desire twist into fear. Mary's desire becomes a river, the living water rising from the place where the curse once fell.

Eve turned away, reaching for wisdom apart from God. Mary turns toward the Voice, receiving wisdom as communion. And in that turning, that simple, trembling pivot, the prophecy of the Seed completes its circle.

The serpent once spoke in a garden and a woman listened in sorrow. Now the Gardener speaks in a garden and a woman listens in awakening. The first garden held the wound. The second garden holds the healing.

The first woman watched the world fall apart. The second woman witnesses the world stand up again. Not because Mary is "better" than Eve, but because the Seed promised to Eve has finally come for her daughters.

Mary does not reverse the first woman's story. She completes it. She fulfills it. She steps into the promise that belonged to both of them. And when she breathes the words, *"I have seen the Lord,"* the ache of Eden exhales.

The prophecy of the Seed stands fulfilled in the garden. And the Bride, long asleep in the story, awakens.

The Morning of All Mornings

Mary's awakening is not peripheral. It is cosmic.

The curse breaks. The ground breathes. The world stands up inside the woman who dared to linger. And the first words of the new creation echo through her voice:

"I have seen the Lord." John 20:18

The Bride is awake.
The Light has risen.
Creation has turned toward its Beloved.

15
EPILOGUE

The Spirit and the Bride Say, "Come!"

Rest now.
You have walked the ancient path
from garden to garden,
from dust to breath,
from striving to stillness.

Eden was never lost;
it was waiting within you
beneath the noise,
beneath the ache,
beneath the endless reaching.

The stone is rolled away.
The veil is torn.
The gate is open.
And the Gardener still walks.

You do not need to chase Him
you only need to turn in.
For every turning toward Love is resurrection.
Every breath surrendered is new creation.

Place your hand upon your heart.
Listen.
That rhythm you feel
is the song that began before the world was formed
and is the pulse of divine rest,
the heartbeat of Wisdom made flesh.

Now let your awareness sink lower.
Beneath the heart, beneath the striving to understand,
there is a deeper stillness.

From this inner place, His living water flows.
Not forced. Not summoned.
It rises because He has been opened within.
This is the well Yeshua spoke of.
The river that does not arrive from outside,
but springs up from within.
Here, creation is not managed.
It is carried.

This is where Wisdom builds.
This is where Love rests and reigns.
This is where you rise.
Qum.
Not by effort,
but by invitation.

The story is still being sung through you,
and its refrain is simple:

"The Spirit and the Bride say, Come."

And all of creation answers:

"Even so, come, Lord Jesus."

Sources

All Scripture quotations and narrative meditations in this book are drawn from the Holy Bible: New King James Version, The Passion Translation, and New International Version. References include, but are not limited to, the following passages, which form the primary scriptural framework of the journey traced in these pages: Genesis 1–3; 4; 6–9; 8:4; 12; 15; 17; 22, Exodus 3; 15:22–27; 16–17; 25–40, Leviticus 16, Numbers 17, Deuteronomy 12; 18, Judges 5, Psalms 19; 24; 68; 84; 132, Proverbs 3; 8, Song of Songs 1–8, Isaiah 2; 9:1–7; 11; 40; 60; 61, Ezekiel 43; 47, Hosea 6:2, Micah 4, Matthew 1–2; 27–28, Mark 8:22–26, Luke 1–2; 24, John 1; 2; 6–7; 10; 15; 19–20, Acts 2, Romans 5; 8, 1 Corinthians 10; 15, 2 Corinthians 3–5, Hebrews 1–4; 8–10; 12, 1 Peter 2, Revelation 1; 14; 19; 21–22

Language, Tradition, and Interpretive Approach

This book is written as a contemplative journey through Scripture, drawing from the Hebrew and Greek languages, Jewish interpretive tradition, early Christian reflection, and the witness of Scripture itself.

Hebrew and Greek word studies (including terms such as *ruach, neshama, nuach, shalom, beten, me'eh, qerev, tevah, kapporet, lehem, lacham, qum,* and others) are offered as windows rather than rigid definitions, not to exhaust meaning, but to invite the reader into the layered texture of biblical thought.

Geographic, numeric, and symbolic themes (such as gardens, mountains, trees, arks, rivers, and Sabbath patterns) reflect longstanding interpretive frameworks within Jewish and early Christian tradition. These elements are presented not as rigid conclusions, but as resonant threads that have long been recognized as part of Scripture's internal coherence.

Typological connections between Eden and resurrection, ark and body, tree and cross, bride and garden are grounded in biblical theology and early Christian reflection, where the story of Scripture is understood as unified and purposeful, culminating in Yeshua the Messiah.

Unless otherwise noted, Scripture quotations are adapted from standard English translations, with attention to original-language nuance where it illuminates meaning.

Sources and Influences

While this work is not intended as an academic study, it has been shaped by long-standing sources and traditions, including: The Hebrew Bible (Tanakh), The Greek New Testament, Strong's Exhaustive Concordance, Brown–Driver–Briggs Hebrew Lexicon, Thayer's Greek Lexicon, Jewish interpretive tradition (including Midrashic and thematic frameworks), Early Christian theological reflection on Eden, the Cross as the Tree of Life, the Ark, and the restoration of creation, Biblical theology of rest, Sabbath, and divine indwelling

Above all, this book seeks to remain anchored in the testimony of Scripture itself, approached not merely as text to be analyzed, but as revelation to be inhabited.

Numbers 6:24-26

"The LORD bless you and keep you,
Y'varech'cha Adonai v'yeesh'm'reicha.

יְבָרֶכְךָ יְיָ וְיִשְׁמְרֶךָ׃

The LORD make His face shine upon you, and be gracious to you;
Yaer Adonai panav eleicha veechooneka.

יָאֵר יְיָ פָּנָיו אֵלֶיךָ וִיחֻנֶּךָּ ׃

The LORD lift up His countenance upon you, and give you peace."
Yeesa Adonai panav eleicha v'yasem l'cha shalom.

יִשָּׂא יְיָ פָּנָיו אֵלֶיךָ וְיָשֵׂם לְךָ שָׁלוֹם

for you, Peter,
until we meet again

www.ingramcontent.com/pod-product-compliance
Lightning Source LLC
Chambersburg PA
CBHW071152130626
46553CB00004B/1629